Praise for *Overflow*

"*Overflow* is an important original work from a new inspired voice in the world of Buddhism. Vincent Thibault presents a well-written and masterfully organised approach to the development of sanity from the perspective of Buddhist philosophy and practice. Through his own studies and practice, he has created a work that is written in the language of our time to encourage us to take the enlightened principles and to make them our own. On the path, it is not easy to notice when we are fooling ourselves. The author makes a point of trying to acknowledge and remedy cultural, psychological and especially spiritual blindspots. Highly recommended."

—Samuel Bercholz, founder of Shambhala Publications and author of *A Guided Tour of Hell*

"I am pleased to recommend Vincent Thibault's *Overflow: A Buddhist Guide to Recovering Sanity in the Age of Information Overload* to anyone interested in how the timeless teachings of the Buddha can be applied effectively to modern life. In language easy to understand and assimilate, he gives us practical instructions on how to cultivate mindfulness, compassion, meditative insight, and other extraordinary qualities of the Dharma that can provide us with unerring navigation through the turbulence and complexity so characteristic of life in the twenty-first century."

—Orgyen Chowang Rinpoche, author of *Our Pristine Mind: A Practical Guide to Unconditional Happiness*

Overflow

A Buddhist Guide to Navigating the Chaos of the Digital Age

VINCENT THIBAULT

Foreword by Traleg Khandro

SHAMBHALA

Shambhala Publications, Inc.
2129 13th Street
Boulder, Colorado 80302
www.shambhala.com

This edition published in 2026

Cover art: SANALRENK/Adobe Stock and Luka/Adobe Stock
Cover design: Daniel Urban-Brown

9 8 7 6 5 4 3 2 1

First Shambhala Edition
Printed in the United States of America

Shambhala Publications makes every effort to print on acid-free, recycled paper.
Shambhala Publications is distributed worldwide by Penguin Random House, Inc., and its subsidiaries.

Library of Congress Cataloging-in-Publication Data
Names: Thibault, Vincent author | Khandro, Traleg other
Title: Overflow: a Buddhist guide to navigating the chaos of the digital age / Vincent Thibault, forward by Traleg Khandro.
Description: Boulder: Shambhala, 2025.
Identifiers: LCCN 2025026722 | ISBN 9781645474982 trade paperback
Subjects: LCSH: Happiness—Religious aspects—Buddhism. | Religious life—Buddhism. | Buddhism—Doctrines.
Classification: LCC BL65.H36 T45 2025 | DDC 294.3/444—dc23/eng/20250910
LC record available at https://lccn.loc.gov/2025026722

The authorized representative in the EU for product safety and compliance is eucomply OÜ, Pärnu mnt 139b-14, 11317 Tallinn, Estonia, hello@eucompliancepartner.com.

— Contents —

— Foreword —
by Traleg Khandro

Overflow is a thought-provoking, insightful, and empathetic book that articulates many of the challenges that accompany us on a day-to-day basis in the 21st century, and it provides essential Buddhist teachings and practices to assist in navigating these challenges in a way that can enrich and stabilize our lives. Thibault addresses many questions of our time.

Within the world of "overload," whether it be from information, crowds, or choices, can we find room to care for and connect fully with others and the world? With the bombardment of information, is it becoming harder to separate the trivial from the important? How can we live with integrity in a conflicted and contradictory world? While we so often look for the cause of our discontent outside ourselves, Thibault encourages the reader to look within. Drawing on the wisdom of many great Buddhist masters, Thibault shares essential aspects of Buddhist teachings and details many meditation practices to assist in enriching our inner journey through life. This book is a triumph in articulating the many challenges we face in our current world, and in marrying their management with the ancient Buddhist traditions.

Overflow

— Introduction —

Clarity, Tenderness, and Integrity in a Fast and Noisy World

Many of us endure day-to-day life, perceiving it as a ceaseless chain of tasks to be completed. Despite an overabundance of data, options, products, and ideas, we're never fully content. Victims of a sensory, social, intellectual, and spiritual overload, we find it increasingly difficult to make decisions and sustain inner peace, let alone be genuinely present with others. Every day, we absorb new information and try to build a meaningful life, and yet we often experience an inner trembling, akin to a subtle but ever-present background noise—a sign that deep, fearless confidence hasn't yet been achieved.

We lead frantic lives, yet we're taken aback by the increasing number of children diagnosed with hyperactivity and attentional problems. To some extent, we actually enjoy being busy, and we occasionally catch a glimpse of what truly matters in life. But we struggle to stay true to our innermost convictions, in deed, word, and thought. It's as if our body, speech, and mind rarely align due to perpetual distractions pulling us in different directions. We treat our bodies like machines, and our minds like computers.

With such an addiction to content, it's no wonder that meditation seems foreign or even absurd if we think its purpose is to "empty the mind." Sure enough, it is legitimate to feel compelled to constantly run when everything seems to go so fast. And then, when we're fatigued, it is understandable to want to shy away from complexity or to apply some quick fix, wondering why life has become so complicated!

But it is possible to develop genuine clarity, ease, and tenderness, even in this fast and noisy world. For that, one needs a spiritual path. Personally, I have chosen to follow the Buddhist path. There is some lucid optimism at play here: Buddhist teachings tell us that though confusion and difficulties are part of the human predicament, we have everything it takes to go beyond our ordinary habits and obsessions, and we can even experience a great deal of joy on the spiritual path towards clarity. This typically involves three stages: first, we learn to relax and tame our monkey mind; then, we train to open our heart; and finally, we soften our very relationship with phenomena, no matter how intense our experiences.

Of course, this is easier said than done, no matter how many quick, alluring recipes are to be found online. Regardless, having the intuition that we are fundamentally out of sync with ourselves and our surroundings is an important first step. As we navigate through our busy days, we may start to wonder:

- How can I live with integrity in a conflicted world?
- How can I make good decisions when there are so many possibilities?
- How can I stay focused and hear my own voice when there is so much noise?
- How can I sustain love when there's so much to do?
- How can I find true serenity when work, unread emails, and to-do lists follow me everywhere I go?

The world can be both dizzyingly vast and painfully cramped, and our own minds may feel crowded, assailed by too much news and input—too many notifications, solicitations, charts, hopes, and fears. I know mine has operated this way for a long time, despite the occasional oasis.

Over years of personal research and upheavals, I have become convinced that the answers to the list of questions above lie in changing our view of ourselves and the world through the practice of meditation—which in Buddhism goes beyond simply following one's breath. If you struggle with any of the above questions, and if you have an interest in Buddhism or are at least open to spirituality, this book is meant for you.

In this book, I discuss the experience of being overloaded and how it afflicts us, for example feeling confused and exhausted due to an overabundance of "content." However, the real problem does not lie with information per se. If that were the case, the solution would simply be to refrain from absorbing information, risking intellectual laziness. The problem is also not in sensory input, but in our constant craving; it is not in concepts but in the way we habitually solidify concepts. And while it is important to examine how we relate to thoughts and projects, there is no intention here to demonise them. What we need is a path to true intelligence. It is a matter of clarity, integrity, and responsiveness. So, in this book, I invite you to explore how the Buddhist teachings and ancient Indo-Tibetan wisdom can help us live with strength, sanity, and compassion in the age of information overload.

— —

This book is divided into seven chapters.

The first chapter, "A Personal History of Frenzy," is a brief memoir that recounts where I have come from, how I have come to understand my experience of raw anxiety in this beautiful and crazy era we are living in, and why I have felt prompted to write this book. Despite the particularities of my journey, you may find that many of the issues I have faced are universal.

The second chapter, "The Current State of Affairs," defines the many problems that arise from our sensory, social, intellectual, and spiritual overload, as well as their main causes. It also offers a glimpse of something else to aspire to.

The third chapter, "Tranquillity," relates to our capacity to find and cultivate peace within. While the previous section is part psychology, part social commentary, and part philosophy, here we actually begin to meditate. We relax the body, let the inner racket subside, and recognize the mechanisms of the compulsive mind.

The fourth chapter, "Processes," explores karma, our relationship with complexity, mindfulness in action, as well as a bunch of seemingly less meditative matters that can help us simplify our decision-making, live with integrity, and stay the course throughout the day.

The fifth chapter, "Tenderness and Warmth," is about love, compassion, and one's sense of duty, which may eventually dissolve into authentic selflessness. We explore how noise and information overload can actually fuel our aspiration to awaken and help fellow living beings instead of distracting us from this natural yearning.

The sixth chapter, "Clear Seeing," proposes a deeper exploration of Buddhist meditation. We start to experience the wisdom aspect of the path and befriend genuine openness.

Lastly, the seventh chapter, "Awakening," evokes further steps we can take on the journey to true freedom, boundless clarity, and unconditional love.

The first half of the book focuses on what Buddhism might consider short-term goals: finding greater happiness and sanity in the samsaric world. The second half is oriented towards the longer-term goal of achieving complete freedom from neurotic habits and perceptions altogether and developing one's full potential to help others. I am not trying to secularise Buddhism. On the contrary, I believe there is great power in tradition: self-made recipes and constant spiritual shopping only get us so far. However, until reaching the ultimate goal of full spiritual awakening or buddhahood, one can and should adopt a balanced approach to deal with daily affairs in an effective, confident, and sane way. Thus, I have no disdain for what could be referred to as "worldly wisdom," as we will see in the fourth chapter. It's all a matter of keeping things in perspective.

We'll find that the overall, longer-term goal of this approach is a unique kind of simplicity: full openness, unimpeded by deleterious mental elaborations, and always imbued with the qualities of wisdom—a capacity to be fully present and caring, in tune with reality, when this reality is not seen through the filters of our own subjective concepts.

— I —

A Personal History of Frenzy

I GREW UP IN A predominantly secular family. My brother and I were both baptised, as were many French Canadians our age, and for a few years, our mum dragged us to the local church on Christmas Eve. But that was pretty much it, and we hardly ever talked about religious matters at home. Dad was a resolute atheist, but of the level-headed type. He never felt the need to embarrass or confront people who adhered to other belief systems, and he was quite respectful of different cultures. To him, religious literature was, well, literature—stories, basically, that nonetheless conveyed valuable life lessons. It was all about symbolism. He was a French literature teacher, and he liked to point out to me the wisdom that can be found in folk tales.

One day, as a child, I asked him what he was if he didn't consider himself a Christian. He pondered for a moment. "If I had to give it a name," he answered, "I'd say I am a humanist." I asked, "What do you believe in then?" "Well, I believe in the human mind. I believe that we have the capacity to explain the world that surrounds us."

I was only a child, but this statement made an impression. There was dignity to it, a sense of awe, and deep respect for the human heart and its capacity to inquire and understand the world. For the first time, I was led to think there was some prestige in having an active, inquisitive mind—in *going towards* things instead of waiting to see what happens.

Despite the fact that there were books all over the house and that Dad mostly lived the life of an intellectual, he also enjoyed more contemplative activities, such as walking in the woods, bird-watching, drawing, and photographing flowers.

Mum was more openly receptive to spiritual matters and teachings. She was a creative and intuitive person who enjoyed the occasional tai chi and qigong lesson, and she had been deeply moved by her reading of a book by a particular contemporary Tibetan Buddhist writer. Though she was hard-working and focused on a demanding career, she always seemed to find time for her children, introducing us to all sorts of sports and arts and crafts. She was also incredibly generous. Celebrating how she would gladly put others before herself, Dad used to say, "Your Mum would give away her very clothes." She taught me a lot about unconditional love, and she never mocked me when I wanted to explore unusual paths—martial arts, alternative healing methods, and whatnot—quite the contrary.

I was born early—before the due date—on the first day of spring, with the umbilical cord dangerously wrapped around my neck. "You were in a hurry to arrive!" Mum would joke. She reminded me of my early arrival whenever I found myself eager to start new projects or showed signs of so-called maturity at a young age. "You're always in a hurry," she would say. That left a mark. She would say it lovingly and somehow she would mean it as a compliment, but at some point, I saw my hastiness as a curse, and it took me three decades to let go of what I thought was defining me. During those years a sense of hurry accompanied me wherever I went, much like a shadow, and I went through all sorts of frenzy, as I am sure you have too.

When I was about eight, the school organised a contest that was meant to encourage children to read more. The idea was to devour as many books as you could during the semester. You had this little almond-coloured card, on which you wrote each title with the date of completion; for every line, a parent or tutor had to sign. I went to the library, picked a bunch of tiny novels, and soon thereafter asked my dad for just as many signatures. My turnaround time was a little suspicious, and so my father looked at me and asked what those stories were about. I remember exactly where we were in the house, and quite a few details, such as the antique wooden furniture in my dad's office and his brass, banker-style desk lamp that had a green glass shade, but the rest of the scene is blurry: there's certainly some denial involved, for I'm pretty sure I lied! Had I read all these books to their very end? Did I invent much? This may have been one of my early experiences as a storyteller! In any case, one thing is sure: that reading contest represents my first vivid memory of experiencing the compulsive mind.

To be more precise, it was a craving for achievement: feeling overwhelmed by too many options (so many books out there!), I liked *having done* more than *doing*. School and society had taught me that the result mattered more than the process, that the destination was somehow distinct from the path. I was just a kid, "with all the time in the world," as the old naïve saying goes, and yet I could not find peace in the present moment.

As children, we frequently experience this blatant mix of agitation and obsessive desire around Christmas. For weeks, you ask for a Batman toy, or a LEGO kit, or a Barbie ranch. You're very specific, reminding your folks about the exact model, circling it and not at all subtly leaving the catalogue by their breakfast cereals. If your demand is reasonable (thankfully it rarely was, for you would have found yourself with an airplane and a robot and a bazooka you would have really had no use for), and if Santa is financially able to provide, you wait for what feels like an eon (one experiences how subjective time is when boxes start to appear under the tree)—but you finally get it. The one and only Batman, complete with his own utility belt! For a moment, the living room is filled with joy and laughter—and shredded wrapping paper. But then, after a cruelly short period of time, you turn the package over, see thumbnails of all the other figurines you could collect, and ask your parents, much to their dread, "Mum, Dad, when's next Christmas?"

I have to confess that I still experience this feverishness once in a while when I wander into a bookstore or peruse the websites of my favourite book publishing companies. I guess that's what catalogues do.

Early on in my teenage years, I had a thirst for knowledge. I was an avid reader with an interest in many different disciplines. High school had barely started when I began experiencing dizzy spells from having to contend with so many career possibilities. Some kids didn't know what courses to choose at school because everything sounded fascinating to them; by comparison, others were indifferent to every subject and seemed to think that the world was a thoroughly boring place. Personally, I thought there was way too much cool stuff! I am not just talking about classes at school, many of which left me unaffected. I'm talking about life. There was an abundance in this world that I found both exciting and frightening. When I shared my anguish with my father, he told me, "You know, being interested in everything—having a curious mind—is a sign of intelligence."

These wonderful words lifted my spirits on several occasions over the twenty years or so that followed. However, as is often the case with common-sense advice, if ego takes over and crystallises it, it can become a problem.

In high school, I had a bizarre relationship with the school system. I felt that I deserved a medal for my absenteeism: I missed physical education to do my own martial arts training, and I skipped French classes to read books that *I* chose—at least that's the version I like to recall. After finishing high school, I started a marginal academic journey, doing only a couple of semesters in *cégep*, a type of college that is exclusive to Quebec. I chose to focus on social sciences, and while I could grasp the notions that were being presented, the format didn't suit me at all. As a young adult, I was mostly a self-taught person. Of course, there was a lot of pride involved, but wanting to live the life of an intellectual while feeling inadequate in an academic setting felt both exhilarating and painful. Still, I kept exploring. I worked in bookstores, had half-baked ideas about launching my own businesses, and tried my hand at writing. I eventually visited different countries—Belgium, France, the United States, Japan, Singapore, and others—and discovered I had an interest in languages. I actually ended up studying many things, later on, as an adult. But the point here is this: since I didn't get much of a higher education at that time, I felt compelled to compensate with a mushrooming of *projects*.

Little did I know, as much as I disliked sitting in a classroom, I was an heir to the rationalistic movement that had been dominating the world of ideas in Europe for centuries. I liked Diderot, Voltaire, and their many endeavours. "I think therefore I am," wrote Descartes, and this seemed to make sense to me: there was a lure to the power of ideas, something utterly seductive about the ability to express thoughts and categorise them. It was as if the compulsive mind was suddenly tamed and given a throne—but its compulsive quality remained. Of course, I wasn't equipped to decipher the nuances of the great philosophical treatises, but there were nonetheless strong mind-habits that were ingrained within me, as if transmitted genetically. This rationalistic approach to dealing with both abstract concepts and things in daily life was invigorating. I just hadn't realised that this clinging to thoughts and ideas came at a cost. Yes, there was something cultural about it—there is something very subtle about Indo-European languages that affects the way we interact with outer and inner phenomena. But it would take years for me to realise that the monkey mind (even if dressed in fancy clothes) is pretty much universal, and does not depend on a specific era, or on one's ancestry or academic background. Admittedly, a great deal of the suffering and confusion that was to come about in my own life was the product of a complicated, materialistic mind. Yet, what I found is that this causal relationship between grasping mind and suffering wasn't something I alone experienced: it was very much part and parcel of the samsaric journey. But one thing at a time! Let's just say that at this stage in my personal history of frenzy, I had found myself in love with thoughts and ideas. Great men and women were all about *raison*, and only one who had awesome intellectual capacities could find Truth. Elitist much?

Fast-forward a few years. I wrote several books, half of which found decent publishing houses. Short stories, novellas, novels, essays, all sorts of odd nonfiction. Again, it was all about ideas and one's ability to stick to them—at least long enough to write them down. French-language Quebec was a small market, and a diluted one; I didn't have any highly dramatic, endearing personal history to tell interviewers; there was nobody famous in the family; I wasn't lucky with launching "the right book at the right time;" and most importantly, no matter how motivated I was, I still had a tremendous amount to learn about my craft. Therefore, despite passable sales, I had not hit the jackpot, and so I found myself thinking that for lack of a bestseller, I had to be more prolific.

In the meantime, my interest in movement training evolved from martial arts to *art du déplacement*, a discipline of French origin related to *parkour* that we often see in movies and TV series, particularly in chase scenes. I eventually trained with some of the founders—the impressive Yamakasi—and started coaching. I cofounded an academy in Quebec and wrote books on the subject.

As my coaching partners and I led classes for children and adults alike, showing them how to jump, run, climb, crawl, roll, vault over obstacles, and most importantly, prepare their bodies to do that safely, we advocated a *culture of effort*. The idea was that if we could find gratification and pleasure in the very process of working towards a goal, we could accomplish a great deal, regardless of the actual results. We may have been a tad ascetic at times, with some peculiarly intense training sessions, but generally, the message was a positive one, part of a wholesome outlook on life. But there was one thing that I simply could not see back then: in placing effort above everything else, we may have been implying that anything of value in this world had to be the result of some stiff intentionality. And yet we clearly saw, for example when walking on a handrail, that we simply couldn't find balance and confidence if the body and mind were too tight.

Coaching *art du déplacement* led me to meet athletes, therapists, experts, and movement artists of all sorts. Fitness is a huge industry, with a proliferation of diets, programs, magazines, research papers, websites, gyms, and studios. I soon realised just how much noise and confusion there was within the wellness industry. There were so many training methods available that it was hard to choose one, let alone persevere with it. Despite the variety of approaches, a common pitfall emerged: a result-driven modus operandi that often turned into an obsession with performance. In this domain, too, materialism and its cousins—cynicism, defeatism, nihilism, and a bunch of other isms—could survive amidst information overload. For all we know, they may have been insidiously fuelled by it.

I also had a vested interest in entrepreneurship and leadership. In this arena, too, there is a prevailing *idée fixe* with results. It's all about productivity, optimisation, and strategies—for better or worse. I was fortunate to meet mindful entrepreneurs, great human beings who were aware of egocentric hazards and who had a nuanced definition of "success." My own research made me learn about goal setting, decision-making, focus, workflow, as well as marketing in a noisy era. Experts had fascinating theories about potential customers, their constant preoccupations, and their limited attention spans. This made me realise how terribly busy most of us are—though whether or not we like to admit it, it's not so much our schedule that is frantic but our mind. On another note, during those few years of trying my hand at launching small businesses, I also discovered that the entrepreneur mindset is commonly held in very high regard, to the point that we are now pressuring nearly everyone to become an entrepreneur—again, for better or for worse.

All the while, I witnessed the arrival and increasing sophistication of the internet. Though I had been enrolled in a special high school program filled with tech—each of us had a laptop for the vast majority of our classes, a provincial first at the time, and the educational methods were based on *projects*—as an adult, I resisted cell phones and social media for some time. I proudly wore a pager when I was 13, but soon ditched it; by my mid-twenties, it seemed everyone but me had a cell phone and a Facebook account. I finally gave in for professional purposes and soon found myself handling numerous pages, websites, profiles, and so on. It was alienating, and I half-heartedly perpetuated what could be described as a love-hate relationship with these tools. A lot of good came from it, but there was so much news and so many notifications, emails, and posts that I occasionally had to withdraw from the racket, not yet fully understanding that the problem lay not with outer phenomena but with our relationship with them. These experiences, these joys and frustrations, contributed to my reflection on noise, overload, and confusion.

At all times, I could still find relative comfort in reading. I had a natural interest in philosophy, psychology, and well-being, motivated by a proneness to anxiety and hypochondria. Many avid readers joke that they have an addiction to a book series or a particular author. Sometimes, I think that this dependence may have been quite real for me: I often had to rely on written words to gain new ideas or to slow down my train of thought. Of course, I immensely enjoyed reading, and it truly made all the difference in my life, but in hindsight, I also have to admit that I dreaded having nothing to do, and my relationship with books was occasionally akin to that of a deluded seaman trying to quench his thirst with salt water.

Reading, writing, publishing, business fantasies, movement training, and coaching … during all those years—and I hope you'll pardon me for wandering to and fro across my personal timeline—there was one thing I could always go back to whenever I needed insight; an anchor, so to speak. For me, this personal oasis was the Dharma. It helped me deal with my own inner over-achiever by allowing me to cultivate a sense of ease and dignity that was not based on my own little, imaginary idea of myself; it also gave me perspective in all aspects of my life, and it continues to do so every single day. Of course, when I first started dabbling in Buddhism, I had no idea what it actually was about, beyond a few romantic ideas and common misconceptions. Be that as it may, I encountered the teachings of the Buddha when I was about 15 years old. I read book after book and eventually met teachers and masters, primarily of the Tibetan Buddhist tradition, both locally and abroad.

Over the years, I connected in one way or another with numerous teachers, receiving teachings and transmissions from all the main schools of Tibetan Buddhism. Such a plurality is rarely necessary—in fact my general advice is on the "less is more" side of things—but that's how my own life situation unfolded. Though I am grateful to all these teachers, the most influential for me are especially connected to the Nyingma tradition of Tibetan Buddhism.

To be more precise, my principal spiritual forefathers particularly hold the Longchen Nyingtik and Dudjom Tersar lineages, and I also have deep reverence for the Kagyu tradition.[1] I find them incredibly profound and powerful—I can't help but feel that these lineages swiftly carry great blessings. Additionally, although both the Nyingma and Kagyu traditions have strong philosophical foundations and offer possibilities to always further one's studies, they are eminently practical, allowing practitioners of all types—notably non-monastics like me—to get to the heart of the matter. However, I suppose it is a matter of personal connection, and of course, all genuine lineages are wonderful, profound, and precious.

Regardless of the specific sub-schools, two preliminary topics explored on the Tibetan Buddhist path are the mind-blowing preciousness of our human life and impermanence—the inevitability of our death and the fact that all conditioned phenomena are bound to change. As we contemplate these notions, we start to feel an urge to actually practice and follow a path. A sense of renunciation—seeing, for instance, that egotistic mechanisms and endeavours are truly pointless and harmful—is essential. Yet, it took me a surprising amount of time to realise that putting too much emphasis on spiritual progress can actually impede it. There is no problem with being inspired and driven; the problem has to do with ego's propensity to claim everything within its subjective territory, and "everything" here includes spirituality. We understand the implications of this when we begin to notice how tempting spiritual materialism is—it truly is a universal tendency. In fact, I think that Chögyam Trungpa Rinpoche's book *Cutting Through Spiritual Materialism* is one of the most vital readings in this day and age. In my case, afraid as I was of spiritual torpor and laziness, it took me years to realise that one could be a serious, genuine practitioner while at the same time being oneself, relaxed and at ease, with a sense of humour, and not playing games. This is easier said than done, as we all have blind spots, and it is not so easy to notice when we are fooling ourselves.

Over the years, I received teachings, discovered numerous practices, and did retreats, and I am deeply grateful for all these extraordinary experiences. In hindsight, however, I have to confess that as authentic, powerful, and precious as those teachings were, I often attended them with a rather compulsive mind. It was subtle, but it was not unlike when I was a little boy fantasizing about owning all the Batman collectibles. At other times, I attended teachings and found myself overwhelmed with an abundance of spiritual methods, making it hard to choose which one to take on and wholeheartedly practice. It was like the teenage version of myself, paralysed by too many options. The ambient noise certainly didn't help to find focus and stay the course. Then, whenever I could finally receive a teaching with a proper intention and stick to it for a little while, oftentimes when I sat down to practice, I would catch myself seeing it as yet another project. That was the old "doer" mentality kicking in: it was the boy trying to get ahead of the reading contest, the entrepreneur, the "optimiser" liking to have done things. I often felt there was a gap between doing and being, and it irritated me, but somehow my strategy to close that gap was to *do* more. The absurdity of it was easy to understand intellectually—I had read about the potential pitfalls of "personal development"—and yet that cerebral grasp too was an addiction, as if not being constantly engaged in conceptual thinking was somehow stupid.

Despite the occasional peace and stillness, everything felt unnecessarily complex!

When I found myself in the presence of masters and genuine, mature Dharma practitioners, I was immediately drawn to their wonderful energy. What I admired about them was not so much what they did (as extraordinary as it may have been) but what they *were*. Some of them seemed to truly embody the qualities of buddhahood. These qualities manifested in myriad ways, and some teachers created a very different atmosphere around them. But there was one interesting common denominator: simplicity. Even when they were commenting on complex philosophical treatises, quoting brilliant masters of the past, there was something disarmingly simple about them, their very presence being uncontrived and unelaborated. They had an open heart that overflowed ceaselessly, effortlessly, like a cascade, in a most direct, unimpeded way. Even if a master emitted a seemingly angry vibe—that can happen, out of compassion—there was some simplicity to it being so precise, like a laser-sharp sword cutting through the veil of ignorance. That power can also be felt in the written words of true masters: no matter how refined and nuanced the subject matter, and regardless of our capacity to understand every bit of it right away, behind it all, we can feel that the author himself or herself is *being* quite simple.

Was this lasting, happy state only attainable by people who practiced meditation full-time for decades in a Himalayan cave? That state certainly was something positive to aspire to, but what if one were a typical, lay, twenty-first century Westerner whose days were filled with emails and notifications? For example, I personally enjoyed meditation and spiritual matters, and yet in between sessions, throughout the course of my personal and professional life, I would often find myself paralysed by too many options and second-guess my own decisions. Sometimes I would take a break from whatever I was working on, and most of that break would consist of "scrolling down" on some social media platform, which tended to leave me bitter and sluggish instead of refreshed, as proper breaks should. I couldn't see the extent to which my multitasking contributed to my neuronal fatigue and how the countless and useless decisions I was unknowingly making throughout the day (such as deciding whether or not that "post" or that bit of information was relevant to me) curbed my clarity and insight when I needed to make more important decisions.

Additionally, behind all musings, oscillations, and inquiries lay one big question: who should I be? Some elements were crystal clear—that the Dharma had an unfathomable value, and that my root teachers represented pure lineages and embodied the qualities of buddhahood—but I still struggled with more mundane matters. There may have been too much "I" in the question "who should I be?" and some delusion as to what "being" involves, but still I remained convinced that one could bring one's own talents and skills to this world and do something meaningful. In my case, it was the specifics that were unclear.

It was in the midst of these many questions that Samuel Bercholz, a Kagyu and Nyingma practitioner who is a good *kalyanamitra*—a spiritual friend who's "been there" (in this case, a very dear companion on the path and one of the great Dharma teachers I have met)—gave me some solid advice: "You have to learn to be simple." He said this to me on several occasions, gently scolding me with unconditional love. Dense as I was (and still am), I have found ways to ask questions about simplicity—ha!

And yet I could tell that he was touching the heart of the matter.

Samuel said this to me several years ago, and I've been on quite a journey since then. That is how this book came into being. Despite all the work I had done and all the tools I had been given, I still regularly experienced an inner trembling, a not-so-metaphorical weight on my chest, an unpleasant background noise. I had trouble seeing things with clarity, handling events with simple and accurate responsiveness, and making decisions with confidence. The stakes tend to rise as one ages, and so I felt a desire to get to the bottom of my restlessness. Most importantly, I came to see that agitation and confusion are universal experiences—characteristics of samsara, the cycle of conditioned existence marked by suffering and delusion. This is not new by any means, but in this overloaded age, filled with noise, distractions, and distortions, it seems particularly prevalent. Clinging and bewilderment permeate all aspects of our lives: that much, I saw clearly. Hence, I felt a deep sense of warmth and closeness for my human brothers and sisters, and a desire to share the fruits of my investigations. I became convinced that though some ideas from classic Western philosophy and tools from modern psychology can indeed assist us, timeless Buddhist teachings and meditations can truly make us close the gap between confusion and clarity, between doing and being—and maybe, if we're lucky, realise that in the end, there is no gap.

Thus, I want to share what I have learned and applied to overcome restlessness, mental tightness, and all sorts of subtle—and sometimes not so subtle—materialistic mindsets, come to terms with the overload of content in the modern world, and better follow my chosen spiritual path with more simplicity and ease, in the hope that it will be useful to you too, dear readers.

— II —

The Current State of Affairs

We like to picture our ancestors living simple lives. Here's how a typical fantasy goes:

They ate the same basic ingredients every day and wore practical clothes that they regularly mended. From their teenage years to their deaths, they kept the same job, stayed in the same house and knew only one spouse. If a machine broke down, they would repair it, for it was a matter of basic mechanics. The sheer number of works of art they could see and musical instruments they could hear in their lifetime was limited. Our ancestors, we like to think, had few pastimes. They enjoyed playing the same game over and over again. And eventually, they transmitted age-old advice and stories to their kids.

Is this accurate or naïve? Regardless, when we are stressed out, we may be tempted to idealise the past—the "good old days." However, previous generations also had to make decisions and deal with complexity.

For example, there have always been individuals who pushed the boundaries of their sensory experiences—such as aristocrats who enjoyed rare delicacies and elaborate ceremonies. Some gifted monastics committed to memory dozens, if not hundreds, of texts. There were also explorers who dealt with a unique kind of uncertainty; to some extent, scientists had to be adventure seekers. The average Jane also had to categorise and prioritise. If you build a house by yourself, there are quite a few things you need to know. If you're likely to spend the rest of your life with the person you're going on a date with, you may ponder things a little more. If you have access to a limited number of works of art, over time you may discover their respective subtleties and enjoy their richness. All these scenarios imply knowledge and thought and decisions and opinions; and so we should be alert to an oversimplification about the past. To the rich and the poor, the world has always had an element of fullness and complexity.

There is no doubt about it: walking through a big modern shopping mall can be an intense experience. But the traditional bazaars that flourished centuries ago in major Eastern hubs were also packed with a dizzying array of colours, odours, tastes, textures, and sounds—not to mention the number of languages and dialects spoken. In rural areas, farmers had a rich and nuanced knowledge of the land. Even nowadays, if you walk in the woods with someone who has truly inherited traditional skills from First Nations people, it's astonishing how they seem to know every tree and plant by its name and can distinguish one rock from another—while to a non-indigenous person, the whole of it is just bushland.

So having to deal with a load of information, conflicting priorities, and even a constant effort to improve one's lot—that's not new. But there *are* differences between our current predicament and that of our ancestors.

We don't need to go far back in time to notice a shift. As cognitive psychologist and neuroscientist Daniel J. Levitin points out:

> Thirty years ago, travel agents made our airline and rail reservations, salesclerks helped us find what we were looking for in stores, and professional typists or secretaries helped busy people with their correspondence. Now we do most of those things ourselves. The information age has off-loaded a great deal of the work previously done by people we could call information

> specialists onto all the rest of us. We are doing the jobs of ten different people while still trying to keep up with our lives, our children and parents, our friends, our careers, our hobbies, and our favourite TV shows.[2]

In fact, year by year, many things seem to increase: sensory inputs, alerts and notifications, noise, things to do, things to remember, tasks we attempt to do at the same time, types of tasks we do in the course of a day, options, decisions, things we own, roads and potential itineraries, bills, memberships, service providers and outsourcing possibilities, small objects to keep track of, software to update, people we know, hours we stay connected, types of medical treatments we can receive, and so on.

In times past, the mailman visited once a day, at best, and that was it. If you were waiting for an important package or news from the front, perhaps you'd catch yourself looking through the window every hour or waiting on the porch. But once the mailman had come, you didn't think twice until the morrow. By comparison, how many times do we check our emails every day? For some of us, the numbers are dizzying, and it is even worse when we take into account other means of communication. For example, reports indicate that about 90 percent of all text messages are read within three minutes![3]

In the sixteenth century, Montaigne was one of the most important philosophers of the French Renaissance—a sceptical, erudite man who liked to entertain doubt, and who was an avid reader. The southern tower of his château held his famed personal library, containing a vast number of books and treatises written by the Greek, Latin, and French masters. We now know that Montaigne's widely celebrated library consisted of about a thousand books. By comparison, nowadays, a relatively small independent bookstore may carry a catalogue of over 20,000 titles. In 2014, we reached the milestone of one billion websites, and despite periods of subsequent decline, the total number of websites has since grown and now exceeds 1.1 billion.[4] Tens of thousands of new sites every day. Admittedly, quantity doesn't always come with quality, and we can hardly compare a ton of websites with the private library of a sixteenth-century philosopher. But here's the thing: flooded as we are with data, it may well be increasingly difficult—whether or not we're aware of it—to decide if new information is relevant for us. We've established that having to deal with an abundance of options and experiences is not new, but there is a specific type of demand on our mind and nervous system that Montaigne probably never had to grapple with, at least not to the same extent.

When televisions hit the mass market, there were few channels, and the broadcasting schedules were limited. Today, if you wanted to watch all the shows people tell you about, you would probably have to quit your day job, and you still couldn't catch up. You could watch professionally produced content 24/7 and still only consume an insignificant percentage of what's available.

Books, works of art, and video content are just the tip of the iceberg. In fact, information specialists have quantified the total amount of data a modern human brain has to deal with. The numbers are hard to believe. As Levitin explains:

> In 2011, Americans took in five times as much information every day as they did in 1986—the equivalent of 175 newspapers. […] Each of us has the equivalent of over half a million books stored on our computers, not to mention all the information stored in our cell phones or in the magnetic stripe on the back of our credit cards.[5]

That quote comes from *The Organized Mind.* It is a telling detail that this book has become a bestseller. Levitin goes on:

> Our brains do have the ability to process the information we take in, but at a cost: we can have trouble separating the trivial from the important, and all this information processing makes us tired. . . . Every status update you read on Facebook, every tweet or text message you get from a friend, is competing for resources in your brain with important things like whether to put your savings in stocks or bonds, where you left your passport, or how to best reconcile with a close friend you just had an argument with.[6]

Levitin explains that separating the trivial from the important can be much more difficult than we imagine, at least from the perspective of tired neurons. *The Organized Mind*, part neuroscience, part self-help, is a great book if you're into psychology. As you will see, *Overflow* is in some ways its spiritual counterpart: it proposes a meditative approach, with elements that aim to bring us beyond simply being more efficient on a daily basis.

In fact, we don't need arduous calculations to understand our current situation. We could do a simple subjective experiment.

Pick a painting, such as a Van Gogh, a Monet, a Hopper, or a segment from the Bayeux Tapestry, and decide to spend just five minutes with it. There's nothing to do: simply spend some quiet time with the painting.

Then set it aside and rapidly flip through a museum catalogue so that you "see" a hundred different pictures in an equally short time. You don't need an actual catalogue; you can just go to Google Images, type "famous paintings," and scroll down for a few minutes. That's it.

Now, which of the two experiences brought about a real sense of what art is—a more intimate connection with the nature of beauty, with the artist's intent? In which case did your neurons seem to tire more quickly? Which experience made you feel like you were actually alive, nourishing true intelligence and sensitivity?

Feeding the intellect with a fast food approach is tempting, as if it were more effective—and as if slowing down were unproductive. But could we really say that spending a couple of minutes with a timeless masterpiece is unprofitable?

This simple (and admittedly subjective) experiment shows two ways we could live our life. It doesn't mean that you should not "cram" and strive to get that PhD if that's your path, or that you cannot occasionally binge-watch, or flip through a catalogue, or simply drink that coffee and finish that thick book! But we have to bring more suppleness and awareness to the way we interact with content. Humans have always had to make decisions, organise information, and deal with stress, but we now find ourselves in a precarious position, with our physical, mental, social, and spiritual health constantly assailed.

I promise we will get to the good news. But bear with me for a few more pages: for now, it is important to find out more precisely *how* the current overload affects us. Sun Tzu, in his classic *Art of War*, strongly encouraged us to know the terrain. In our case, we may realise that discovering the extent of the problem can initiate the healing process. It was, after all, the approach used by Shakyamuni Buddha when he taught the four noble truths—the first being the truth of suffering—that ultimately led to genuine lasting joy, peace, love, and clarity.

The Difficulties Associated with the Current Overload

Here is a list of the many areas in which we may currently experience problems, sometimes unknowingly. As we will see later, we should be wary of spiritual materialism and the tendency to use meditation as a mere tool to become more efficient in mundane affairs. However, I do believe that meditation—if understood correctly—can be of tremendous help in the following areas.

Decision-making

An increase in options, agitation, and distorted perceptions makes decision-making difficult. We can experience this on a daily basis: on the one hand, the number of products available at the supermarket is now staggering; on the other hand, we don't know who and what to believe anymore when it comes to healthy eating. Hundreds of thousands of books have been published this past year (in all likelihood, more than 300,000 in the US alone),[7] and on YouTube more than 500 hours of content are uploaded every minute.[8] If you ever found yourself arguing with your partner after a long day of intellectual work ("No, *you* pick the movie, I can't decide! Just pick one already!"), you know how neuronal fatigue can contribute to sluggishness and lack of clarity. Many of the choices we make in those situations have limited consequences, but making informed decisions about our career or spiritual path can be trickier. We can also find ourselves in dire need of unbiased clarity when it comes to choosing between different medical treatments or political parties, for example.

Physical and Mental Health

Surely you have heard about the effects of stress on our heart, or that of blue light exposure on the quality of our sleep.

But one thing we should talk about more is the myth of multi-tasking—where the materialistic, doer mentality teams up with the monkey mind. Every time we switch between two tasks, no matter how simple they seem, it takes a little while for us to get back to optimal focus, and the constant, rapid-fire adaptation places a burden on our system. No matter how productive we think we are in the moment, more often than not it is an illusion and a great recipe to feel tired and lumpish.

Another indirect and insidious effect that content overload has on our health relates to our relationship with performance. If we are constantly bombarded by unrealistic images outwardly and guilt-ridden chatter inwardly, we may become obsessed with performance, at the risk of losing the many benefits of joyful exertion. For example, someone can initially derive tremendous pleasure and gratification from an art form, or life passion; but over the years, after seeing countless, disproportionate "success stories" online, they may succumb to a competitive mentality, causing their whole approach to their craft to feel contrived and exhausting.

I often see this with sports, where people focus so much on the results that they lose the benefits of joyful movement. Instead of making our bodies stronger and more resilient, extreme and inadequate fitness programs can have the opposite effect, or we may end up forsaking physical exercise altogether. Both extremes are possibly linked to content overload, as it distorts our perception by radically altering our reference points. For the ascetic, the "click-bait" content leads one to believe that quantifiable performance is what matters most; while for an unhealthy person who tends to feel overwhelmed, the images of a small but over-represented elite take up so much space that they eventually eclipse any sane middle ground that could be within one's reach. Such influences are not always blatant, so in this area too, we need to be discerning.

The Ability to Hear Oneself

There seem to be so many outstanding benefits to silence that we could spend a whole book exploring that one topic. Conversely, according to the World Health Organization, excessive noise can cause cardiovascular and psychophysiological effects; it may increase the risk of hypertension, impact mental health and contribute to a bunch of other health problems.[9] The scientific details can be found elsewhere, but here we are taking a particular interest in how it relates to our spiritual health.

In an interview, Buddhist author and teacher Elizabeth Mattis Namgyel recalls how she mostly stayed silent for a year and a half while on retreat:

> I found that it really enhanced my practice, because when we use words often, it kind of solidifies our experience a little. It's like you're objectifying things and not having a full experience: you're labelling things right away. I found that by not labelling things or putting words on them, you can experience fullness. It's like you usually put a lid on it, or judge it, or try to subdue your experience, but [now], you have this incredibly full experience, just in the moment, in a very simple way. I found that was wonderful. [...] When I started to talk again, I appreciated language so much. I don't think it's been the same for me since then. It's so wonderful that we can communicate in this way! But somehow, it's not such a chatty situation anymore.[10]

Of course, we don't have to refrain from talking for such an extended period of time to enjoy the benefits of silence. Little pockets of silence here and there throughout the day can go a long way.

Concentration and Productivity

In Buddhism, meditation is not seen as mere mental gymnastics. Nonetheless, it does cultivate attention, and since attention deficit is a widespread concern these days, we will explore how we can improve in that area in another chapter. Not only will we discover simple tools that can boost our focus on a daily basis, but we will also unveil a delightful irony: we tend to become more efficient when we stop obsessing over the results.

Here's an example. There is this person who likes to get things done. She enjoys checking things off her list—the faster, the better. She has a lot to do every day, so she keeps her emails short and sweet. But nine times out of ten she forgets an important detail when giving a task to her graphic designer, which results in a considerable waste of time, energy, and money. These things happen all the time. Whether such occurrences are due to a lack of attention or to an obsessive desire to rapidly check off a to-do list, they are certainly not alien to our current overload.

The Bottom and Surface of Things

Our inability to experience things fully is often due to inner agitation, which in turn is aggravated by our incapacity to deal with the current overload of information, expectations, and sensory input.

We understood this earlier with our simple experiment when we took the time to look at a painting. In one of his *Letters to Lucilius*, the Roman Stoic philosopher Seneca (c. 4 BCE—65 CE) takes this a step further and gives the following advice:

> The primary indication, to my thinking, of a well-ordered mind is a man's ability to remain in one place and linger in his own company. Be careful, however, lest [the] reading of many authors and books of every sort may tend to make you discursive and

> unsteady. You must linger among a limited number of master thinkers, and digest their works, if you would derive ideas which shall win firm hold in your mind. Everywhere means nowhere. When a person spends all his time in foreign travel, he ends by having many acquaintances, but no friends. And the same thing must hold true of men who seek intimate acquaintance with no single author, but visit them all in a hasty and hurried manner. Food does no good and is not assimilated into the body if it leaves the stomach as soon as it is eaten; nothing hinders a cure so much as frequent change of medicine; no wound will heal when one salve is tried after another; a plant which is often moved can never grow strong.[11]

That doesn't mean we cannot explore new places, discover new authors, or learn about new topics—simply that too much, too fast, only gets us so far. This is true when it comes to career, education, spirituality, or just about any area. On a larger scale, a "skimming through" culture can have terrible social effects if we don't bother to go beyond preconceived ideas. Our relationship with content is more subtle than it seems, and sadly, though we don't mean to, we often contribute to misinformation. For example, someone we know shares an article on social media, we read little more than the title, and later that day we catch ourselves spreading the word. The more overloaded we are, the more these things are likely to happen.

The Value of Time

Isn't it easy to run around like a headless chicken? I know I often do! When we are constantly distracted, we tend to lose sight of the value of time. This has nothing to do with the state of flow described by Mihaly Csikszentmihalyi, in which we are so fully immersed in an activity that we tend to ignore temporal concerns.[12] Rather, what I am referring to here is the opposite of mindfulness: being *distracted* and barely noticing it. Distracted from what? Not only from the task at hand; often, we are distracted from what we know truly matters. We keep busy in an attempt to reify ourselves, then when we finally have nothing "important" to do, we tend to fall into numbness, remaining idle and perhaps feeling guilty about it.

However, as the French writer and Buddhist monk Matthieu Ricard writes:

> Time often resembles a fine gold powder that we distractedly allow to slip through our fingers without ever realizing it. Put to good use, it is the shuttle we use to pass through the weft of our days to weave the fabric of a meaningful life. It is therefore essential to the quest of happiness that we be aware that our time is our most precious commodity.[13]

Whether we kill time or complain about the lack of it, our relationship with time is rarely optimal. But when we acquire a few good habits (a training that will one day lead to the state of *no habits*), and most importantly, when we change our outlook on life, we suddenly find more time for what truly matters, and the whole process becomes more enjoyable.

As the great eighteenth-century master Jigme Lingpa wrote in his *Treasury of Precious Qualities*:

> Tormented by the summer's heat, beings sigh with pleasure
> In the clear light of the autumn moon.
> They do not think, and it does not alarm them,
> That a hundred of their days have passed away.[14]

The Capacity to Express Ourselves Clearly

There is a timeless image: we inadvertently drop a key in a pond. If we grab a stick and stir the water in an attempt to locate the small object, the water will get muddy, making our task all the more difficult. For us to be able to see clearly, first the mud has to settle at the bottom.

This analogy can be used to describe the dawn of clarity, and more specifically, the relationship between tranquillity and insight (two subjects that we will explore in chapters 3 and 6 respectively). But here, I am using this image to showcase how our current habits diminish our capacity for skilful communication. If our mind is agitated and overloaded, it will be hard to express ourselves clearly and fully, with all the nuance or impact that's required. We may find it increasingly difficult to clarify our own beliefs and dispel our doubts, to ask relevant and precise questions, and to truly share and connect with others.

Presence for Others and the Capacity for Empathy

Imagine you're walking down a crowded street on a busy day. It doesn't have to be the famous, hectic Shibuya Crossing in Tokyo. Any place in which hundreds of people move about will do.

At some point, you may realise that to most of these people, you are not a human being, but rather an *object* that stands between them and their destination. The area is so crowded that you do the same: no matter how smart you are, you encounter a "cognitive scope limitation," a limit to the number of distinct pieces of data your brain can process. Beyond that data limit, information tends to be processed in abstract terms: when there is too much to assimilate, we unconsciously bundle everything into categories. Unless you pay attention to them with awareness and a tender heart, the people crossing the busy street are not individuals anymore, each with their own lives and personalities; they are, collectively, a *crowd*.

Dunbar's Number, first proposed in the 1990s by the British anthropologist Robin Dunbar, suggests a "cognitive limit to the number of people with whom one can maintain stable social relationships."[15] The number regularly quoted is 150. Other studies suggest that it is higher: for example, the Bernard-Kilworth median is 231.[16] Experts surely would argue over the exact figure. In any case, author Josh Kaufman warns us:

> The same thing happens to executives of large companies. Rationally, they may be aware that they're responsible for hundreds of thousands of employees and millions of shareholders, but no matter how intelligent they are, their brains simply aren't capable of processing the magnitude of that reality. As a result, executives can hurt a lot of people without even realizing it. [...] Personalizing an issue is a way to hack this universal limitation.[17]

Regardless of the actual numbers, we may find it increasingly difficult in this day and age to be genuinely present for others. Our listening skills wane. There are so many things we're asked to pay attention to, and we are so frequently solicited, that we tend to become thick-skinned and indifferent.

And yet, in Mahayana Buddhism, mature spiritual practitioners can be sensitive to the suffering of an inconceivably vast number of beings and actually work for their benefit without ever feeling disheartened. There is not the slightest doubt that until we get there, we can learn to be gradually more present to the people around us. We will explore this theme in chapter 5.

Creativity

Wonderful works of art can bloom in the most chaotic situations—that is, if the artist knows how to channel their energies.

For many of us, however, the more boisterous our inner environment, the less creative we tend to be. When our world is tumultuous, we often rely on sweeping generalisations in order to keep our bearings. In an attempt to compute our experience, we resort to clichés and, often enough, to delusions. But attachment to categorising is *not* the way to true simplicity, and extreme conceptualisation doesn't foster creativity; it impedes it.

For example, if we cling to the idea that situations are permanent, there won't be any room for things to evolve—at least in our view. If we lose our capacity to *care*, we are unlikely to experience fullness: the richness of the phenomenal world won't penetrate the armour of our thick-skinned indifference. If our relationship with outer and inner phenomena remains cold and superficial; if we're too stiff, as if all our thoughts and perceptions were rocklike and existing in and of themselves in isolation; if, feeling overwhelmed by too much input, we build more and more sophisticated defence mechanisms; or even on a relative level, if we never take the time to enjoy texture, colour, light, and shade—then it will be difficult to generate powerful creativity, or to express the type of genuine and liberated spontaneity that true wisdom allows.

I'm referring to the possibility of enlightened arts, but it isn't just about that. Even in our daily lives, if we lack openness and inner space, we'll tend to always go for the same (or "the same but different"). We'll sow the same seeds and expect different fruits—like a snake biting its tail. At work or at home, we'll try to find solutions to improve our lot or to deal with a situation that has come up, but we'll feel sluggish, uninspired, unsatisfied, or shameful. Though we know that we can't solve problems without clarity, we often waste a tremendous amount of energy struggling, as in the image of the pond used earlier, where a person agitated the water with a stick in a failed attempt to retrieve their key.

Regardless of how much of an artist we are, some suppleness is required to live one's life fully and face challenges. There is some creativity involved on any spiritual path.

Memory

Without clarity, awareness, and attention, the two essential aspects of memory—storing information and accessing it—may fail. The more overloaded we become, the harder it will be to trust our own knowledge—and quite possibly, our intuition. It will also be difficult to establish new and relevant connections between different ideas and elements. Thankfully, we can develop clarity, awareness, and attention.

Transmission

Earlier, we broached the topic of misinformation and of how we can sometimes unknowingly spread it. The more confused *we* are, the more we're at risk of adding to the ambient confusion. This goes beyond the short-term effect of idle gossip. We have to take a stand and decide what values and skills we want to pass on to future generations. Do we want to bequeath a culture that compounds neuroses, or one that is all about presence and kindness? A culture that is based on alienation, agitation, and sheer individualism or one that is founded on resilience, suppleness, and true communication? These questions have to be answered in one's heart of hearts. And they apply regardless of whether or not we have children or grandchildren, for transmission occurs both vertically and horizontally—in other words, in both time and space. How we live matters. It has more impact on others than we think. We live in an interdependent world, and within us lies the capacity for boundless love, tenderness, clarity, and insight. It's time we learned to let it shine.

The Environment

Our inability to be simple and content may accentuate our environmental footprint, as does the number of things we use, perhaps just a few times, before we throw them away. The connection between our level of contentment and our ability to care for the environment may seem far-fetched, but if we take an honest look at how our states of mind influence our consumption patterns and our general behaviour in both social and private settings, we will see that this is a serious issue.

By comparison, there is often something utterly beautiful and natural in the way a mature, lucid, and warm-hearted spiritual practitioner interacts with the world around her.

As Dza Kilung Rinpoche says:

> Once meditation becomes a part of your life, you may notice that the practice radiates positivity to others—its gentleness and peacefulness influence the whole environment. [...] If we want peace on earth and to heal the environment, first we must look inward and heal ourselves, and then expand this positive influence outward.[18]

I like to think that in this quote, "environment" can be interpreted literally as well as metaphorically. We can have a positive impact on the outer environment, both natural and built, but we can also purify our psychological landscape and heal our social "space" as well as the way different areas of our lives interact and fit together.

Recognising Our True Nature

In Buddhism, there are countless means to attaining relative freedom and happiness—the short-term goal of finding more sanity within the samsaric world—but the Nyingma tradition teaches that ultimately, to fully awaken and to reach the long-term goal of buddhahood, we need to recognise and familiarise ourselves with our true, innermost nature. Sometimes, if we're lucky, as we go about our daily lives, we may catch a glimpse of the open nature of things: it is like we are standing some distance away from a window and seeing how beautiful, vast, natural, and bright the landscape is outside; we don't fully experience it yet. For example, we may sometimes come to an understanding that everything is workable and arising in dependence on ever-changing causes and conditions. But these brief insights typically don't last long, partly due to our perpetual distraction. Surely, there are meditators who have reached high levels of realisation in the midst of chaos—they've found boundless wisdom at the very heart of confusion, like sudden light in the darkest of pits. Lotuses do grow in the mud. But generally speaking, the more unstable and agitated we are, the harder it is for us to experience genuine openness, let alone familiarise ourselves with it. Even if we read traditionally restricted materials containing the highest philosophical views, our clinging and addiction to concepts may lead us to intellectualise them. Even if we are in the very presence of a qualified master who lovingly points out the deepest truths to us, we may remain impervious if we grasp at hopes, fears, and preconceived notions of what is and is not. Our own wisdom wants to shine forth, but first we have to be receptive and surrender, and our present incapacity to deal with the current overload gets in the way.

Buddhist meditation definitely helps us in that regard.

Shakyamuni Buddha said that he's shown us the path, but it is up to us to follow it. As powerful as the fully awake buddhas are, we must be receptive to their blessings and wisdom teachings if we want to follow in their footsteps. For any progress of that sort to happen, we have to learn to be simple.

The Causes of Our Current Overload

The Buddha taught that when causes and conditions come together, effects inevitably follow. When we suffer, it is up to us to identify and remedy the causes and conditions of our suffering.

This may sound simple, but we tend to overlook its profound implications. For example, we repeatedly produce the same causes, expecting different results, like someone who continues to plant beans, hoping for an orange tree to grow. I am not necessarily referring to our odd little ways, but to our larger approach to life: we all want happiness, but we keep looking for it in all the wrong places, hoping that the next conditional, material, or temporal solution will bring unconditional, immaterial, lasting contentment. As well, when a problem arises, we often put all the blame onto what we think is its exclusive, independent cause, forgetting about all the other elements that contributed to the situation we find ourselves in. Indeed, the conditions and contributing circumstances are plural, and there are many life situations for which it would be presumptuous to claim that we clearly see *all* the factors involved. (As astronomer Carl Sagan put it, "If you wish to make a pie from scratch, you must first invent the universe.") Of course, strictly speaking, knowing all the factors involved is not necessary for us to function, so we generally just do our best.

In this spirit, I will do my best to summarise, in a couple of pages, what could be the causes of our mind being currently so overloaded. We will start with the most contemporary elements and gradually move on to the timeless ones.

Generational Factors

We have already mentioned the proliferation of possibilities and categories: apps, options, products, packages, and so on seem to be multiplying at an exponential rate. Additionally, there is a growing concern with how we perceive our own image and that of others, how we *think* we are perceived by the world at large, and how we are encouraged to assert identities categorically using dramatic statements, visual means, and all sorts of numbers and badges. Add to that a culture of performance, the myth of autonomy, and the lure of multitasking: certainly a part of our neuronal fatigue, back-burner anxiety, and spiritual unavailability is linked to elements that are fairly new in our history as a species.

The Achiever's Dream (and Nightmare)

Socially, we admire people who do a lot. And why wouldn't we? Greatness is not just in *being*. This idea, by the way, is not solely Western. In Mahayana Buddhism, while we do value solitary retreat and emphasise the need to renounce harmful pursuits, we are also wary about a so-called "static nirvana," or any kind of elevated ivory tower in which one would refrain from any involvement whatsoever with the world at large. There are long lists of abilities that the buddhas and high-level bodhisattvas acquire, and these lists do serve to inspire. Additionally, in Tibetan Buddhist communities, wondrous da Vinci-like polymaths such as Mipham Rinpoche, Jamgön Kongtrul Lodrö Thayé, and Thangtong Gyalpo are greatly revered—even more so for their spiritual qualities, admittedly, but their massive undertakings in areas as diverse as art, medicine, diplomacy, and civil engineering certainly are motivational.

Of course, their endeavours were not purely worldly; their actions were carried out from a spiritual point of view and motivated by a tremendous compassion for all living beings, not by self-cherishing.

(In fact, to the extent that one's egotistic clinging diminishes, one's capacity for compassionate action increases.) In any event, there is no problem with rejoicing in meaningful projects. There is, indeed, beauty in having a vision and making things happen. The problem arises when there is a widespread glamorisation of busyness. In some professional circles, much respect is given to unending, break-less workdays and weeks, even when it is clear that this is detrimental to one's health. In some circles, contemplation is actually considered idle (though perhaps this isn't said aloud). Thankfully, more people are starting to discover that meditation is one of the best ways we can spend our time and one of the best things we can do for both ourselves and others. Still, for many of us, at first the notion seems counter-intuitive.

Novelty Bias and Addiction to Complexity

Have you ever heard that potato chips trigger an addictive reaction in our brain? Whether it's the crispiness, the salt, or the carbohydrates, few people feel content after a tiny handful! Sometimes it's like that: new bits of information create a feedback loop in our brain. Our mind races, it's gratifying to feel like we are doing *something*, and it is quite pleasurable until we find ourselves exhausted—and then, much like after we've eaten a whole bag of chips, we suddenly shy away from complexity altogether.

Funny comparisons aside, "simple" often feels shallow, too easy, and unsophisticated. This is connected to the lure of constant "progress" deeply ingrained in the dominant, modern narrative, which suggests that more is always better. This bias poses a problem for people interested in spirituality: our inability to relax our conceptual hang-ups prevents us from fully experiencing things, and it may lead us to constantly seek other, "higher" teachings. But the core legacy of the great spiritual guides of this world is both profound and simple. We may not always fully grasp it, but we could!

The Nature of Samsara

This is a profound point that will be explored in more detail further down the road, but a basic understanding of some Buddhist notions can be helpful at this stage. According to Buddhism, samsara and nirvana are not geographical locations but states of being, or more precisely, states of mind. "Samsara" inevitably implies suffering—including its most subtle and latent forms—while "nirvana" refers to the state beyond suffering, a truly unconditional, selfless, and lasting happiness. If we have doubts about the possibility of such spiritual realisation, it may be due to a misunderstanding of what it means. By studying the lives of the masters, we may find that this realisation has indeed been attained again and again over generations by devoted meditators.[19] Nowadays, some people claim to teach a so-called "secular Buddhism" that sometimes involves materialistic ideas and a lack of actual spirituality. For now, let us just say that one of the important elements of Buddhism is the belief in enlightenment and the trust that there are undeceiving sublime beings that can show us the path to enlightenment.

Now, according to Buddhist teachings, our suffering—including anguish, mental stress, lack of clarity, guilt, self-contempt, egoism, obsession, hatred, jealousy, arrogance, agitation, and other emotional problems—is rooted in ignorance. In this context, "ignorance" does not refer to a lack of intellectual knowledge about geography, history, or any suchlike topic; rather, it is a confusion about the nature of things—the nature of our mind, the nature of the world, and so on. For example, ignorance is at work when we look at or think of outer phenomena and believe them to be permanent, independent, indivisible, constricted, when in reality they are impermanent, interdependent, divisible, and open.

Certainly, no one walks around thinking in these very terms—"I believe that every phenomenon I come into contact with is independent, autonomous, permanent, and endowed with an inherent, lasting existence"—but our emotional reactions to events are definitely based on such erroneous, deep-seated beliefs and habits. Put another way: our experience of the world seems objective, while it is, in fact, subjective. As the Kagyu teacher, the Third Jamgon Kongtrul Rinpoche, summed it up: "Samsara actually means 'clinging'—it means deludedly clinging to whatever appears as though it were an independent existent."[20]

We ceaselessly grasp at objects of all sorts as if they are static and inherently real; but while they are not entirely *non-existent*, there is a gap between the true nature of things and the way we think they exist. So, Buddhism is not nihilism; in fact it considers that nihilism is an extreme, deluded, and harmful outlook. What Buddhism says is that our view is currently askew.

We will return to this concept, but the immediate take-away is that even though it seems like a contemporary problem, at its most fundamental level, our current overload is directly linked to the very nature of samsara.

That being said, Buddhist teachings do acknowledge that some things are getting worse globally. In fact, it is often said that we now live in a decadent era, "the age of fivefold degeneration." There is the degeneration of our lifespan: even though we seem to be living longer, time feels compressed, there are more distractions, and more things threaten our health. There is also a degeneration that relates to our emotions: mental toxins are said to increase. Additionally, there is the degradation of beings' make-up, which makes it difficult to help them. There is also the degeneration of outer circumstances, with the arising of wars, famines, and so on. And the fifth aspect of this fivefold reference has to do with deluded beliefs, which rapidly spread.

Such masters as Guru Rinpoche (Padmasambhava) foretold many of the problems the world faces today with chilling accuracy: environmental disasters, epidemics, the increase of toxicity in foods, polarisation, radicalisation, waves of nihilism, and so forth.[21] Thus, many problems do increase, and it is important to remain lucid. It is not only environmental activists who sound the alarm; some spiritual seekers also raise flags.[22] But if anything, contemplating the state of the world—if we do it with the proper attitude and if we use the tools that we will explore in this book—can fuel our compassion, our joyful determination, and our desire to extract the essence of our precious human life.

Not only is alienation *not* a new thing, but it may also be increasing. However, this does not mean that there is no hope.[23] Also, the fact that something feels more present at some point in time doesn't mean that it is exclusively attributable to current, outer circumstances. It bears repeating: although it seems like a modern issue, when we examine it closely and look for its roots, we find that our current overload is directly linked to the very nature of samsara. This distinction is important because it sets this book apart from many self-help books that focus on stress, productivity, and similar topics.

Part of this samsaric process goes like this: In an attempt to preserve our identity and keep our bearings, we label *everything*. These labels can be useful at times, but we end up taking them too seriously and literally, which limits our view. We place layers and layers of concepts between ourselves and the world, as if the objects of our experience were totally separated from some kind of experiencer that exists "on its own side." As a result, we become numb, cloudy, and judgemental. How can things be workable if we compulsively crystallise them?

Regardless of whether agitation and sorrow are timeless or recent, prevalent or latent, subjective or objective, the central idea is this: we can deal more effectively with all problems if we heal our relationship with our own mind, thoughts, emotions, beliefs, and habits.

I am convinced that the way to do so lies not in purely intellectual pursuits, but in the actual practice of meditation. Then—from a place of clarity, simplicity, and tenderness—meaningful action can arise naturally.

As the Nyingma meditation master, Orgyen Chowang, writes:

> So long as we are addicted to external conditions, when we engage with the world we [may] feel good, but when we try to rest without external stimuli we can be lost, anxious, and confused. We do not know how to remain in connection with who we really are. This is why we compulsively engage in so many activities, one after another. With meditation, we break through our addictive habits. Then we can remain in touch with our true nature very comfortably, and we can engage as we need to engage, in a very healthy way.[24]

Something to Aspire To

Trained swimmers have wonderful technique. They don't seem to go against the water; instead they rely on it, or use it, with a grace, a certain freedom, and an efficiency of motion that can only come with experience. By comparison, I am often reduced to some laborious variant on the doggy paddle. Laugh all you want, but it gets me from point A to point B (eventually).

All jokes aside, the dog paddle has been taught in the army when a silent stroke is needed,[25] so there must be a way to do it that doesn't involve depleting all of your precious calories at an alarming rate. Nevertheless, my variant on the doggy paddle is a good metaphor for our time in samsara: we alternate between frenzy and exhaustion.

> He had been a man among men and he had been bustling about like all of them, hustling through the crush, sometimes softly, sometimes fiercely, without knowing where he was going.[26]

This is how the Belgian writer Georges Simenon describes one of his characters. We can't help but feel a kinship with the busy and weary protagonist.

By comparison, the great Nyingma master Longchen Rabjam writes:

> What a relief it is for the burdened man who has long walked through the world of suffering to lay down his heavy and useless load.[27]

This echoes the fundamental teachings of the Buddha on the four noble truths (a more accurate translation of which could be "the four truths of the noble ones," since these truths, once fully realized, lead one to a state of nobility): the truth of suffering, the truth of the cause of suffering, the truth of the cessation of suffering, and the truth of the path that leads to cessation.

Once we have acknowledged the problem, we identify its causes. The third truth then follows logically: if we uproot the causes, the effect will naturally cease. In teachings that could be considered part of the "causal vehicles" of Buddhism, the attainment of cessation also has a cause, relatively speaking.[28] Thus, we follow the path that leads either to the cessation of subjective suffering and turmoil or to full enlightenment, according to our understanding, motivation, and capacity.

Every now and then along the path, we can rekindle our motivation by asking ourselves what our life would be like if we possessed boundless clarity, the ability to discern perfectly, and the capacity to love unconditionally. Please take some time to think about this. For example, how many times have we found ourselves wanting to help others but felt powerless due to confusion and not knowing what to do? What would our experience of the world be like if we had a flawless mix of genuine wisdom, tenderness, and fearlessness?

There is, however, a risk in listing our many problems and then hoping for some form of panacea or deliverance—particularly when we turn meditation into yet another project, with an "achiever" mentality. In *Cutting Through Spiritual Materialism*, Chögyam Trungpa Rinpoche warns us:

> We have many expectations, especially if we seek a spiritual path and involve ourselves with spiritual materialism. We have the expectation that spirituality will bring us happiness and comfort, wisdom and salvation. This literal, egocentric way of regarding spirituality must be turned upside down.[29]

If we get too hung up on expectations, we constantly struggle, and we start to live in the future. As Trungpa Rinpoche points out, "one's whole practice should be based on the relationship between you and nowness."[30]

Even if we keep this warning in mind and learn to let go and open up, we may still occasionally need a healthy dose of inspiration. At some point, love and compassion will primarily motivate us, and practice will hopefully become more and more selfless, perhaps even effortless. But for now, it is legitimate to envision something to which we can aspire. In time, we will let go of our expectations, loosen our conceptual grasping, and dissolve our tendency to materialise our experience. For now, a genuine desire to find more clarity and freedom can provide us with fuel. In this way, yearning and concepts can temporarily be used on the path to non-conceptual wisdom—a profound, fully open wisdom that does not rely on discursiveness and goes beyond mental grasping. As the masters tell us, we can go from negative to positive, then from positive to perfect. Going straight from negative to perfect is extremely hard, so for beginning practitioners especially, it is worthwhile to use positive phenomena and feelings as sources of inspiration to persevere on the path.

Thus, again and again, reflect on how precious this human life is. Contemplate death, consider all the time you've been wasting in futile agitation, unwholesome emotions, and egotistical cravings—and make a decision.

— III —

Tranquillity

A FRIEND OF YOURS MAY say something like: "I don't mind washing the dishes; it's my meditation." Highly experienced meditators can arrive at a point where there is no distinction between meditation and post-meditation—between sitting practice and going about their daily life. However, beginners like us should remember that we can hardly call it "meditation" if there is no actual awareness. While it is certainly great to approach daily chores with a positive mindset, what your friend means is that washing the dishes brings her some kind of relaxation, perhaps an opportunity to daydream and let go of the day's physical and mental stress. That is healthy, but it is not exactly meditation.

Or maybe your friend mentions a hobby, like playing golf or painting, as her own form of meditation. But while just about any path—from martial arts to gardening—if pursued wholeheartedly, can bring about some self-discovery, generally speaking we need to practice actual meditation if we want to reap the benefits of meditation.

So what is meditation then?

Since we talk about overload in this book, we could note the irony: in English, the suffix *–ation* often suggests an action. Meditation could then turn into yet another thing we have to *do*, another project, especially if we like to keep busy and grasp at tangible goals. However, while meditation can require and develop vigour, and while most meditation techniques involve "doing something" (insofar as they emphasise a method of some sort), our approach in this book is aimed at keeping it simple and genuine. That is, extraordinarily ordinary, alive, and wholesome, instead of materialistic, stressful, or overly conceptual.

I find that the Tibetan etymology is more explicative. One of the words used in Tibetan to talk about meditation is *gom*, which means "to familiarise oneself." With what, you might ask? It could be with an understanding, such as the truth of impermanence, or with a state, quality, or natural ability of the mind that we need or wish to cultivate: tranquillity, clarity, compassion, openness, joy, wisdom, and so on. Eventually, one familiarises oneself with, and rests in, the true nature of enlightenment.

Of course, there are countless types of meditation. For example, we sometimes read about conceptual and non-conceptual meditation. But the gateway to those types of meditation is calmness: for genuine insight, loving-kindness, and enlightened qualities to unfold, first we need to quiet the mind.[31]

This chapter surveys the theoretical information one is likely to need in the Tibetan Buddhist tradition, interspersed with seven guided meditations. The next few pages provide some nuance and warnings to clear up common misconceptions. They also include some general advice on the place and time, posture, and preparation for meditation, according to traditional sources. However, feel free to go straight to the first meditation (under "Awareness of the Breath") or to jump back and forth between sections as needed. Additionally, the practical key points for a basic "calm abiding" session are summarised at the very end of the chapter.

General Considerations on Mindfulness

Nowadays, most people have heard of "mindfulness" in one context or another. Since this term is often being used in very confusing and vague ways, I will try to clarify some misconceptions surrounding it.

Mipham Rinpoche, a celebrated Tibetan polymath from the Nyingma school, gives this definition:

> Mindfulness is not to forget a familiar object. Its function is to prevent distraction.[32]

In general, when we practice mindfulness meditation, we train our *attention* by continuously bringing it back to a chosen object. Although there are "objectless" meditations that also involve mindfulness, we usually start from the ground up: there is an object (such as our breathing) to which we turn our attention, and whenever our mind wanders, we gently bring our attention back to it. Over time, we start to notice the effect of being either too tense or too loose, and as we find a balance, the mind settles. As we gain more experience with this practice, we start to recognise distractions for what they are, which, in turn, paves the way for deeper insight. That's the general framework.

Now, our mind staying with its chosen object involves *attention*, whilst our mind's capacity to notice that it is wandering off is called *vigilance*, or alertness. Some people use the terms "mindfulness" and "awareness." The great Kagyu master, Traleg Kyabgon, explains the difference between the two:

> Mindfulness (Skt. *smrti*; Tib. *dran pa*) and awareness (Skt. *jneya*; Tib. *shes bzhin*) are distinct but related features of the mind. Mindfulness is something we apply more or less deliberately in order to become more cognizant, while awareness is a gentle way of simply being present. The meditation literature describes mindfulness as the opposite of forgetfulness. [...] Awareness, on

> the other hand, according to the *Abhidharmasamuccaya*, is a state of mental and physical pliability that gradually develops as we remove mental sluggishness and clear away all obscurations, drawing the mind toward a state of integration. [...] The basic difference between mindfulness and awareness is simply that the former is deliberate and the latter spontaneous. According to Buddhism, being aware is not something we habitually tend toward; it is something we have to learn through meditation.[33]

Both mindfulness (or attention) and awareness (or vigilance) work and develop together. Strictly speaking, mindfulness alone is not sufficient, at least if one is aiming for full awakening in the Buddhist sense. However, we typically start by deliberately training our attention.

It is important to also note that all schools of Buddhism practice two types of meditation: *shamatha* and *vipashyana*. These Sanskrit terms can be translated as "calm abiding" or "tranquillity" meditation, and "insight" or "clear seeing" meditation. Although the different Buddhist schools have different views and methods of training, they consistently refer to these two types of meditation. In this chapter, we focus on tranquillity; insight will be explored in chapter 6. Although both types of meditation involve attention and vigilance, in the present chapter we will mainly look at training our attention to foster tranquillity, which will, in turn, prepare the ground for insight.

Further Clarifications on "Mindfulness"

Now that we have established a framework to understand what mindfulness means, we can dig a little deeper. The term is so polysemous that it is well worth taking the time to explore its meanings and importance.

In tranquillity meditation, mindfulness helps cultivate and maintain stillness of mind. However, the term "mindfulness" is sometimes also used to refer to discipline, meaning "not forgetting what should be adopted and not forgetting what should be abandoned." Etymologically, the Sanskrit term *smriti*, commonly translated as "mindfulness," connotes memory or recollection. Simply thinking of the Buddha or your teacher as you go about your daily affairs, or bringing loving-kindness to mind as you walk to avoid crushing insects on the ground, is a form of mindfulness.

Interestingly, in the Abhidharma[34] teachings, mindfulness is classified among the "five mental functions allowing discernment." While this may not mean much to some of us, it highlights that the capacity to remember the quality of an object is something we all possess. It's not something we need to import from another source, like installing software on our computer. This is extremely important and contributes to a sense of confidence and dignity: mindfulness is a natural ability of the mind. And to some extent, we all make use of that capacity; but the question is, what are we mindful of?

The four foundations of mindfulness—mindfulness of the body, mindfulness of feelings, mindfulness of the mind, and mindfulness of the objects of the mind—are essential contemplations in Buddhist studies. These can be found in the Pali Canon (the early Buddhist sutras attributed directly to the Buddha), and they permeate countless texts and teachings. Whatever form it takes, mindfulness is a fundamental practice at every stage of the path and in all vehicles of Buddhism.

Some people may claim that they can skip mindfulness and focus on "higher" meditations. Others may believe that mindfulness is a defining characteristic of the Theravada tradition, and not as relevant in Indo-Himalayan forms of Buddhism. However, the accomplished adepts of tantric Buddhism also value these teachings.

For example, Nyoshul Khen Rinpoche, a consummate Nyingma master of the second half of the twentieth century, wrote:

> Mindfulness is the root of the Dharma,
> Mindfulness is the path's main practice,
> Mindfulness is a fortress for the mind,
> (...)
>
> Lacking mindfulness, we're overcome by negative forces.
> Lacking mindfulness, we're beset by laziness.
> Lacking mindfulness, we commit every wrong.
> Lacking mindfulness, we fail to accomplish our aims.[35]

So we should take mindfulness seriously and find joy in practicing it.

Depending on the context, the word "mindfulness" can refer to different things: awareness of one's commitments, remembrance of the teachings, antidotes to laziness, and so forth. It can also refer to being aware of our behaviour and of what's going on in our mind (though in that particular case it is more akin to vigilance), and as such it relates to wakefulness. However, to simplify, in this book we will mostly equate mindfulness with attention.

In any case, it's clear that what is commonly referred to as "mindfulness" in popular culture is just one aspect of our practice, and that there is more to meditation than just learning to focus one's attention. In Buddhism, the topic of mindfulness is a rich subject that can help us understand the meaning of phrases such as "meditative equipoise," "abiding in evenness," and "boundless openness." But it all starts with the fundamentals.

These fundamentals are about being present and not judging. It's about paying attention, but in a thoroughly non-aggressive way.

Eventually, mindfulness teaches us to see things as they are, without being distorted by our compulsive thoughts, disturbing emotions, and habitual tendencies, which often go unnoticed.

For example, in this chapter, we will explore meditating on the breath. Cultivating mindfulness of the breath (or of the body, for that matter) does not mean that we deliberately block all the other foundations of mindfulness—that of feelings, the mind, and the objects of the mind. It simply means that we use the breath as an anchor. Buddhist meditation teaches us to let go of all fixations, but we do need an aid: the breath. While advanced and objectless meditations are wonderful, it is helpful for beginners to train with an object; otherwise, it is hard to notice when we are distracted. In this exercise, we pay attention to our in-breath and out-breath without forcing anything. When thoughts, memories, or fantasies come up—and they will—we acknowledge them and return to the breath. It's simple, but we need this training, for we often are desperately mindless. The exercise will also help us improve our concentration and our capacity to notice what typically goes unnoticed. While our thoughts may seem to increase at first, meditation on the breath will help us appease the ceaseless mental chatter.

It is concerning that so many people nowadays approach mindfulness with a materialistic, if not downright nihilistic, perspective. Materialistic, in the sense that one uses meditation as a mere tool to become a superficially more efficient person while ultimately reaffirming one's ego; nihilistic, in the sense that one doesn't believe in immaterial wisdom. Misunderstood, mainstream "mindfulness" can serve to solidify our relationship with phenomena. When we cultivate a type of attention that is overly tight, we overlook the fact that—at least from a Buddhist perspective—concentration alone does not suffice and should be accompanied by wisdom and openness. While it is important to learn to observe, feel, and listen, at some point we also have to learn to dissolve dualism, or the deeply ingrained belief that subject and object are truly separate, a delusion that perpetuates suffering.

In other words, learning to be in the here and now is wonderful—but if we are too rigid in the way we observe, and if we lack openness, we can be "present" when peeling potatoes or mending a shirt, yet turn it into some *thing* that is strangely cerebral, preventing us from simply and joyfully blending with our experience. Chögyam Trungpa Rinpoche also warned us against becoming too introverted, constantly observing ourselves, to the detriment of a direct and supple relationship with the world. Regardless, training in mindfulness can be highly beneficial, especially when we approach it with a tender heart and an open mind.

Our busy, ordinary mind constantly races with thoughts: "and then after this, and then after that, and if this, then that . . ." As a human being, you owe it to yourself to learn to actually and wholly experience things. Be entirely present with whatever you do, but do so in a relaxed manner, allowing yourself to view phenomena as they are in the moment without feeling the need to constantly label them. This element of non-judgement is essential: if you stay mindful and aware, thoughts, memories, concerns, and ideas will still surface, and occasionally some of them will be useful, but you won't be automatically and blindly carried away by them.

Mindfulness is not about being rigid and drab, nor is it *solely* about being in the present moment; it is about finding some fundamental freedom. It is the first step to acknowledging, claiming, and celebrating our birthright—a boundless source of happiness, love, and healing energy to be discovered within.

The Place and the Time

It is often said that we can meditate anywhere, such as on the bus. This is true: from Kyoto to Los Angeles, and from the boreal forests to the urban centres, we can always reconnect with a sense of dignity, calmness, and loving-kindness. Throughout this book, we will hopefully be inspired to bring some openness to this world, and not just hang out forever on our meditation cushion. However, formal practice is essential, and for beginners like us, the Buddhist traditions advise finding a proper place for our meditation sessions.

We are still very much affected by outer circumstances, and so a peaceful place will help develop tranquillity and clarity within ourselves. Meditation in nature or group practice at a centre can be wonderful, but ideally, we also have a designated place inside our own home. It is a gentle way to commit—we can't blame the weather!—and to invite positive energies into our daily life.

Ideally, your meditation space should be removed from noise—a dedicated room is great. It doesn't have to be big, but it should feel intimate. If you live in an open space or share a small apartment, you can choose a quiet area and delimit it with a screen or some kind of partition that is suitable and doesn't encroach on a communal area. A window can be a plus, not as a distraction, but for natural light and fresh air. Keep the space simple, clean, and inspiring, maintaining a sense of respect for it.

Having a sacred space in the home can be incredibly beneficial. If you feel comfortable, you can discuss this with your roommates or family members, letting them know they are welcome to use it if they feel the need. Zen master Thich Nhat Hanh writes about the benefits of having a "breathing room":

> We have a room for everything—eating, sleeping, watching TV—but we have no room for mindfulness. I recommend that we set up a small room in our homes and call it a "breathing room," where we can be alone and practice just breathing and smiling, at least in difficult moments. [...] [For example], when a child is about to be shouted at, she can take refuge in that room. Neither the father nor the mother can shout at her anymore. She is safe within the grounds of the Embassy. Parents sometimes will need to take refuge in that room, also, to sit down, breathe, smile, and restore themselves. Therefore, that room is for the benefit of the whole family.[36]

A meditation room should be an inspiring and quiet place with few distractions, one that you won't associate with naps, but where you can sit straight, breathe, and focus. Add a meditation cushion or bench, or a chair, and perhaps some flowers. Buddhists typically have an altar, with representations of the Triple Gems (Buddha, Dharma, and Sangha) or of the body, speech, and mind of the Buddha. But contrary to what is often thought in the West, Buddhism is not about idolatry. As Thich Nhat Hanh beautifully says:

> [P]lacing a statue of the Buddha on the altar is a reminder of our own capacity to be mindful, awake, loving, and accepting. Creating and maintaining a home altar is a way to pay respect to the world around us, our ancestors, and the natural world, and to remind us that whatever we love and respect is also within us.[37]

Keep it simple and sincere. Don't get lost in fantasies of having a big, golden shrine room; what matters is your receptiveness and your willingness to actually practice.

Regarding the time, any time will do, but regularity is more important than intensity. It is much better to start with as little as ten minutes a day, every day, and gradually increase it, rather than trying to cram in two hours straight once in a while. Of course, it is great if you can do longer sessions every day—an hour or more—but if you are just starting, it is good to end your sessions feeling inspired rather than fed up. As with any apprenticeship, meditation may involve some challenges at the beginning, but if you maintain good motivation, most difficulties quickly dissolve.

Routine also helps. You can set a fixed time—for example, in the morning, or in the evening, or both if you like to "bookend" your day. Early morning sessions are great: your mind is fresh, the outer environment is a little quieter, and you can start your day with positive energy. But choose whatever time works best for you.

Relaxing the Body

Many of us see contradictions where none exist. For example, we often think that there is a fixed opposition between the intellectual and the physical.[38] However, Buddhism advises that the mind and the body should work together instead of against each other.

Sure enough, the Buddha said:

> Mind is the main factor and forerunner of all actions.[39]

This is a fundamental teaching in Buddhism: a peaceful and wise mind leads to peaceful and wise actions; and we can always work with the mind, regardless of external circumstances. We will come back to this. But when we start to learn to meditate, it is worthwhile to learn to relax the body. There is some interdependence at play here: just as a healthy mind promotes a healthy body, a relaxed body helps to foster a relaxed mind.

Below, we will explore three things we can do to relax the body. As we do so, let's keep in mind that our goal here is not just to "feel good," but to actually foster a wholesome and regular meditation practice.

Adopt a Healthy Lifestyle

We already know that daily habits have a significant effect on our mindset. While details can be found elsewhere, it's important to remember that there is a connection between the way we typically spend our days and nights and the quality of our meditation. For example, if we nurture counterproductive emotions such as hatred between sessions, we might find it harder to settle our mind as we sit down to meditate.

Aim for a healthy lifestyle that promotes relaxation, joy, gratitude, empathy, and other positive emotions. Make sure you get enough sleep—but not too much—and dedicate time to truly meaningful activities. Also, choose your friends wisely. This advice goes beyond common sense; it deeply impacts one's spiritual path. As the great fourteenth-century Kadampa master, Tokme Zangpo, wrote in *The Thirty-Seven Practices of All the Bodhisattvas*:

> The practice of all the bodhisattvas is to avoid destructive friends,
> In whose company the three poisons of the mind grow stronger,
> And we engage less and less in study, reflection and meditation,
> So that love and compassion fade away until they are no more.[40]

Additionally, one of the most overlooked aspects of our lives when it comes to meditation and clarity of mind is what and how we eat. Although elation and dullness are mostly experienced by the mind, the way we fuel our body does have an impact, especially for beginners. Over the upcoming weeks, if you have never done so, pay attention to how your eating habits affect your energy level, and consequently, your capacity for tranquillity and insight.

You might notice that some types of food don't suit you all that well. For example, too much caffeine tends to make one nervous; alcohol, while it may relax the muscles if taken in small amounts, is likely to have a depressant effect. Good fats can be a lasting source of fuel, but may have the opposite effect if combined with sugar. Perhaps too much sugar gives you a high you can barely handle, followed by a crash. Eating too fast makes one uncomfortable; eating too much makes one sleepy.

So it's not just about what we eat, but also how we eat, and how much. As the great second-century Indian Buddhist master, Nagarjuna, says in his *Letter to a Friend*:

> Take food as medicine, in the right amount,
> Without attachment, without hatefulness:
> Don't eat for vanity, for pride or ego's sake,
> Eat only for your body's sustenance.[41]

There are traditional sources that discuss food for spiritual practitioners,[42] but one could also rely on contemporary findings, practice moderation, and follow some basic yet effective advice, such as favouring fresh foods and varying the colours. This approach allows for a wider array of vitamins and nutrients and has the added benefit of incorporating more vegetables to one's diet.

In any case, feeding ourselves should not be a source of stress; instead, we should aim for a flexible, simple, and healthy relationship with food.

Often, we take these things for granted.

Enjoy Mindful Movement, Stretching, or Massage

While too much physical exertion can make us tense, too little can make us apathetic. Try to incorporate mindful movements throughout the day, such as simple stretching or mobility exercises. These activities will help you feel alive and refreshed. We all know sports can bring many benefits, but simply walking can also do wonders to relieve tension. If your mobility is limited, try to get closer to trees or plants, or find a window where you can see the open sky.

If you've been tensing up for months and years, consider making an appointment with a reliable physical therapist. You could also learn simple self-massage techniques, perhaps using a foam roller or a lacrosse ball. Regardless of whether you choose to stretch or self-massage, be cautious: stay mindful and keep it safe. The idea is not to perform acrobatics but simply to relax.

Do Some Simple Breathing Exercises

While the previous two ways of fostering a relaxed body—a healthy lifestyle and joyful movement—help you relax more generally, there are specific steps you can take as you sit down to meditate. Turn off distractions and notifications, and find a comfortable sitting position. We will get to the proper meditation posture in a moment, but for now, just focus on relaxing.

Traditional teachings include specific breathing exercises that help purify the body's channels and energies. These exercises are best learned from a qualified teacher. Some people attempt intense pranayama exercises—or yogic breathing techniques—without proper preparation or reliable instructions, or even with a materialistic intention or a sports-like performance mindset, which I really don't recommend. However, there are simple breathing exercises that you can do safely to help you relax.

For example, imagine that as you breathe out, all your physical tensions are melting away. As you mindfully inhale through the nose, breathe in light, simplicity, confidence, and inspiration. Don't force it—breathe naturally. When you exhale, release all your negativity, doubts, and counterproductive emotions, letting go of any mental tightness. If you feel tension in a particular area of your body, visualise the cycle of your breath gently soothing it. You can practice this for a minute or two at the beginning of your session.

In the Buddhist tradition, there are many meditation exercises for health and well-being.[43] For now, as you sit down to meditate, simply let go of tensions in whatever way feels natural to you.

The Posture

The physical, earthy aspect of meditation is often overlooked, but it is essential to befriend your body and learn to relax. In formal meditation, a good posture is particularly important. While it shouldn't become an obsession, your posture should ideally have both resilience and suppleness. You shouldn't move at every small discomfort, but you can adjust your position if needed during the session.

In other words, it's good to build up endurance without turning the practice into asceticism; we should remain alert but comfortable. Additionally, your posture should convey dignity—not pride, but a quiet strength and self-respect, coupled with humility and openness.

You may read elsewhere about the classic "seven-point posture:" (1) legs crossed, (2) hands resting in the lap, right palm on top of the left, facing up,[44] (3) spine straight, (4) shoulders spread and relaxed, (5) chin slightly lowered, (6) tip of the tongue touching the palate, and (7) eyes gazing past the tip of the nose.[45]

Feel free to experiment with your meditation posture. Regardless of the specifics, there are three key elements to remember, as highlighted by Will Johnson in his book *The Posture of Meditation*: alignment, relaxation, and resilience. Keeping these three elements in mind during practice can help you maintain a proper and effective posture.

Most important is to keep the back straight—erect, not stiff. There should be verticality and stability while respecting the natural, slight curve of the lower back. This prevents the upper part of the spine from compensating and slouching forward. Imagine a sapling, a young tree reaching for light but remaining flexible. You can sway slightly from side to side a few times to sense and find your balance. The chest should not feel compressed, and the belly should be relaxed.[46]

If you are feeling stressed out or overworked, closing your eyes for a moment may help you settle down. However, in the Nyingma and Kagyu traditions, we also learn to meditate with our eyes open. Typically, we lower the gaze—a soft gaze—at a 45-degree angle, looking roughly six feet in front of us. If we feel lethargic, we can raise the gaze; if we feel agitated, we can lower it.

The Motivation

As they sit to meditate, Buddhists usually take refuge in the Triple Gems.[47] Practitioners of the Mahayana tradition also cultivate *bodhicitta*, which is the altruistic intention to fully awaken for the sake of all beings, or to bring all beings to enlightenment. We will revisit this concept later, but if you are just beginning, try to adopt a purposeful mindset as you start your session. For instance, you could acknowledge the tremendous amount of suffering and confusion in this world, and recognise that to do your part in cultivating true discernment and unconditional love, you first need to tame the monkey mind. Thus, even a simple calm abiding session can help you slowly open your heart and adopt a broader perspective.

If that sounds like too much for now, at least try to have a positive motivation. For example, instead of thinking, "I will increase my concentration to be more productive at work and thus bring in more money," you might think, "I will allow myself to relax in order to tread the path to genuine happiness; and I will slowly improve my clarity in order to make better decisions and cause less harm to myself and those around me."

Appreciate the opportunity you have to practice, and make a decision about what matters for the next few minutes. This will help you stay focused during the session.

Awareness of the Breath

As mentioned earlier, the four foundations of mindfulness form the basis of Buddhist meditation practice. The first foundation is mindfulness of the body, often beginning with the exercise of mindfulness of the breath. In a sense, this practice is incredibly simple. At some point, it may become effortless, and striving itself may become a hindrance; but initially, it requires patience and perseverance. If our old "doer" mentality kicks in ("Meditation feels too passive! I'd rather accomplish some-*thing*!"), we can motivate ourselves by remembering the benefits of the practice.

When we become more open, serene, and more aware of both our surroundings and our own body, it is easier to be resilient, strong, and stable. Strong, even when vulnerable. And when the inner fuss subsides, it leaves room—a boundless space—for creativity and positive energy to manifest.

As you move through this book, you will discover various aspects and benefits of mindfulness, along with different traditional exercises to cultivate it. Any phenomenon, sense faculty, or object can be used to practice mindfulness. For example, Buddhists often use an image of the Buddha, which is full of blessings. Here, we will use the breath. Mindfulness of the breath has been used for ages in many traditions. Choosing the breath as our object of focus has numerous benefits. For example, it is always available, regardless of who or where we are, and it is neutral, in the sense that it is unlikely to evoke attachment or any other strong emotion.

Exercise: Discovering Mindfulness

Staying mindful of the breath is both easier and harder than it seems. It is not a breathing exercise *per se*, as we don't try to control the breath. Instead, we simply pay attention and feel the breath.

Sit comfortably and keep your back straight. Respect the natural, slight curve of the lower back, but keep the rest of the upper body comfortably erect, with shoulders open. You can close your eyes for a few seconds, but then try to keep them open or half-closed if you can. Find the right balance between tension and relaxation: being too loose can increase sleepiness, and being too tight can increase agitation, so adapt as you go along. If you can, breathe through the nose.

Inhale . . .

Exhale . . .

Simply be aware of the air coming in and out, especially at the opening of the nostrils . . .

Inhale . . .

Exhale . . .

Feel how your abdomen and diaphragm move through a cycle . . .

Inhale . . .

Exhale . . .

Don't try to control it. Your breathing can be long and quiet or rough and shallow. Just observe. We spend our whole day—our whole life—judging and rationalising. Give your conceptual mind a much-needed rest. Here, not judging is the kind thing to do.

At some point, your mind will wander away. You will think about work, dinner, a message you have to write, or an advert you've seen. Simply come back to the breath.

Thich Nhat Hanh invites us to use these simple phrases if we need:

> I inhale, I know that I inhale . . .
> I exhale, I know that I exhale . . .

Keep going for a while.

There is nothing else to do for now: just relax and observe the breath.

Distractions can be subtle. If you think, "My, I'm getting good at this!" you're already straying from the very sensation of the air coming in through your nostrils. Whenever your mind wanders, gently escort it back. Don't judge yourself. If you catch yourself judging, just smile, acknowledge it, and escort the mind back to the sensation of the breath.

Obstacles and Solitude

The literature on *shamatha*—calm abiding or tranquillity meditation—is abundant. For example, you can learn about the nine stages in the development of shamatha, also called "the nine ways of resting the mind."[48] There are also discussions on the five faults or defects (laziness, forgetting the instructions, dullness and agitation, failure to apply the antidotes, and over-application of the antidotes) and the eight antidotes to these five obstacles. However, don't intellectualise too much; focus on familiarising yourself with the exercise we just did. Occasionally, refresh your session by tuning into your posture or rekindling your motivation, then return to the main object. Avoid constantly wandering, but don't be too uptight either. The point is to keep the mind focused, yet relaxed and fresh.

First-time meditators are often overwhelmed by how many thoughts they have: they are under the impression that thoughts suddenly proliferate when they meditate, that this is bad, and that they are "not made" for meditation. But in this situation, thoughts are generally not more numerous than they were; we are simply becoming more aware of them, and that in itself is an important first step. We are finally starting to befriend our mind. After all, creativity is a natural ability of the mind, and meditation is not about forcefully blocking thoughts or becoming numb.

To develop shamatha, it is often advised to secure the "three solitudes": solitude of body, solitude of speech, and solitude of mind. This typically involves going to a secluded place, remaining silent, and keeping the mind free of mental poisons such as obsessive desire, hatred, and greed, and not worrying too much about our usual preoccupations such as the hope for gain and praise and the fear of loss and blame.

But at the same time, though it definitely helps to have fewer activities, the practice also embraces thoughts, emotions, and difficulties of all sorts. If we think, "I am only really practicing when my mind is perfectly calm, clear, and happy," we misunderstand what it's about. The same applies to boredom, which is ironically fascinating: allowing ourselves to fully experience boredom is very much part of the path to joyous freedom. In fact, if we approach boredom with an open mind, we can learn so much from it. We can observe our habit of constantly trying to do something in an attempt to reify our existence.

As we will see in chapters 5 and 6, whatever arises can be part of the practice. There is no need to beat ourselves up when we face agitation, fogginess, or any other obstacle.

Exercise: Staying Focused

Concentration is typically developed in relation to an object. For example, we can visualise the Buddha sitting in the sky before us, try to remember the details of our chosen representation, and sustain these details as clearly as we can. It is then relatively easy to evaluate our level of focus based on how blurry or vivid the mental image is, while also relaxing and remembering that it is a visualisation, not a material object, so we do not focus too much on the eye consciousness. When visualising the Buddha, it is said to be beneficial to see him as utterly pure and resplendent; rather than having a usual body of gross flesh and bones, he is an enlightened figure made of golden light.

To improve our focus, we can also do the following exercise, which is a variation of the first one where the object of our attention was the breath. The main difference here is that we will count the cycles. While we will eventually let go of our obsession for quantifiable goals, counting the breath can serve as an effective anchor, especially if we feel agitated at the beginning of a session.

First, sit comfortably with your upper body erect, and adopt a positive motivation. Then, as you breathe in through your nose, count "one." As you breathe out, count "one." That completes one cycle. Next, as you breathe in again, count "two," and as you breathe out, count "two."

Decide whether to start with sequences of 5 or 10 cycles, and stick with that for the bulk of your session. Once you have gained some experience, move on to 20 breaths (or 21, as I usually recommend and as is often done traditionally). Don't force, control, or contrive your breathing; just observe and gently come back to it whenever your mind wanders. If you lose count, simply start over with "one."

At the end of your session, take a moment to fully relax, letting go of any reference points. Feel gratitude for having taken the time to befriend your mind, regardless of how you feel the session went.

Follow-up Exercise: Relaxed Focus

After some time working with the previous exercise, when you notice you can do several sequences in a row—for example, all the way to 21 cycles without losing count, with freshness and clarity but without agitation—you can stop counting. However, continue to maintain awareness of the breath. It's like learning how to write: children hold their pencils tightly, and as an adult we may need to pay more attention to our grip if our hand is sore or if we are very tired, but generally, we need to relax our grip to write properly.

So, without counting or commenting, simply rest your mind on the breath.

With time and experience, you can expand the scope of your awareness to include your environment, while still using your breath as an anchor. This means not focusing too tightly on your breath but letting it be a steady point of reference. You could then be riding the breath as smoothly and confidently as riding a friendly, tame, and healthy horse on an open plain. However, in the initial stages, keep your focus primarily on your breath. If you feel dullness or elation, you may find it helpful to return to counting your breaths as in the previous exercise.

Resting Versus Seeking

In English and French, the word "meditation" has different meanings, one of which is to *plan mentally*. This involves strong, deliberate thought processes—or cogitations. In Buddhism, although there are analytical or investigative meditations, the previous exercises focused on tranquillity meditation. In tranquillity meditation, we typically start with setting an altruistic motivation, and we might rekindle it occasionally, but during the core of the session, it is beneficial to let go of any particular ambition. The distinction between motivation and stiff intentionality may seem subtle, but experience helps us differentiate them. The main points of the previous exercises were to observe, and then to befriend our innate ability to be precise and relaxed. Excessive effort can become a hindrance.

A famous teaching illustrates this point. A zither player seeking advice on how to meditate went to see the Buddha. In the course of their discussion, the Buddha asked the musician how he tuned the strings of his instrument. The zither player replied, "I make sure they are not too loose and not too tight." Our approach to meditation, the Buddha said, should be like that: neither too loose nor too tight.

Generally speaking, rather than trying to force things, it is healthier to walk the spiritual path with simplicity, humility, and a sense of humour. The desire to find happiness and avoid suffering is human and legitimate. But when we cling too tightly to such dualistic categories as "happiness" versus "suffering," or "spiritual" versus "mundane," we risk meditating to seek altered states of consciousness or to become someone else, perhaps someone "spiritual" or someone more "successful." That is one of the many facets of spiritual materialism.

As we sit, we simply sit. It's straightforward and earthy. We establish a frank and open relationship with ourselves and our world. Aside from keeping a balanced posture and gently riding the breath, there's nothing we have to do in particular. There's no need to pretend. And when we catch ourselves pretending—I know it often happens to me!—we can just smile and return to the breath.

Four Essential Contemplations (I and II)

Tibetan Buddhists practice "the four thoughts that turn the mind away from samsara," or put another way, the four contemplations that turn the mind towards Dharma and sanity. These could also be called the four contemplations that steer one away from insanity and neuroses—away from the cycle of suffering and delusion. They are considered important preliminary practices in Tibetan Buddhism. Regardless of what we call them, they consist of meditations on 1) the difficulty of finding a precious human life endowed with freedoms and advantages, 2) the impermanence of life, 3) the defects of samsara, and 4) the interplay between causes and effects (which relate to karma). Serious practitioners should study these from the classic texts, such as *The Words of My Perfect Teacher* by Patrul Rinpoche (1808–1887), and deepen their understanding through repeated contemplations. An overview might prove useful here, as such meditations, while not considered shamatha exercises per se, can only help develop calm abiding, as well as all other spiritual skills and qualities. Indeed, when we keep the many concerns of this life in proper perspective, it becomes easier to stay focused, remain at ease, and let go of our inner chatter.[49]

In this chapter, we will work with the first two contemplations—this precious human life and impermanence. Karma will be explored in the next chapter, and the defects of samsara will be considered in chapters 4 and 5. While these meditations involve reflection, at some point, we leave the cognitive effort aside and simply rest. We merge with the feeling that has arisen from using reasoning and metaphor. Then we can go back and forth between analytical and contemplative meditations whenever the need arises.

Contemplation: The Extreme Rarity of a Precious Human Life

Sit in a stable and comfortable manner. Relax your body and mind. Focus on your breathing for a minute or two. Then slowly contemplate the following:

We often take this human life for granted, but there are many states of existence in which there is no opportunity to practice an authentic and complete spiritual path.

Some beings endure unimaginable suffering, trapped in hellish experiences, violent conflicts, or enslavement. Many endure scorching heat and intolerable cold, and are subjected to all kinds of harm, without any chance to stop, reflect, and see the light. Pause and contemplate this.

Countless beings experience constant hunger and thirst, both physically and mentally. Some are so utterly dissatisfied that they can never appreciate what they have—sometimes unable to even see it. Contemplate this for a moment.

We might think that house pets live comfortable lives, but such thinking is naïve. Animals that are not eaten or enslaved often live in a state of relative stupefaction, and cannot wake up one day and decide to cultivate spiritual qualities. For example, under exceptional circumstances, a dog might assist a blind person or perhaps even save a child from drowning, but this isn't really comparable to the scale at which a human being can consciously and eagerly do good—or harm, for that matter. Many animal species also live in constant fear.

In contrast, some beings live in god-like bodies and divine settings, seemingly enjoying tremendous ease and prosperity. But they may be so distracted by ceaseless pleasures that they never see the most profound truths or feel prompted to genuinely practice a spiritual path. When death inevitably comes, they experience indescribable terror and remorse.

Others live in bleak lands or in communities that condemn

spiritual life or at a time and place where no enlightened beings have taught. Many have incomplete faculties that hinder their capacity to study and practice.

Some others have deeply ingrained, extreme views—particularly tenacious and unwholesome concepts that prevent them from seeking, understanding, or practicing a healthy spiritual path. Some take refuge in hatred and violence, or are manipulated by deceitful or confused teachers.

Even among humans that look just like us, countless have harmful lifestyles or live in conditions that are unfavourable to Dharma practice. Most go through life at a dizzying speed, never really taking time for what truly matters, swinging between attachment and aversion, elation and depression. Months, years, and decades fritter away in a mix of ambitions and idleness, hope and fear.

This isn't about feeling contempt for beings caught up in those situations; it's about feeling disdainless compassion—simple, humane, heartfelt tenderness. The main idea is to recognise how incredibly fortunate we are. The sheer number of microscopic insects found in a cubic metre of soil is mind-boggling. Considering the whole world, having a precious human life filled with freedoms and advantages—with the conditions, capacities, and interest for spiritual practice—is absolutely astonishing. All things considered, it is much rarer and much more precious than winning the lottery.

Contemplate how marvellous that is, until you feel grateful beyond words. When you do, rest with that experience—let go of reasoning and metaphors for a moment, and just let it permeate you.

Contemplation: Impermanence (A)

Sit in an erect and comfortable position, and relax your mind for a while. Then contemplate the following:

Everything compounded is impermanent. In other words, anything that is made of parts and that relies on causes and conditions is transitory. This includes buildings, mountains, rivers, forests, fauna, seasons, weather conditions, governments, borders, bank accounts, emotions, discursive thoughts, relationships, the state of scientific knowledge, war and peace, and all social and material phenomena.

Things break, things get repaired, and eventually things lose their repairability. Parts of things, in turn, break up. At a subatomic level, there is ceaseless movement. Some phenomena seem to last, and as we live our lives, we naturally apply useful concepts and labels, but it is all relative. Everything is in flux.

When you see that everything changes, contemplate that for a moment.

At first, the notion of impermanence might seem a little fuzzy. We might get an inkling that things are more fluid than we usually assume. We can stay with this feeling for a moment, with a healthy sense of awe. As a component of wisdom that sees phenomena as they are, impermanence helps slowly hack away at our delusion and loosen our obsessive attachment. Releasing our grasping and dispelling ignorance are the way to true happiness.

Contemplation: Impermanence (B)

Sit straight and comfortably. Define your motivation—for example, reaffirm your intention to courageously tread the path to clarity, for yourself and the sake of others. Settle your mind by focusing on your breathing for a minute or two. Then, slowly contemplate the following:

With the gift of birth comes but one certainty: death. Despite our attempts to forget about death, and cherish our bodies, we are all dying. It is a process that simply cannot be stopped.

The greatest philosophers and logicians, the most devout religious practitioners, the most talented artists, the strongest athletes, and the richest kings and queens of the past have all died. Those of the present will die too, and so will those of the future. We can maintain a healthy lifestyle, have access to wonderful facilities, and perhaps gain a few extra years—but our bodies are impermanent. When our time comes, no matter how powerful, witty, or wealthy we are, we cannot fight, reason, or bribe our way out.

We may think we still have some time. But that is hope, not fact: countless people have died at a much younger age than we have currently reached, and many of these people were not so different from us. Every day, people die without planning to. There are accidents and sudden diseases. Even what we enjoy most can turn into a cause of death: sports, tasty food, or travel. People die in the middle of a phrase, during daily chores, or while engaging in their favourite activities. Some even die while making love.

Even if we are blessed with a long and healthy life, time can go so fast. As we age, we look back on our life and stand gaping: "Where did it all go? It feels like it was all just yesterday; I thought I had all the time in the world."

And so there are three certainties.

1. Death is inevitable.
2. Its timing is unpredictable.
3. At the time of death, the only thing that will matter will be our spiritual maturity—our capacity to remain loving, open, and confident, with some understanding of the mind.

Since this is the case, let us not waste time in idleness and egotistic patterns. Contemplate the three certainties until you feel moved. You may even feel horrible and anxious—but promise yourself that you will not stop there and that you will keep reading and practicing. The anguish will pass and transform into confident determination as you tread the path of peace and joy. There are indeed major upsides to impermanence. But for now, contemplate the three certainties until you feel a sense of urgency.

Contemplation: Impermanence (C)

It's natural to feel fear, and in one way or another it is often what motivates us to seek a spiritual path. But we should also be wary of our tendency to look for a cocoon, don armour to protect our ego, or shy away from harsh realities altogether. The purpose of this contemplation is not to deny the sense of urgency generated in the previous exercise, which is indeed important. Instead, it is to embrace the raw, rugged quality of life and to see the bigger picture. There is no spiritual Band-Aid here, yet we can learn to befriend our predicament.

Keep your back straight, relax, and slowly contemplate the following, taking the time to rejoice in the positive implications of impermanence.

When an object of attachment fades or breaks, it is easier to deal with it if we are familiar with impermanence. This doesn't mean that we can't feel sadness. Some situations will still feel cold and incisive, but we won't feel compelled to add a sense of injustice to our suffering.

More importantly, the impermanence of compounded phenomena makes the cessation of suffering possible. Our egotistic patterns, habitual delusions, compulsive behaviours, and the skewed views tying us to cycles of pain and dissatisfaction are not permanent.

Our state of mind, and thus our very perception and experience of the inner and outer world, can change completely throughout a single day. Think about how our state of mind could change over our lifetime with proper training and guidance.

Also, if impermanence and death bring value to our lives, it is even more important to recognise their inevitability. Whatever happens, we can be fully present, less inclined to resort to hypocrisy, defence mechanisms, or elaborate philosophical subterfuges. Our spiritual practice is about openness—and occasionally magic and poetry—but not escapism.

We simply cannot befriend life unless we befriend death. The inevitability of our passing can be like a loving mentor who constantly reminds us: "Don't lose your time in paranoid little scenarios and complicated, selfish schemes; learn to stay open and aware; learn to relax and cultivate love; in brief, tread the path of uniting wisdom and compassion." When we truly and properly befriend impermanence, we befriend ourselves, and we become more loving towards others.

Thus, remembering death can tremendously simplify our life and bring much joy to it.

Additional Notes on the Four Contemplations

As mentioned earlier, the "four thoughts" that turn the mind away from the cycle of suffering and delusion include contemplations on 1) the difficulty of finding a precious human life, 2) impermanence, 3) the defects of samsara, and 4) the interplay between causes and effects (which relate to karma). So far, we have explored the first two. We will delve into the other two later in the book.

These four topics are incredibly profound and helpful. We should let ourselves be inspired and nourished by these four companions, day after day. If we do, they will help us deal with our cognitive, emotional, spiritual, and even physical overload. As we discussed earlier, our experience of overload may seem like a contemporary problem, but it fundamentally relates to the very nature of samsara. In other words, the "too much" and the "can't handle" feelings we often experience are symptoms of an unenlightened lifestyle.

Contemplations on these four topics, combined with other exercises found in this book, will help develop a sense of renunciation.

"Renunciation" is one of the most commonly misunderstood concepts in Buddhism. Although some paths involve abstaining from contact with objects likely to arouse inner turmoil, and while it is sometimes worthwhile to keep our distance, many approaches to Dharma make it clear that it is not the experiences themselves we renounce, but our attachment to them and our distorted ways of viewing them. In other words, renunciation is not about forsaking joy but about letting go of our clinging and about recognising the poisonous quality of self-cherishing patterns.

To give a crude example, let me quote the classic *Lethal Weapon* action films, in which veteran detective Roger Murtaugh has a catchphrase: "I'm too old for this shit!" Funnily enough, that's one of the ways the four contemplations can make us feel about samsara. Our capacity to laugh and fill up with wonder has not run dry, not by any means, and we're never too old to enjoy time with children and animals and flowers and good books; what we're fed up with are self-delusions of all sorts. Of course, we may say to ourselves, "From now on, day and night, I will devote myself only to virtue," and then feel our determination wax and wane because old habits die hard. But that very instability, as well as the lure of a holier-than-thou attitude and the pitfalls of laziness, can all be part of the journey.

In any case, we need to give ourselves time to regularly explore the four topics with a fresh and open mind. Otherwise, we risk misunderstanding and mixing these teachings with our own neuroses or with nihilist or eternalist concepts.[50] If we feel contempt for other types of beings because they don't share our spiritual values or through some subtle form of prejudice because Buddhism is not prevalent in this or that country, we have misused the teachings on the precious human life. If we find ourselves being constantly grim when talking with friends or thinking, "This is all purposeless, we're all going to die anyway," we likely have misunderstood the meaning of impermanence.

A surprising amount of joy can result from the four contemplations that turn the mind away from an ego-driven life: they keep things in perspective, bring simplicity to our existence by clarifying what truly matters, help us feel a more intimate connection with fellow living beings, and buoy us up on the path.

Calm Abiding Meditation in Brief

- Preliminaries: In a quiet environment, sit comfortably but keep your back straight and your eyes preferably open to stay alert. Take a few deep breaths, relax your body, feel grateful for the opportunity to practice, and decide to let go of your worldly preoccupations, at least for the duration of the session. Then reaffirm your motivation. At this point, Buddhists take refuge and recite a prayer to cultivate bodhicitta, thus connecting with a vast, long-term goal.
- The gist of it: Start paying attention to your breath, especially to the feeling of air gently coming in and out through your nose. Just observe, without judging. Don't force your attention too much—not too loose, not too tight—just remain aware of your breathing.
- Optional: You can count the cycles of your breath (a cycle being defined as an inhalation and an exhalation), for example in sequences of 21 cycles, gently starting back at "one" when you lose count.
- Important: Don't deliberately control your breathing; let it come naturally and ride it ever so gently. When you catch yourself wandering off or mentally commenting,

simply acknowledge it and kindly escort your mind back to the breathing.

- Conclusion: In Mahayana Buddhism, we end each session by mentally sharing the benefits of our practice with all beings. For example, we could wish, "Any virtue generated here, I dedicate to all. May we all ultimately achieve full spiritual realisation and, in the meantime, happiness and well-being."

— IV —

Processes

WHEN WE FEEL OVERLOADED, it becomes harder to make decisions. We lack clarity and desperately seek the right course of action. On those occasions, the very principles of causality—the driving forces in our life—may seem blurry. But, by studying and understanding these principles, we can distinguish between what matters and what doesn't, and between what should be done and what should be avoided. Conversely, if we never reflect on causes, conditions, effects, and interdependence, we may end up chasing rainbows or feeling powerless, thinking we are mere victims of circumstances.

While actual meditation sessions matter—and we will explore this further in the next chapters—the spiritual life does not just happen on the cushion. Our daily lives are filled with countless opportunities to open our hearts, develop clarity, and catch our self-deception in the act. So, we should not disregard the importance of day-to-day affairs.

When we discover beautiful, ancient spiritual teachings, we often have a knee-jerk reaction to the harshness of existence. We might want to turn our back on the turmoil of the world, becoming distant and disdainful. That can be a big problem. Perceiving the futility of ego-driven habits can be a sign of maturity, but we need to remember that the problem lies not so much in the temporal world as a collection of seemingly outer phenomena, but more in the way we relate to it.

While occasionally it's necessary to secure some form of solitude, it is crucial to realise early on that the spiritual life is not an ivory tower—something disconnected from the world and our fellow beings. This is why the Buddhist teachings don't just expound meditation; they also speak of ethics and discipline and contain abundant counsel on how to lead a meaningful and compassionate life.

Be that as it may, this chapter is somewhat unorthodox. While it does attempt to demystify some traditional teachings, especially pertaining to *karma*, part of it serves as a suggestion box—a bunch of seemingly random and less spiritual ideas that might nonetheless help us find clarity, live with integrity, and heal our relationship with complexity. We will examine some ideas in vogue in the "popular psychology and well-being" department, to see if we can use some of them, occasionally raising a red flag or analysing them from a Buddhist perspective.

The first couple of pages will require a fair amount of concentration. However, take heart, as it will soon become more apparent how this theoretical information relates to our main concern: to genuinely simplify our lives. After this initial effort, the subsequent pages will be more fun and concrete. Also, I recommend continuing to practice the exercises and contemplations presented in the previous chapter.

The Meanings and Characteristics of "Karma"

This is a wonderfully deep, rich, and important subject; unfortunately, it is also one of the most commonly misunderstood. "That's my karma," people say, often tongue-in-cheek. While this is not necessarily false—whatever happens must have had causes—the phrase is often uttered with a somewhat eternalist understanding, hinting at some vague concept of "soul," or taking karma as some rigid "destiny," as if our very present and future have always been written in stone.

In some traditional communities, being born into a particular caste meant you were bound to stay in that caste. Such thinking easily leads to some form of pessimism that is alien to the Buddhist understanding of karma. While the present depends on the past, it also contributes to conditioning the future. In other words, we can sow seeds that affect our personal and collective experiences to come.

But let's dig a little deeper.

Logically, the "future" largely depends on *its* past, which includes *both* our current present and the past. In other words, in a linear approach to time, C depends on B, but also on A. It would be naïve to believe that the future solely depends on any given present. That may seem verbose, but understanding that the past, present, and future are all connected is crucial. For example, sometimes we start a project but become frustrated when the desired result doesn't come about. We may end up blaming something immediate, such as a client, the weather, or our handling of things, while the problem may lie elsewhere. Essentially, the fact that the desired result didn't manifest is due to the necessary causes and conditions not being gathered, which may imply some influence from a distant past or location or from an element so subtle that we can't see it.

For example, if A is any previous situation, B is your effort, and C is the experience of an undesired result, you cannot just blame B and pretend that A didn't have *any* influence. But you cannot solely blame A either. This is not to say that we can never identify a main cause for a given problem; but it is healthy to remind ourselves that things are in a state of flux and are more subtle than we typically imagine. Effects can have a primary cause, but the latter can only bear fruit if the proper contributory circumstances are present. So let's try not to jump to hasty conclusions. After all, history is an endless chain of interdependent occurrences.

To see the myriad implications of everything that exists, one would have to be a buddha. But perhaps we don't need to understand *everything* in detail; perhaps instead we could rely on some general guidelines that explain how causality works. This is where the teachings on karma come into play. They unveil how the principles of causes, conditions, and effects relate to happiness and suffering, as well as to confusion and liberation. In this way, they show us how to live and navigate our lives with discernment.

In Sanskrit, the root of the word *karma* means "to act" or "to do," but *karma* can also refer to an action.[51] When Buddhist scholars use this term, they often imply a twofold definition. *Karma* can connote a "movement"—a momentary intention, a force that drives the mind towards an object. It can also evoke an "imprint"—like a seed sown by an intention, or like a trace of potential energy left in the mind. When the necessary circumstances are gathered, this potential energy manifests and produces a result of a similar nature. Bundles of traces form tendencies, and the mind tends to follow these habits.[52]

Buddhists believe that karma has four essential characteristics:

1) Karma is determined: the nature of its result is specific and is primarily determined by the intention behind the action. For example, orange trees don't grow from apple seeds. Similarly, a burst of destructive emotions, no matter how seemingly satisfying in the moment, ultimately leads to suffering unless it is transformed through spiritual means.
2) Karma grows: unless purified or neutralised, karma develops until its result manifests when the required circumstances are gathered. This is similar to interest at the bank or like an ongoing quarrel that gets inflamed. At the very least, traces can bundle up, and thought patterns of a given sort can start to proliferate.

3) If we don't perform a given karma, we won't experience its result. This is not the carrot and the stick approach; it is simply a reminder that effects cannot come about without their causes. If we don't sow apple seeds, there may be weeds and mushrooms and other plants and fungi growing, but there won't be any apple orchard.
4) Once performed, a karma does not just disappear: unless purified or neutralised, it will produce a result. If we throw a ball, it is bound to land somewhere—no matter how high it flies or how long it stays in the air.

Some texts are astonishingly thorough when discussing the different types of karma—positive, negative, and neutral—or when examining the rationale behind these characteristics, the types of results, the forces of karma, the support of it all, and the ways to neutralise or purify it. I don't have any such ambition to cover all that in this book, nor do I possess the wisdom to do so properly. However, the key idea here is to realise that, despite life's uncertainties, things are not entirely random. Though we must live with the effects of some unknown past causes, we are not mere victims and can indeed influence our future. This can be achieved, at the very least, by becoming more aware of our mental habits and by changing our perception of events.

When we feel foggy and powerless, stuck with a conundrum or seemingly arbitrary situations, we can find some comfort and clarity by contemplating the following key points:

- Causes have effects.
- Effects have causes.
- If there is no cause, there is no effect.
- A cause also needs contributing circumstances to produce the effect (just as a seed needs soil, water, sun, and so forth).

- The nature of the cause and the nature of the effect share a common quality (flowers don't grow in the sky; hatred fuels violence).

From this last statement, we can extrapolate a fundamental notion in Buddhism: negative or counterproductive emotions (such as hatred, attachment, jealousy, arrogance, and confusion) lead to suffering, while positive emotions and qualities (such as love, compassion, humility, wisdom, and openness) contribute to happiness. Of course, at some point, especially in Vajrayana Buddhism, we can learn to transform our relationship with all emotions, whether typically considered positive or negative. However, cultivating wholesome emotions and learning not to be blindly carried away by unwholesome ones provide a safe guideline to lead a meaningful and fruitful life.

In any event, we don't study the principles of karma to become obsessive spiritual planners. The idea is not to fixate on results and start living in the future, but to be more aware of how things are and to learn to be more skilful and responsive in relation to ourselves and others. As Zen master Thich Nhat Hanh beautifully puts it, we start to discover how things *inter-are.*

Okay, So Now What?

Understanding karma can help us gain clarity, simplify our lives, and act with integrity. Take negative actions, for instance. In Buddhist teachings, we commonly find a list of ten non-virtuous actions: killing, stealing, engaging in sexual misconduct, lying, sowing discord, speaking harshly, gossiping, mentally engaging in covetousness, harbouring ill will, and indulging in wrong views. This may sound like a list of absolute "don'ts." However, many are circumstantial. The most important things are one's motivation or state of mind and the effect on the happiness or suffering of living beings.

For example, if a murderer asks if you've seen his next potential victim, whom you know is hiding nearby, and you say you haven't, this is technically a lie, but the karmic effect is certainly not the same as lying for egotistic reasons. You may even have protected two people: one from dying, and the other from committing an irredeemable act of violence.

Another example: one could use harsh speech in a compassionate manner, or as a skilful means to help or awaken someone, without much, if any, of the results typically associated with hatred. But for that to be the case, it would have to be done in a selfless way, at the right time, and with clarity, precision, wisdom, and most importantly, unconditional love.

Thus, in the end, we could consider that there really are just two categories: the first is thoughts, words, deeds, decisions, and endeavours that are ego-driven, and the second is those that are based on genuine love, insight, and openness. Taking some time to understand the implications of this is fundamental to truly being able to simplify our life.

There are many ways to approach spirituality or religion. For instance, we could focus on memorising countless rules, or we could focus on how we appear to others. What Buddhism emphasises, rather, is observing our own mind. However, this approach only works if we are willing to cut through our self-delusions. Otherwise, we become self-centred or allow spirituality to be absorbed into ego's territory without our noticing. Practicing Buddhism isn't about constantly observing ourselves as if we were the most fascinating subject. Instead, it's about understanding our mind and relating to the world with frankness, freshness, and accuracy.

Here's an example. Imagine you're leading a team for a project. In the privacy of your home office, you suddenly come up with a brilliant idea that could revolutionise the whole operation. But this new direction has many implications that you need to consider. It might cost more money, require you to rearrange your schedule, make tons of phone calls, and redo the visuals. Some team members might disagree with the new approach. Even though you haven't left your home office or made any decision yet, your mind feels incredibly crowded! Is this idea worth it? How can you make a decision when the possibilities are so overwhelming? Now, you could make lists, heaps of lists, of pros and cons, and sometimes that works. But you could also look within. Why is this idea so appealing? Is it because it would allow you to prove a point, establish yourself as a powerful leader, or demonstrate your out-of-the-box creativity? Or is it because the project would ultimately be more gratifying for the people involved and the end-result more beneficial? In short, is this about self-aggrandisement or actual service?

On the one hand, we have dozens of questions; on the other, we have just one. Sometimes, answering the one question is scarier, but it can help deal with this type of overload. It's important to consult friends and partners, but it's equally, if not more important, to learn to see through our own smokescreen.

In such a situation, if we finally decide to adopt the exciting idea and give the project a whole new direction, there will inevitably be some complexity involved—those phone calls, budget amendments, and other tasks will still need to be handled. However, we will now have the courage, vision, and confidence to move forward and manage the many tasks ahead.

Building Trust

The practice of calm abiding, which we began to explore in the previous chapter, allows insight to emerge. We will revisit the relationship between tranquillity and discernment in Chapter 6. But, if you are anything like me, there will be many occasions when "looking within" does not immediately bring insight. Until we have the maturity to fully see through our self-deception (and ego is sneaky and fantastically clever in its constant battle for self-preservation), we should rely on ethical guidelines. In fact, even great masters pay close attention to karma. The wondrous Buddha Padmasambhava, also known as Guru Rinpoche, said, "My view is higher than the sky, but my attention to actions and results is finer than flour."[53]

Familiarising ourselves with the principles of karma and refraining as much as possible from the ten non-virtues is far more helpful than believing we live in a completely random world. Having *some* frame of reference is healthy. While we may someday let go of our attachment to concepts, in the meantime, we need some bearings. It is wiser to abide by those trusted by generations of sages.

If we second-guess the principles of karma, we are likely to learn the hard way. We might think we can get away with "white lies" and devious behaviour, but eventually we will have to face the hard facts.

The Buddha and other masters pointed out that when causes and conditions come together, effects inevitably follow. This simple yet powerful point is undeniably true. Still, we shouldn't take such counsel at face-value; it's perfectly okay to test it first—just as one would test the authenticity of a bar of gold before acquiring it, as the texts say. This applies to all Buddhist teachings. Is it true, for example, that hatred, arrogance, and greed bring suffering? Is it true that altruism and openness contribute to happiness and inner strength? To find out, we could look both within and without. We can examine our own life experiences and phenomena happening globally. This examination will reinforce our understanding and confidence.

Additionally, to better appreciate karma and its implications, it is helpful to understand the interrelated nature of the world. Familiarising ourselves with interdependence, even on a simple level, will instil trust and understanding in our lives. With this in mind, let us engage in another contemplation.

Contemplation: Interdependence

To explore the interdependence of phenomena, let's engage in a preliminary exercise related to the third of the four contemplations that turn the mind towards sanity.

Sit in a stable and comfortable manner. Feel content and relax your mind. Focus on your breathing for a minute or two.

Take a simple object, such as an apple you bought at the supermarket. Look at it deeply, with an open mind.

Consider the apple's origin: it came from a tree.

The tree depended on water, light, warmth, soil, and nutrients.

The land's type, orientation, soil density, and the proximity of rocks and so on influenced the tree's shape. Weather, seasons, and countless insects and animals interacted with the tree during its lifetime.

Countless people also worked for the apple to reach your home. We may think "countless" is a bit of a stretch, but let's take a closer look.

Take the orchard owner. She had employees, helpers, mentors, teachers, lenders, or partners, and she had parents, who also had parents . . .

But there's no need to go too far back in the genealogical tree just yet.

Focus on one aspect of her life: her food. In order to work and operate that orchard, she herself had to eat.

Consider just one of her many meals, her breakfast, and just one element of it: bread.

She bought the bread from a local bakery. The baker, like her, had parents, ancestors, mentors, and countless influences. The bread's journey involved countless living beings and material factors that made it possible to arrive at the orchard owner's breakfast table.

The apples were transported in a van from the orchard to the market. While it may have been an old, battered pickup truck, it nonetheless represents a marvel of engineering—generations of designers and manufacturers, a baffling number of trials and errors, and a dizzying assortment of ideas and components coming together from all over the world. Somehow, this very truck is linked to various factors, from violence and conflicts in petroleum-rich regions of the Middle East to the health of local populations of bees and other pollinators.

Think about the pollinators, the wooden apple crates, or the supermarket cashier. Each object, each sentient creature has a myriad of factors contributing to their existence.

If we had the time and inclination (and either the omniscience or the creativity), we could fill entire books on how this apple came to be in our hands. Imagination can be used on the path: this is one of those contemplations in which we can almost daydream, and marvel at the infinity and interdependence of things.

Keep contemplating until you glimpse the interdependence of phenomena. As Buddhist author Elizabeth Mattis Namgyel phrases it, "Everything leans."

When you feel joyful openness, new understanding, or a sense of awe at the interrelated nature of all things, don't force the experience; just relax for a moment and merge your awareness with that experience.

— —

We can practice contemplations like this every now and then, using different objects such as a table, a book, or a teapot. This is especially helpful when we feel constricted, isolated, or narrow-minded. When we notice our tendency to cling to the "self" of phenomena—for example, when we see that our mind believes things are permanent, autonomous, and independent—we can alternate or combine meditations on interdependence with contemplations on impermanence, as we did in the previous chapter.

Contemplation: Karma

Here is a third contemplation to help turn the mind away from insanity and neuroses.[54]

Sit in a quiet environment, keep your back straight, and

relax. If you have the time and inclination, you can review the first contemplations—the rarity of a precious human life and impermanence—but you can also devote a session solely to karma.

Once you have settled your mind, slowly take each of the five or six elements that follow (the sixth being an extrapolation of the fifth), and come up with at least three concrete examples for each. These examples could be particular episodes from your daily life, generalities from common knowledge, or a mix of both. They can be tragic or amusing, and on any scale. Choose anything that works best for you and that helps you understand the principles of causality.

- Causes have effects.
- Effects have causes.
- If there is no cause, there is no effect.
- A cause also needs contributing circumstances to produce the effect.
- The nature of the cause and the nature of the effect share a common quality.
- Negative (counterproductive and egotistic) emotions lead to suffering; positive emotions and qualities contribute to happiness.

If you encounter a challenging counterexample—an event that seems to have happened without a cause or a so-called negative emotion that seems to bring happiness—allow yourself more time, open your heart, and keep observing with a non-judgemental mind. Trust your own intelligence, but also give yourself enough time to dig deep.

Eventually, switch from an investigative approach to a more contemplative mode, and simply rest. Over time, you may develop a more intimate understanding of karma. If, at this point, you rekindle your motivation—such as committing to treading the path towards clarity, integrity, and tenderness for your own sake and that of all living beings—you may feel an urge to live with more awareness from now on. If you feel that urge, let it permeate you without crystallising it: experience it openly, and rest.

The Power of Small Things

The four contemplations help us re-establish our priorities in life. When we have a clear direction and strong determination, distractions don't affect us as much, allowing us to focus on what truly matters.

This principle applies not only to our spiritual journey but also to our daily affairs. By prioritising, we realise we don't have to be pernickety all the time and can discern where to invest our time and energy. In fact, efficiency often involves letting go. While performing a task, there is a law of diminishing returns—a threshold after which further effort brings limited value, if any. Highly effective people have a talent for determining this threshold: they do what needs to be done without waste. This isn't about glossing over details or not "going the extra mile"; it's about recognising when enough is enough in order to move on with the day. There are many situations where no perfect solution exists, yet we still need to decide on a course of action. Interestingly, in the 1950s, the American political scientist Herbert Alexander Simon coined the term "satisficing" for this skill—a portmanteau of *satisfy* and *sufficing*—for a strategy where decision-makers reach an acceptable threshold and then move on.[55]

In short, we don't need to split hairs all the time. That being said, we often underestimate the power of small actions, especially when it comes to spirituality.

For example, the list of the ten non-virtues we discussed earlier includes "idle gossiping" alongside more obvious negativities like stealing and killing. We may wonder if gossiping is truly harmful or just a small, negligible thing. But if we look closer and stay brutally honest, we see that worthless chatter almost inevitably drifts into remarks that fuel confusion, attachment, or aversion. Thus, not only do we waste our precious time and that of our interlocutor, but we also reinforce unwholesome mind habits that have ripple effects. As Shantideva said:

> Self-aggrandizement,
> Scorn for others,
> Blather about the pleasures of this world:
> Always, the madman receives from the madman
> Something harmful.[56]

The problem is not in having a simple and joyful conversation with a friend or stranger. If we desperately hope for "nuggets of wisdom" when we first meet a lama, we may find it unsettling if he or she starts talking about the weather. The problem lies in ego-driven thoughts, words, and actions that are based on or reinforce confusion, partiality, and aggression. Nothing is smaller than a thought or a word, yet these can be incredibly powerful.

Again, the power of small things is not limited to the so-called "spiritual life." It manifests in our day-to-day affairs as well.

Take emails, social media, and notifications of all sorts: as harmless as they seem, they insidiously gnaw at our neuronal energy. As previously quoted from Daniel J. Levitin's *The Organized Mind*:

> Our brains do have the ability to process the information we take in, but at a cost: we can have trouble separating the trivial from the important, and all this information processing makes us tired.[57]

Our system struggles to prioritise decisions, and when overloaded, we become more stressed and confused, leading us to make bad calls. Strangely enough, obsessing over tangible results and "perfect" solutions can also cause stress. While a healthy dose of stress can be useful, clinging to it or becoming overly self-conscious makes us tense and unnatural. Clumsy decisions and awkward data-handling make us more anxious, causing us to become more self-absorbed and less empathetic. As our lucidity declines, so does our emotional, relational, and spiritual health, creating a vicious circle. I have noticed this in my own life: when I am distraught and unnerved, I seek comfort and pay less attention to the people around me.

With this in mind, we should periodically examine our priorities in life to discern what is worthy of our attention. We should also be wary of multitasking, which leads to neuronal fatigue, and use discipline and any tool that can simplify our daily affairs. For instance, it is usually much more efficient to group together small tasks of the same nature. For example, we could check our emails once in the morning and once in the afternoon when we have the mental space to take care of incoming messages, instead of interrupting our workflow a hundred times a day and overusing the "mark as unread" button, leaving yet more unfinished business nibbling at our attention. We should also learn to unplug. In any case, it's important to remember that our mind follows habits, and it is up to us whether we develop wholesome or unwholesome habits.

Since small things tend to accumulate, shouldn't we commit to building clarity and altruism? If we consistently sow seeds of complications, we will reap the same fruits.

Enjoying the Process

Earlier we mentioned that familiarising ourselves with the principles of karma should not nourish our self-serving attempts to gain worldly success. We don't study the mechanics of causality for mundane strategic purposes or to "optimise" our chances of becoming rich, strong, and superficially happy. Instead, the point is to gain more discernment and avoid perpetuating harmful patterns.

Once we learn to trust the principles of karma, we can relax a bit. This doesn't mean we become lackadaisical or act as if we're squeaky clean. Rather, it allows us to maintain greater awareness of our mind and behaviour, enjoy spiritual training more and more, and multiply our meritorious deeds. Once we ascertain that we are acting in accord with the Dharma, there is no need to be anxious or depressed if the results of our actions are a long time coming. We should every now and then check our motivation and refresh it as needed, but generally, we can enjoy the journey, quite simply.

The phrase "trust the process" has become commonplace in some circles. In America, some sports fans attribute it to a general manager of the Philadelphia 76ers, a US basketball team, but there have undoubtedly been other occurrences and variants of this slogan throughout history. A good coach might say, "Focus on the process and the results will take care of themselves."

There is some wisdom to that, but it's important to recognise that such advice can be understood and applied differently by different types of people. For example, there is a difference between the stubbornness of the know-it-all, the perseverance of the prolific artist, and the healthy confidence of the spiritual devotee. The first case is a matter of pride; the third is ideally a matter of humility; the second can be either. To prevent misunderstandings, inner authority must be coupled with openness; matched with arrogance, it only leads to suffering and delusions of grandeur.

With a healthy dose of leadership in our lives, we can aim for the long term and stay the course. This is true for meditation: when practicing shamatha, for example, we can simply stay in the freshness of the present moment, without worrying about improving or achieving some future state of enlightenment. The same principle applies to work and projects of all sorts: once we've established our priorities, we can focus on doing our best with the task at hand, without constantly preoccupying ourselves with the next step or the end result.

As we will see in the next chapter, it is even more important to let go of our expectations when they are focused on the small self. As Dzigar Kongtrul Rinpoche writes:

> When we let our ego get hooked into relatively petty expectations, we make it that much harder to get free. The taint of self-importance severely limits the effect of our practice.[58]

Thus, in both our work and meditation, enjoying the process of putting in the effort and exploring is best done with humility and a simple, kind heart.

It is also interesting to note that honing the process, while having no particular expectations and attaining a relaxed focus in nowness, is an approach also found in martial arts. Additionally, in some meditative traditions, the path itself *is* the goal. The main idea here is that we are perfectly allowed to enjoy the path. There is no need for self-flagellation or constant misgivings.

A Word on Contentment

Nagarjuna, a great master who lived around the second century and was one of the most revered commentators on the Buddha's teachings, wrote:

> Of all the great wealth, contentment is supreme,
> Said he who taught and guided gods and men.
> So always be content; if you know this
> Yet have no wealth, true riches you'll have found.[59]

Other traditions also celebrate contentment. For example, in a lecture given in Bouguenais, France, in 1999, the contemporary philosopher André Comte-Sponville explained that the common definition of "desire" is problematic for leading a fulfilling life. If "desire" is defined as wanting or wishing for something we *don't* have, then by definition, once we obtain that object, we cease to desire it. We are then doomed unless we redefine our notion of desire to appreciate what we already have.[60]

From the Buddhist point of view, any form of clinging leads to suffering. We could live a simple life in a grass hut and still be a slave to our emotions, attached to false concepts, partial towards things we like, and aggressive towards anything that threatens our comfort. But being able to appreciate our present circumstances can be healthy, especially if it dampens the fire of our consumerist hunger.

There are many reasons why the term "Zen" has become so popular in Western languages. We often say, "This is Zen" about something that has nothing to do with the Chinese, Japanese, or Korean Buddhist traditions, meaning it is peaceful or uncluttered. The word "Zen" is often used by marketers, and of course that might be inconsiderate at times, but it speaks volumes that it has become so trendy: it shows that simplicity inspires us and makes us feel good. Some authors have even had tremendous success writing books about how outer order can contribute to inner well-being. "Declutter your life," they say, and who would argue back?

There are some examples of Dharma kings and wonderful devotees who lived among riches and used their resources wisely, as they would use any energy that manifested in their lives—without attachment, in an altruistic way—and who managed to remain serene and humble. But for those of us who don't yet have that level of spiritual maturity, aiming for a simple life makes good sense. We don't necessarily have to move to a cave or a minuscule dwelling, but there is something eloquent about the tiny house movement: these small and affordable houses, aside from being adorable and hopefully reducing one's ecological footprint, hold the promise of simpler days to come. A lot of good can come from such trends and philosophies, at the juncture of ecology, economy, and sometimes even civil disobedience. Conversely, an uncompromising focus on economic growth comes at a cost, and things such as planned obsolescence should be considered crimes.

Still, from a spiritual point of view, it may be worthwhile to examine our desire to declutter our lives. The aspiration is fine, of course, but the "why" will vary from one person to the next, and we should be frank in our investigation. Are we simply fed up with over-consumption, or is it that we can't handle content and haven't learned to be at ease with our own being, regardless of outer circumstances? Are we shying away from complexity altogether, in denial about the ruggedness and unpredictability of life? Are we chasing rainbows? Are we becoming disdainful? Such questioning is harder to face than just retiring to some place in the countryside (which is legitimate) or cleaning our house and getting rid of whatever doesn't bring joy or meaning (also totally legitimate). But although we don't have to constantly question ourselves, it may be good to do the occasional check-up.

We constantly hope for more space. But what is space, really? What if the experience of spaciousness was subjective and its source was within?

What Matters Most

With so many things to do on any given day, it would be logical to start with what matters most. But distractions abound, and so do reasons to do *something else*. Experience may have shown us that starting our day with a meditation session is beneficial; maybe it makes us calmer, more empathetic, and resilient at work. Or maybe it's a walk outside or some physical exercise that helps us kick-start our day, but for some reason, we are tempted to scroll down on some social media platform instead. Or maybe we have an important life project, something creative and fulfilling, but it requires a lot of effort, which catapults us out of our comfort zone, so we watch TV instead, thinking ". . . just another episode." I'm not judging, for I often do just that! With the crazy shifts we put up with at our jobs and the constant hurriedness, aren't we allowed some nonchalance? Of course, we are! But the demarcation line between a true need to relax and pure laziness may blur . . . And at some point, we're shocked by how time flies and how little of it is left.

So, on busy days, it may be worthwhile to write down your most important tasks—reasonable ones, that is, and a reasonable number of them—and slog away. If you manage to complete two-thirds of them in the first half of your working day, when your energy and inspiration are higher, then you're in business.

Of course, that's just one way to proceed. Adaptation is key. But say we have a colleague, boss, or project manager who defines the priorities for us at work; how do we determine what matters most in our spare time? Tal Ben-Shahar, a best-selling author in the area of positive psychology, suggests the following exercise.

We draw a table with four columns: "Activity," "Duration," "Pleasure," and "Meaning." In the first, we list our regular activities (for example, training at the gym, playing with the kids, meditation, social media, television, reading . . .), and in the second, we note the average duration (30 minutes, 2 hours). In the other two columns, we assign a value, say, from 1 to 5. The "Pleasure" column reflects our immediate enjoyment; the "Meaning" column relates to the longer term, the benefits for ourselves and others, or a general sense of direction and contentment in life.

To clarify the possible combinations of enjoyment and value, Ben-Shahar gives the analogy of four hamburgers we could choose from:

- An unhealthy burger that tastes bad.
- An unhealthy burger that tastes good.
- A healthy burger that's somewhat flavourless.
- A burger that's both tasty and nutritious.

In this exercise, the duration of activities also brings interesting nuances. We can spend a week or two filling out the table, making amendments if needed. Then, we examine it to see if there's anything we can learn from the experience.

Naturally, a law of diminishing returns applies to some activities, and we cannot only do what brings us immediate pleasure. Also, the results may vary as we age or as we progress along the spiritual path, particularly once we step onto the Mahayana, which we will discuss in the next chapter. But the exercise may be worthwhile: it sheds light on how we could align the way we spend our days with our personal values.

Over time, when we study the Buddhist teachings, what matters most to us becomes clearer, especially as we familiarise ourselves with the four contemplations that turn the mind towards the Dharma and as we cultivate compassion. But Buddhism is about one's inner experience, not mere intellectual understanding, so it is up to us to relate to our current situation and to decide what matters and what doesn't.

A Calling?

These days, we have so many options it's easy to feel confused on a fundamental level: the question isn't just, "What are my priorities today?" but also, "Who should I be?" Sometimes we don't even put it into words, but if we pay attention to people's speech and behaviour, we notice a widespread anguish. Many of us have lost our bearings, and we suffer.

From a Buddhist perspective, losing one's bearings isn't necessarily a bad thing. If we remain humble and receptive, the experience can teach us a lot about our attachment to concepts. For example, if we have always identified as a carpenter and then injure our hands, we're forced to let go of an identity that we thought was solid. It's quite a shock, and we may have to go back to school and reinvent ourselves. Even without such an obvious manifestation of impermanence, there's often a persistent dissatisfaction in our life. It's hard to wake up every morning and find the motivation to go to the office and work on that spreadsheet, so much so that we begin to question our lifestyle and career path.

From the Buddhist point of view, suffering is inherent to samsara. As long as we cling to dualistic concepts, there will be pain and sorrow. As long as we reinforce an egotistic sense of self—the illusion of a permanent, autonomous, and supremely important "I"—we will awkwardly live in cramped quarters, like a magnet for distractions and a target for attacks. So-called enemies and problems will gnaw at our cherished comfort. As the traditional texts say, we will drink salt water in an attempt to quench our thirst, using deluded strategies to try to find happiness. Though we occasionally find some relative peace, suffering will always be latent within it. When we've had enough of that exhausting cycle, we may turn to the fourth noble truth, the path that leads to the cessation of suffering.

The fact that there is all-pervading suffering in samsara doesn't mean that we shouldn't try to improve our lot. Renunciation is not the same as resignation. While samsara, or a deluded and ego-driven experience of the world, is bound to be messy and painful, we don't need to add more suffering to our current load. Meditation teaches us that part of the problem is our constant struggle, but it doesn't negate the fact that it's perfectly human to try to figure things out, for example when it comes to our career path.

As we reflect on our occupation and place in the world, the words "vocation" and "calling" come to mind. We seek a raison d'être, a way to live and work in harmony with our beliefs and unique set of talents. The Japanese have a word for this: *ikigai*, which refers to what makes life fulfilling and gives us a reason to wake up in the morning.

Many contemporary authors have written on ikigai. For example, in 2009, *National Geographic* reporter Dan Buettner suggested that it contributes to the longevity of elders in Okinawa. Regardless of how much of an actual thing the concept of ikigai is in Japan, and of how much Western motivational speakers have tailored it, there's an exercise now commonly mentioned online which can help clarify our professional orientation. We draw four interlocking circles labelled "things I love," "things I'm good at," "things that society needs," and "things I can be paid for." According to this model, any combination or overlap of two elements brings an interesting but incomplete scenario; our ikigai is found at the very centre of the diagram, where all four circles—passion, mission, profession, and vocation—meet.

This concept is so stimulating. It's no wonder it has caught on. If it can help you find a career path that is both sustainable and inspiring, one that allows you to use your skills to serve your community, by all means, try it! However, given the exercise's popularity, I feel compelled to add some nuance and provide advice from a Buddhist practitioner's point of view.

Firstly, career planning of this sort is best done with a kind heart. It shouldn't be yet another way to self-serve, but a way to connect with others and foster a flexible and meaningful relationship with the world.

Secondly, there's always a risk of clinging to our so-called raison d'être: we may think we're on a "mission" and take ourselves too seriously. A sense of direction can add a healthy dose of confidence to our lives; it could help us avoid distractions and become more competent workers, coherent thinkers, or well-rounded artists. But ego can get in the way and derail the train: we can become ideologues, fundamentalists, or fanatics, thinking that our way, our *ism*, is the best and the only way, and feel the need to spread the "sacred message." That's a dangerous path. If we notice that we have this tendency, it may be safer to use the diagram to find our trade—such as graphic designer, hairdresser, or translator—without adding too much ideology into the mix.

Finally, any exercise that aims at integrating one's personality should be done with a tender heart, a sense of humour, and an awareness of impermanence. It's not just that our ikigai or career can change over time. We're really touching the heart of the matter here, and an essential lesson from the present book: real clarity has an element of openness. If we think we see all the details of a situation but cling to these details—as if they were independent, permanent, or only defined in relation to our sense of a solid "I"—or if we become upset when these details cease or change, that is mere intellectual understanding, not wisdom. Therefore, we shouldn't look for our vocation to cling tighter to our identity; rather, we should do these exercises knowing that change is allowed and, in fact, inevitable.

From a Buddhist point of view, there's a fundamental problem with trying to impose meaning on everything in a way that is always self-referential. We spend our lives wandering about, trying to reaffirm our sense of a solid self, thinking: "Is this me? Is this truly me? Is this who I am?" Though it can bring us some temporary comfort when we seem to find a "good fit," the whole exercise, if applied compulsively, causes us to suffer continually. As we construct this "autobiographical self," we become overly selective and we inevitably lack objectivity. Over time, we add layers of confused concepts, getting lost in our thoughts, storylines, and projections. We oscillate between acceptance and rejection, attachment and aversion. This tendency to classify the world in this way is somewhat aggressive, exhausting, and illusory. We build ourselves a psychological prison by thinking there's fixed meaning to our identity. Buddhas show us how to be completely at ease without such fixations. They show us the path to true freedom, freedom from all bondage.

There's a huge difference between getting to know our nature and imprisoning ourselves in any given concept of what we currently think of as our "self." We can and should develop and integrate all aspects of our personhood—as long as we don't confuse personhood with some kind of static, lasting, autonomous identity.[61] That there is no fixed self doesn't mean subscribing to a pessimistic and nihilistic notion that there's no meaning in life. For Buddhists, the openness of the world, its fluidity, has a wonderful, freeing quality, fostering a cheerful sense of awe and deep appreciation. The implications of this will become clearer as you keep reading and meditating. For now, just relax and take heart: it is perfectly legitimate to use the notion of ikigai and other such tools from popular psychology or any other approach for that matter; only, let's do it with some humour and openness.

Paralysis by Analysis

From Hamlet's celebrated monologue:

And thus the native hue of resolution
Is sicklied o'er with the pale cast of thought,
And enterprises of great pith and moment
With this regard their currents turn awry,
And lose the name of action.

Shakespeare's character has a tremendous quality: he thinks and doubts. It's also his curse. Aren't we just like him?

Overanalysing a situation can halt forward momentum. If we overthink an issue, we may end up lacking perspective: we may speculate endlessly, adding layers of concepts and projections onto the situation, further distancing ourselves from its actuality. We may become so tense that things become blurry, making it hard to find the clarity and insight required to make a decision. Sometimes, it's not so much overthinking but the sheer number of options that overwhelms us. Regardless of why we're paralysed, there are many things that can help us.

One of them is silence. Not silence that allows us to cogitate more, but silence that creates a sense of *space*. Calm abiding meditation helps. In the previous chapter, we explored the outer and inner conditions conducive to clarity. As we will see in chapter 6, meditation can help change our relationship with thoughts and concepts. When there is more space, we can have an open and positive relationship with our thoughts. This makes us more likely to reconnect with our true intelligence.

Space helps, but so does time. "Discernment," a wise friend once told me, "is not only about *going towards* things, ideas, and solutions; sometimes it's about letting them come to you." If we are impatient (I know I often am!), it may be healthy to remember that when the proper causes and conditions come together, the effect inevitably follows—and that time may be one of the required conditions. For example, when we have a eureka moment, finally finding the solution to a conundrum, it's not that we were being dumb before, but simply that our brain needed to process the information and make new associations.

Decision-making can also be facilitated by paying attention to the earthly aspects of our experience. That is where mindfulness of the body comes into play. Often, our physical sensations can tell us a lot about the soundness of a decision. If I am offered an opportunity, and whenever I think about it my stomach hurts—not in a pleasant, exciting way, but in a something's-not-right kind of a way—I should slow down and look at the opportunity more closely before jumping in. Paying attention to the earthly aspects of a situation can also involve stepping down from the world of mental cogitation to reconnect with the elements at hand. Sometimes, our discursive thoughts take us so far away from the actual situation that there's an unhealthy distance, a blurriness. It doesn't mean that we can't think in abstract terms, only that we should be aware of when we're overdoing it to a point that serves no purpose. Buddhist meditation helps us see the distinction between discernment and discursiveness. When we realise that we've been carried away by conceptual thinking, it can be helpful to reconnect with the physical environment—matter, textures, and so on. The wisdom lineages tell us that we can establish a frank, direct relationship with the world, and that it's unnecessary to always live in the realm of ideation.

Another technique to avoid paralysis by analysis is *satisficing*: we don't need the best, just something good enough.[62] If you go to the supermarket and need a grapefruit for a recipe, you don't feel all the grapefruits to find the best one; you just pick one that seems ripe and wholesome enough and get on with your day. If you're considering buying a gadget that does 99 percent of what you need at half the price of another model, and if the remaining 1 percent isn't a deal-breaker, you've got your answer—assuming the materials are equally sustainable, because that's also an issue. Of course, in some areas, a "good enough" culture can lead to laziness, negligence, or pollution, so "satisficing" is not always advisable.

In other situations, if we're paralysed, a good scare does the trick. Meditation on impermanence helps put things into perspective. If I knew I only had one month to live, what would I do? Perhaps I would try to finally let go of my arrogance, attachment to trivialities, negative thoughts about the past, and expectations about the future and start to live more in the moment. Perhaps I would love unconditionally. Or perhaps I would simply let go of that petty project and give everything I have to this other one. That might sound drastic, but sometimes that's precisely what's needed. Is it worth it to spend 45 minutes deciding which restaurant my friends and I will go to? If this was the last time I'd see my mother before she passed, deciding whether or not I should let her off the hook for something she said years ago would be a no-brainer, wouldn't it? And so on.

So, silence, space, time, attention to the feelings of the body and to the physical aspects of one's experience, satisfaction with what suffices, and awareness of impermanence: all of these tools can help us deal with paralysis and make tricky decisions.

A posteriori acceptance and humility may also be required: each and every one of us will make bad or painful decisions at some point.

Humility and a Sense of Wonder as Antidotes

In a short story written by the great Argentinian writer Jorge Luis Borges, we learn about the anguish of a book lover:

> Like all those possessing a library, Aurelian was aware that he was guilty of not knowing his in its entirety.

Guilty as charged! In any case, the library is a powerful metaphor. Such a feeling, the awareness of "being guilty of not knowing our library in its entirety," could be a manifestation of our neuroses. Like a thirsty man drinking salt water, we're never content. We define ourselves by the quantitative heap of theoretical knowledge we amass, but it never seems to be enough. This leaves us lacking self-esteem, unable to enjoy the process, the sheer joy of discovery, and fosters a strangely bulimic relationship with content.

However, acknowledging our limitations can lead to a liberating sense of wonder. It is joyful to realise there is so much we don't know, for it means that there is infinite room for exploration. Most importantly, accepting that we can't and don't need to know everything allows us to relax. There is still enjoyment and a good dose of curiosity for the many great books out there in the vast libraries of the world, but our relationship with reading changes for the better. We rid ourselves of complexes and finally understand French writer Daniel Pennac's *Rights of the Reader*: the right not to read, the right to skip pages, and all the others. How joyful! How freeing!

We don't have to be perfect, know everything, or stubbornly cling to our concepts. We can live with more openness and fluidity, realising that humility can liberate us.

Sometimes, we're paralysed by too many options or lack of clarity. When we just don't know what to decide, fully acknowledging the not-knowing is essential. Only then can we approach the situation with a fresh mind, free from preconceptions that cloud our seeing clearly. This may take time, but humility also means accepting that we can't control the timing and scheduling of it all. We need to be able to tolerate doubt and relax amidst uncertainty.

The French psychiatrist and author Christophe André, in his delightful book translated as *Looking at Mindfulness*, devotes a chapter to accepting mystery. He writes:

> What can we do in adversity, we who are incapable of Christ-like certainties? We must seek refuge in the present moment and train ourselves to make room for feelings of not knowing, not being able or not understanding. We must observe how uncomfortable these feelings are, how they try to suffocate us

> with waves of distress and chaotic impulses: "Stir yourself, do something, don't just sit there." We must cultivate and develop our tolerance for this experience, just as, when we listen to a friend, at certain points we need simply to listen, without feeling duty-bound to solve the person's problems for them. We must free ourselves from the pressure to find a solution, which may make us unable to listen properly. We must do the same when we examine our own worries. Let's gently assess the state we are in, here and now, before tensing up around the need to take control—there will be time enough for that.[63]

Indeed, giving up the desire to control the situation and any heavy-handed tendency to understand and "fix" things is often very healthy. Sometimes, it is okay to "lean into the mystery" and accept that there is more to life than meets the eye—or more to it than meets the conceptual mind.

That being said, Chögyam Trungpa offered an interesting comment on our relationship to mystery. While his profound book *Cutting Through Spiritual Materialism* was written in a different context, there is still a relevant point to consider here. From Trungpa Rinpoche:

> [...] eventually the believer in eternalistic doctrines may become disillusioned with a God he has never met, a soul or essence he cannot find. Which brings us to the next and somewhat more sophisticated misconception of reality: nihilism. This view holds that everything is generated out of nothingness, mystery. Sometimes this approach appears as both theistic and atheistic assertions that the Godhead is unknowable. [...] The universe takes place mysteriously; there is no real explanation at all. Possibly a nihilist would say that the human mind cannot

> comprehend such mystery. Thus, in this view of reality, mystery is treated as a *thing*. The idea that there is no answer is relied upon and dwelled upon as the answer.[64]

Here, Trungpa Rinpoche is discussing eternalism, nihilism, and *shunyata* or "emptiness." We will revisit these topics in subsequent chapters. If this paragraph seems hard to relate to, don't worry. The point is that if "mystery" or the "unknowable" is turned into yet another *thing* we cling to, we may feel temporary relief, similar to when we are relieved of a duty or responsibility, but that relief will be superficial and short-lived.

Bearing that in mind, it can be good to relate to the world with childlike wonder—not naivety, but a playfulness and a capacity to occasionally say, "I don't know."

A No-disdain Policy

When we discover the joy of meditation and find comfort in spiritual texts and conversations, our interest in trivial things may decline—especially as we become more aware of impermanence and the suffering around us. We want to focus on what truly matters, and that is a step towards sanity. But we can also become hypercritical or contemptuous of "mundane affairs" or anything that doesn't align directly with our own spiritual path. When this happens, we risk reinforcing a narrow-minded view of spirituality, seeing it in opposition, as something very sacred opposed to our daily schedule packed with many things that just seem to get in the way. Instead, wouldn't it be better to learn to integrate the two, to dance with the energies of life? If we bring discernment, awareness, relaxation, and compassion to our activities, nearly anything can be part of our spiritual journey.

There are many fields of knowledge we can explore, many subjects that can inspire us and help us connect with fellow living beings, many tools that can help us understand ourselves and the world better. The importance of meditation doesn't mean we should neglect everything else in our lives. In other words, meditation and the activities of our daily life are not mutually exclusive—at least not necessarily. Unless we're full-time meditators in retreat, our "post-meditation" time represents the bigger fraction of our days. So we might as well approach these opportunities with an open, positive mindset.

Chögyam Trungpa Rinpoche taught some of his students how to put on a tie, study *The Art of War*, and practice proper Oxonian English elocution. These activities may initially seem remote from spiritual priorities. However, Trungpa Rinpoche—who I am confident never for a single instant lost compassion for his students—showed a path to mindfulness in action and a more enlightened way to navigate the world.

Therefore, we can integrate many contemporary elements onto our spiritual path. While Dharma is infinitely vast and includes everything we need to reach enlightenment, it is okay to use tools and ideas borrowed from different disciplines. For example, although Dharma contains many beautiful and powerful healing meditations, sometimes one needs to see a doctor. While Dharma includes countless profound pieces of advice on dealing with emotions, sometimes one needs to see a psychologist. Likewise, we can adopt any tool that helps us with clarity, time management, and professional savvy. We can use journals, lists, registers, apps, diagrams, mind maps—whatever works for us. It's also beneficial to have a system for monitoring and off-loading the burden on our memory. This way, we can keep track of unfinished business. We can use any of the tricks of the trade of the twenty-first-century worker. If needed, we can also heal our relationship with money and learn to be more optimistic.

However, while it's beneficial to use various tools and ideas in our lives, we should not confuse the mundane and the spiritual. Sometimes, motivational authors and some elements of the personal development sector blur these lines, incorporating all sorts of stuff into homemade systems that are supposedly spiritual. Yet, some ideas and methods are simply not spiritual. Some are even contrary to spirituality, in the sense that they subtly deny immaterial wisdom, focusing solely on optimising the material brain's quantifiable capacities, which is not the same as mind. While these tricks and theories may help us gain some understanding, they are no substitute for actual meditation, and they cannot provide spiritual refuge. Masters of wisdom may eventually dissolve the distinction between meditation and post-meditation, but it's safe to say that's not what most modern personal development authors are talking about. In any case, real equanimity requires time, focus, dedication, and the ability to recognise how tempting strategies aggravate our tendency towards spiritual materialism and self-aggrandisement.

It's all about perspective. The key is to keep an open mind, while acknowledging the difference between what brings temporary ease and what contributes to fundamental health and long-term spiritual freedom. To paraphrase my friend Samuel Bercholz's great advice: "Don't mix your metaphors." Ideally, we learn to spot nihilism, materialism, and eternalism over time, discerning how Buddhism differs. We also learn to distinguish what provides spiritual refuge and what doesn't.

For now, we should try to find a middle way. On the one hand, we can respect other schools and philosophies, genuinely care for others, and stay open to learning different things. On the other hand, we should keep concepts in perspective, avoid overloading our mind with countless trivial theories, and refrain from constantly looking for external answers. Instead, we should sit and meditate with a clear mind and relaxed focus. To attain the joyful simplicity, genuine clarity, and lasting happiness that come with true spiritual freedom, we must first tame the monkey mind, and for most of us that is much easier when we stop chasing every new trend.

Later in this chapter, we'll discuss taking refuge in Buddhism. The key take-away for now is that while models and theories like Pareto's principle, or the Hero's Journey as popularised by Joseph Campbell, or business management insights, or tactics to improve one's mood from the personal development sector can be interesting and at times helpful, they are not objects of ultimate spiritual refuge.

Humour and Lightness

Remember Buddha's advice to the zither player? Not too loose, not too tight?

So far, we've been talking a lot about how to avoid being too loose. For example, we've discussed how to adopt a good posture, motivate ourselves, safeguard against spiritual naivety, detect prevarications of all sorts, and distinguish between what matters and what doesn't.

But if we focus too much on these things, we might become too tight. There is often a fine line between discipline and rigidity. That's where relaxation comes in. We've talked about physical relaxation, maintaining a relaxed focus in meditation, cultivating a sense of wonder in daily life, and letting go of the heavy-handed tendency to want to control everything.

In addition to these methods, something particularly helpful in easing our physical, mental, emotional, and spiritual tensions is a sense of humour. In fact, one of the best pieces of advice one of my spiritual teachers ever gave me was: "You're too fucking serious!" And holy macaroni, was he right. Such good advice! While many of us take everything so seriously, there's some humour in the dynamic energies of this world, some drollness to the way thoughts and concepts dance and seem so solid, and some dramedy in ego's paranoid, chipmunk-like attempts to constantly secure its territory.

Funny videos of obstinate animals abound online: squirrels hoarding nuts, cats obsessing over some moving object . . . Some of these videos are great metaphors for the samsaric mind. Watch one with this in mind and you'll see. It can be like looking in a mirror!

And so, mocking ourselves—gently, tenderly—can sometimes be healthy. Especially for people like me, for whom one of the predominant mental poisons is pride. It's good to put ourselves in situations which can crack our shell. This can happen with friends and teachers who see right through our little games, or during solitary meditation when we suddenly catch a glimpse of our childish patterns.

As well as humour, simply smiling can alleviate tensions, allowing us to lighten up. As Tulku Thondup Rinpoche writes in *Boundless Healing*:

> Smiling is a very simple way to feel good. It's amazing how you can lift your mood instantly just by smiling. It may sound too easy or simplistic, especially if you're someone who mistakenly believes that the wisdom of life should always be somehow obscure or unattainable, but the simple act of smiling makes uncommonly good sense. It also fits into the Buddhist practice of positive perception. By smiling, the body is giving your mind and heart a positive message. You feel more lighthearted, as if the world had suddenly become more enjoyable.[65]

The Venerable Thich Nhat Hanh also wrote on the wonders of smiling. "Our smile," he says, "affirms our awareness and determination to live in peace and joy."[66]

In fact, smiling and having a healthy sense of humour can be so powerful that it could be one of the most important pieces of advice in this whole book: it helps de-dramatise situations, heals our relationship to complexity, provides freshness to the body and mind, keeps our arrogance in check, paves the way to creative solutions and out-of-the-box thinking, and facilitates benevolent communication with others.

Personally, when I feel too tight, obsessed, or narrow-minded, and when I start to get stressed out about the most trivial things, I like to think of some of the Chinese poets of old, the Taoist vagabonds who would gladly sleep on a riverbank and chat with the frogs. It seems to me that these guys knew how to enjoy a cup of tea and the soothing shade of a tree. That nonchalance bordering on crazy wisdom, that lightness of being, that inner freedom and harmonious relationship with the energies of life: perhaps that is a cliché or an oversimplification, but the idea nonetheless appeases me.

Another method to relax the monkey-mind is to try something new. A simple game, a new artistic medium, a fun coordination exercise such as juggling . . . We're not obsessing over novelty like adrenaline seekers. We're just willing to explore—and fail.

"Coming to our senses," literally, can also do wonders, adding some lightness to our day. For example, gently stimulating a sense—mincing rosemary from the garden or smelling freshly ground coffee or cinnamon—can often stop the flow of overly conceptual thinking. Looking at the stars with childlike wonder can also bring a sense of how relative our self-importance is. In shrine rooms, we can often hear a gong or a bell: the crisp quality of the sound can provoke sudden openness within and bring us back to the freshness of the present moment. Of course, there's always a risk of clinging to the sense object, but it can be done very simply, again with some fundamental sense of humour.

It's all in the dosage: neither too tight nor too loose!

Precommitment

The prefix might sound redundant here: isn't some chronology already implied in "commitment"? Possibly, but here we want to distinguish between being fully present while doing an action and committing ourselves in advance or for the long term. For example, if we are trying to develop a new habit or to get rid of one, there are ways to make our lives easier. If we are to quit smoking, we can ensure there is not a single cigarette left in the house and avoid situations that might put us amidst active smokers. That is a form of precommitment: at the very moment we decide to quit smoking, we make a decision for the morrow—we know we will have a craving at some point and decide in advance *not* to have the option of lighting a new cigarette. We know that if the option is readily available, it is much harder to make the decision not to smoke. In other words, we prepare the ground for more clarity and sanity by limiting our options. Asking a friend to take you for a jog every other morning is a precommitment. So is telling everyone around you about your weekly poetry blog.

One of the greatest examples of precommitment in the history of literature comes from *The Odyssey*, the Greek epic attributed to Homer and one of the oldest extant works of Western literature. It tells of the hero Odysseus and his journey home after the fall of Troy. In a famous scene, Odysseus and his sailors must skirt the land of the Sirens, whose enchanting songs cause passing mariners to steer towards the rocks and ultimately to their deaths. The clever hero wants to enjoy their chant but knows that as soon as he hears it, he will lose control of himself—so he has his sailors plug their own ears with beeswax and orders them to tie him to the mast and leave him tied up no matter what. Clever Odysseus knew there was only one way to both listen to the beautiful songs and survive: he made sure that plunging to his own death was not an option.

We all have romantic ideas about freedom, and we all like to have plenty of choices. But what if there were situations in which limiting our options was the best thing to do?

Even for such things as personal finances and office work, *automation* is often worthwhile. For example, if we decide to put some money aside in a savings account every month, we can automate the transfer, so we don't have to think about it. Put another way, we remove the option of deciding to put it off. Not only will this preserve some of our energy by offloading the process onto an external system, making a little more space for other matters, but it will also help us avoid the temptation to use the money on some impulse buy we may later regret.

Mindfully, wisely, and deliberately limiting our options often paves the way for more clarity. This is perhaps one reason why many practitioners enjoy taking vows: there is much power in this. Correctly understood—that is, not as an extreme asceticism or as a means to further strengthen our sense of a solid and all-important self, but as a middle way to sanity—vows can be extremely freeing. Of course, the meaning of vows is much deeper than just limiting our options to make things easier; it has to do with wisdom, devotion, and compassion. But the idea here is that, generally speaking, precommitment can simplify our lives. Especially if we're not too stubborn and can show some resilience and understanding when things don't go as planned.

Refuge

At some point, we may feel we need a deeper commitment: we want to commit to our spiritual path. Perhaps we seek some form of protection. We may have shopped around and tested the waters here and there, but now feel some urgency. We have meditated on impermanence and recognised the extent of our self-deception. We have become more sensitive to the suffering within and around us, and we feel a desire to make the most of our precious human life. We feel compelled to do something both drastic and kind, both simple and profound, something true—a gesture towards authenticity and sanity. In Buddhism, this is when we seek refuge.

We officially enter the Buddhist path by taking refuge in the Three Jewels, or Triple Gems: the Buddha, the Dharma (teachings), and the Sangha (spiritual community). We take the Buddha as our ever-reliable teacher, the Dharma as our way out of ignorance towards the union of wisdom and compassion, and the Sangha as our companions along the path.

In the Tibetan Buddhist tradition and others, *lineage* also assumes particular importance. If a living teacher represents the Buddha for us, it is best to ensure that they hold an authentic lineage, are wise and selfless, and embody the qualities generally required to teach. We may request a refuge ceremony, after which we renew our determination and confidence every day: we courageously and joyfully commit to cultivating fundamental health and openness. The lama or spiritual friend who leads the ceremony typically gives us a Buddhist name (there is no need to change our passport or anything!), and we are likely to develop a special relationship with that person. However, he or she is not necessarily our one and only teacher. Additionally, our understanding of the Three Jewels may vary according to the vehicle we practice—Hinayana, Mahayana, or Vajrayana—and we may unveil unexpected richness and symbolism as we progress along the path. Regardless, we can always trust Shakyamuni Buddha and his teachings.

We will return to this topic, but it is worth noting how refuge helps with both calm abiding meditation and clarity in our day-to-day affairs. Essentially, as we become a Buddhist, *we stop taking refuge in samsara*. We now clearly see that destructive emotions and self-centredness do not contribute to happiness. This doesn't mean we will never experience conflicting emotions again (if only!), but it does mean we are less inclined to deliberately cultivate them, which in turn alleviates the intensity of our mental chatter. By paying attention to our thoughts, words, and actions throughout the day, the inner rambling eventually becomes less noisy. We also begin to see that phenomena are not independent, autonomous, permanent, and constricted—or at least we try to remind ourselves regularly that they are not as solid as we think they are. This adds a little fluidity to the way we interact with the world. As we continue practicing, we impart less importance to conceptual thoughts or, more accurately, we give them the relative importance they deserve—when they deserve any—and we stop solidifying them. This helps us keep the inner racket in proper perspective and develop more clarity and insight, which we will explore in chapter 6.

Importantly, ceasing the reliance on mundane concepts, material objects, and self-aggrandisement doesn't mean our heart dries up. Quite the contrary. To live a meaningful and happy life in this fast and noisy world—and ultimately transcend confusion altogether—tenderness and warmth are essential. These are the subjects we will explore in the next chapter.

— V —

Tenderness and Warmth

There is a beautiful interdependent relationship between love and clarity. One fosters the other and naturally leads to it. How is that?

Clarity implies the capacity to see the big picture. To do this, we need to shift our focus from the small self to other realities. We need to be able to see other possibilities beyond the self-referential scenarios we tend to build in our head. For example, if we have an issue with a co-worker, sticking only to our way of viewing things gives us only one side of the story, which can hardly bring true clarity, regardless of who is "right." We need to be open and empathetic, able to imagine ourselves in our colleague's shoes.

Understanding different needs and points of view is important on any scale, whether dealing with our family or the world at large. This understanding provides insight into what to do and what to avoid and often yields unexpected, creative, and effective solutions to problems. Being empathetic, open, and even loving also tends to simplify things: often, the complicated mind is an egocentric mind, lost in its concepts, attachments, and frustrations. Truly loving people frequently make sound decisions, and when they don't know something, they simply say so, instead of improvising just to save face, which only sows further confusion. These loving people inspire many, showing that altruism and wisdom often go hand in hand.

Since it reduces the effects of the egocentric mind, our capacity to care for others fosters clarity. But it works both ways: the clarity we develop also improves our ability to care for others. Over the course of our meditative journey, we first learn to relax and quiet the mind. Eventually, our relationship with thoughts, emotions, and fixated references softens. This leads to a growing sense of freedom and clarity. The less "polluted" our mind is, the easier it is to love: fewer rigid concepts and emotional hitches get in the way of establishing genuine and caring relationships with others. This is evident in the way some accomplished meditators seem to immediately connect on a deep level with almost anyone they interact with. It's very inspiring.

Meditative clarity makes it easier to get a sense of what people are going through, either in the moment or in general. We begin to see that we are all in the same boat. It provides insight into the nature of human suffering and unveils everyone's desire to find happiness. It also shows us that everyone—despite the current state of affairs, mental illness, emotional warfare, or extreme views—has the potential to awaken, even if that potential is buried deep within their heart-mind. We can then treat everyone with respect, dignity, and even camaraderie. In short, if more clarity means fewer distortions, the progressive removal of our egocentric filters makes it natural and eventually effortless to have caring and meaningful interactions with ourselves and others.

It seems obvious that there is a relationship between clarity of mind and an altruistic heart. Unfortunately, with so many distractions nowadays, it is hard to get a sense of how to develop either of these qualities. When we are overloaded, we tend to tense up and solidify our views, making it even more difficult to cultivate true clarity and unconditional kindness. The wonderful news is that we can train in both. In this chapter, we will explore some of the many benefits and practices related to love, tenderness, and warmth, while clarity and insight will be explored in the next chapter.

A Thousand Ways to Love: Definitions

In the West, the word "love" often carries romantic connotations. However, figures like Jesus, Francis of Assisi, and many saints and accomplished spiritual devotees have taught a much broader and more selfless concept of love. Unfortunately, nowadays, "love" is often confused with attachment. In fact, attachment is often seen as something positive, such as being attached to one's family or country. Psychologists often regard a safe and supportive attachment to close caregivers as necessary and beneficial for child development. So, whenever engaging in dialogues between different traditions, such as between Buddhism and Western psychology, it's crucial to address terminological issues. In the Buddhist tradition, fostering caring relationships between a child and her family is not considered negative. On the contrary, respect for one's parents is often emphasised, and the image of a caring mother is frequently used as the quintessential example of a loving person. It is also said that the love and peace we want to see in the world must start at home before they can spread to the neighbourhood and beyond. Thus, when we aim to cultivate impartiality and train to love all beings equally, it is understood that some people will naturally be more prominent in our thoughts and lives due to karma and circumstances.

The Buddhist understanding of "attachment" shares parallels with one posited French etymology of the word, *estachier,* an old French term from the eleventh century which means to fasten or tie something to a stake or a pole. That's just my two cents as a writer, but my point is that in Buddhism "attachment" usually implies bondage. For example, if we are attached to an extreme belief, we may become a slave to it. Or if we get overly attached to our own body, we will inevitably suffer when it undergoes significant changes.

Here lies a common misunderstanding about Buddhism: some people, when they hear of a spiritual path that is wary of attachment, think it involves relinquishing all forms of pleasure. However, as we mentioned earlier and will explore further, the problem is not with pleasure, happiness, tasty food, inspiring works of art, or any lovely experience. The issue lies in clinging to and entertaining delusions about subjects and objects. "Attachment" does not refer to our capacity to enjoy things, but rather, to the stickiness we bring to the situation. One is allowed to enjoy chocolate or a beautiful sunset. Buddha is not asking anyone to become grumpy. In fact, we might even argue that we temporarily use the very mechanism of attachment on the spiritual path: we get attached to spiritual practice and spiritual phenomena, using positive concepts until we can let go of conceptual clinging altogether.

In any case, the "love" we refer to in this book is not what is typically called attachment. We are more interested in an increasingly impartial love, one that is not so much based on ourselves as it is on every being's legitimate yearning for happiness and comfort. In this context, love and compassion can be seen as two sides of the same coin: love is the wish that beings be happy and compassion is the wish that beings be free of suffering.

Matthieu Ricard, in his authoritative 900-page book *Altruism*, brilliantly defines a diverse set of concepts: empathy, emotional contagion, compassion, self-interest, selfless altruism, and so on. As for us, we've named this chapter "Tenderness and Warmth" because we see an interesting nuance between the two terms.

Tenderness can have an element of sadness: we connect with someone's suffering, which makes our heart a little sore—like a tender spot. Sometimes, even the mere experience of something cute can crack our shell: we see a small child or an adorable animal, and despite the elation we feel, deep down there is also an acknowledgment of the fragility and evanescence of life. In and of itself, sadness doesn't sound too appealing, but when we stop seeing it as something inherently negative, we understand that it doesn't negate our own happiness and freedom—quite the contrary.

Warmth is more on the joyful side and more expansive; it is a stable, impartial, and protective joy, a sheer presence that can be quieter and more tranquil than the "shell-cracking" of tenderness. It can also be more active at times. Sometimes it resembles a shelter where an animal might find refuge: the shelter has an equanimous quality, for it does not make itself prettier when the refugee is a colourful bird or uglier when it's a skunk, and it doesn't feel abandoned or victimised when the guest leaves after the storm.

As far as I know, traditional Buddhist teachings don't distinguish "tenderness" and "warmth" in the way I have described above. These are just my own musings. In fact, "warmth" can have other meanings in some Buddhist contexts. But the key point is that these two elements are interrelated: first, we find our soft spot, then we open up more and more. So this chapter is not so much about what words to use or their etymology, but more about our actual experience of loving-kindness. We could read and talk for ages, but in the end, experience is what matters. In the case of enlightened masters, their loving-kindness is impartial, unconditional, effortless, and exactly as active and creative as the situation requires. For us, this may sound like a remote ideal, but we can take heart in knowing that it is achievable, and we can trust that any step we take in that direction will be worthwhile.

Mahayana Buddhism and Bodhicitta

The historical Buddha taught continuously for several decades. In contrast to the caste system, he disagreed with the view that only an elite were worthy of spiritual guidance and freedom. Thus, he gave teachings to all—men and women, young and old, healthy and sick, rich and poor, kings and bandits, merchants and monks. Consequently, it would be absurd to insist on a one-size-fits-all approach to spirituality. While there are some universal truths that need to be realised in order to find freedom—such as the truth of suffering and the impermanent nature of relative, conditioned phenomena—we all have different backgrounds, personalities, needs, goals, and capacities. This is why the Buddha gave different teachings to meet the capabilities of his listeners. From these teachings, different paths developed, leading either to personal liberation or to boundless awakening. Over the centuries, countless devotees have reaped the fruits of their practice, and have legitimately taught the Dharma according to the needs of the people in their eras and socio-geographical locations. In the last chapter of this book, we will discover some tools that can help us establish the validity of a teaching. The point here is that an astonishingly wide variety of Buddhist teachings have appeared in this world.

There are many ways to divide these teachings, one of which is to speak of "vehicles" or *yanas*, each implying a difference in terms of view, practices, and fruition. There are many classifications into such vehicles, but the most common system is that of three vehicles: Hinayana, Mahayana, and Vajrayana.

The Hinayana, or so-called "basic vehicle," is often equated with the Theravada—which evolved from the only extant school of eighteen schools of ancient Buddhism and is still influential in Sri Lanka, Burma, Thailand, Laos, Cambodia, and parts of Vietnam. However, a closer look reveals that this is somewhat inaccurate and problematic. Some people might use the term "Hinayana" to refer to old schools of Buddhism that disappeared from India, but that is not how we use it here. When Mahayana practitioners use the term

"Hinayana," they often refer to the goal of personal liberation and the common path that leads to it, which is closer to our definition. As Traleg Kyabgon Rinpoche writes:

> For the purposes of understanding the yana system [...], we can safely understand Hinayana to include the fundamental doctrines of the Buddha, including the Four Noble Truths, selflessness, dependent origination, karma and rebirth, and individual salvation within nirvana. When we are on this spiritual path, there are many things that we might notice within ourselves that we do not like, want, or need—excessive anger, excessive jealousy, extreme forms of selfishness, self-centeredness, violence, hatred, and so forth. In order to rid ourselves of these things, to displace them from our consciousness, we renounce them in favor of a more caring attitude.[67]

So *renunciation* is a key element of the Hinayana, which includes foundational teachings.

The Mahayana, or "great vehicle," builds on the foundation of renunciation but decides that striving only to liberate oneself is not enough. Since all sentient beings experience suffering, we should strive for the awakening of all beings. Mahayanists are wary of a "static" nirvana and instead seek a complete enlightenment or buddhahood, which would allow us to effectively help others. The Mahayana path is one of love and courage, involving training in vast, meritorious, and altruistic activities. It is also a path of profound wisdom, further exploring the notion of emptiness.[68]

The Vajrayana, or "adamantine vehicle," builds on the fusion of altruism and wisdom and offers more expedient means to cut through delusion. Motivated by renunciation, compassion, and a sense of urgency, the practitioner works with meditative techniques that are both more powerful and subtle. Therefore, proper guidance and a certain level of maturity and understanding are required to prevent mistaking the energetic methods for materialism, the iconography for eternalism, or emptiness for nihilism, which could have detrimental effects. Vajrayana involves esoteric practices that need to be learned from an established lineage and in a proper context. This uncommon, indestructible vehicle is preserved in Indo-Tibetan Buddhism and practiced in Bhutan, Nepal, and wherever there are Tibetan and Himalayan diasporas. There are also Vajrayana traditions in China, Japan, and elsewhere. It is mind-blowingly deep and varied, but it always builds upon the union of love and wisdom, making Vajrayana very much a form of Mahayana.

The practitioner's relationship with difficult emotions evolves through the three yanas. In the Hinayana, we tame the mind to avoid conflicting emotions. In the common Mahayana, instead of merely trying to avoid them, we work on purifying them, which involves a more accommodating or encompassing way of training the mind. Whilst in the Vajrayana, we are more concerned with transforming so-called negative emotions into their opposite wisdoms and qualities.

Tibetan Buddhism integrates all these teachings in a comprehensive and coherent manner, allowing us to safely and progressively refine our understanding. Over the course of a practitioner's life, many wonderful things can happen. One of the most pivotal moments, after taking refuge, is when the practitioner takes the bodhisattva vow. While taking refuge is common to all vehicles of Buddhism, generating an altruistic motivation is what propels one into the Mahayana path.

A bodhisattva is a spiritual practitioner who formally aspires to bring all beings to enlightenment. They tread the path to full awakening for the sake of all sentient beings. Although it may sound ambitious, it is precisely the opposite of egomania. This motivation is often referred to as *bodhicitta*, sometimes translated as "the mind of enlightenment," or "the awakened heart."

Bodhicitta eventually becomes the cornerstone of our spiritual practice. No matter how awkward, forgetful, selfish, or impatient we may be, we try to return to cultivating it with an honest and open heart. In fact, bodhicitta is the most important subject of this chapter. It arises when we meditate on suffering, the nature of samsara, love, compassion, impartiality, and empathetic joy. It also relies on our gathering positive circumstances or energies (or "merits") that encourage and propel us along the path to sanity.

We could argue that significant differences exist between Hinayana and Mahayana when it comes to philosophical views and actual practices. But, unlike other systems of classification, the Hinayana-Mahayana distinction is more about one's motivation than about distinguishing specific doctrinal schools. As Traleg Kyabgon explains in *Integral Buddhism*:

> The basis or the determining factor remains the motivation, irrespective of the tradition one follows. If we are following the Theravada tradition and we have bodhicitta—even if we do not call it "bodhicitta"—if we want to attain enlightenment for the benefit of others, then we are following Mahayana. If we think we are following Mahayana teachings but our motivation is not that of a Mahayanist, then we are not following Mahayana.[69]

To get a sense of how important bodhicitta is, we can quote Tsongkhapa Lobsang Drakpa (1357–1419), the founder of the Gelug school of Tibetan Buddhism. Tsongkhapa, an erudite scholar, wrote lengthy treatises but also composed a concise text in fourteen verses entitled *The Three Principal Aspects of the Path*. What are those three? According to this tradition, the three principal aspects are renunciation, bodhicitta, and wisdom. As well, Patrul Rinpoche, an illustrious Nyingma master of the nineteenth century, wrote and taught again and again about the importance of love and bodhicitta, as do many contemporary masters such as Dzigar Kongtrul Rinpoche, Shechen Rabjam Rinpoche, and others. In fact, all Tibetan teachers acknowledge the importance of bodhicitta.

So it is clear that a vast and altruistic motivation to cherish all beings and cut through our own delusion for their benefit is immensely valuable. It is important to note that bodhicitta encompasses not just compassion, but also the wisdom of emptiness. We will revisit this concept, but the idea is that there is an interplay, and eventually a union, between compassion and wisdom. A genuine realisation of the true nature of things brings about a truly boundless, impartial, and active form of compassion.

Currently, we are suffering, and so are all living beings, but we don't know how to truly help ourselves or others. In order to do that, we need to cultivate wisdom and awaken to our true, ultimate nature. We can begin by being wary of suffering, egotistical patterns, rigid thinking, and extreme views. Then, we can train in tenderness and love. Finally, we can learn to see things as they are, with clarity and insight. Renunciation, bodhicitta, and wisdom are all linked and reinforce each other.

Spiritual Clarity: Finding the Essence of All Teachings

Our experience of the world starts with our mind. Consequently, if we are to skilfully navigate any area of our life, we need mental clarity. However, as we accumulate knowledge, traumas, and all sorts of information and experiences over the years, we may lose sight of what matters most. In the context of Mahayana Buddhism, it is safe to say that training in bodhicitta is what truly matters. Once we start to cultivate it, everything becomes clearer (though not necessarily easier), and every life situation can be viewed through this lens and used as a support for practice.

Bodhicitta has several aspects and levels, summarised here by the great master Dza Patrul Rinpoche:

> Generally there are said to be two levels to bodhicitta, the relative and the ultimate. *Relative bodhicitta* is the mind that is intent upon attaining perfect enlightenment for the sake of others, and *ultimate bodhicitta* is the wisdom that directly realizes emptiness.
>
> Relative bodhicitta itself can be further divided into *aspirational bodhicitta*, which is like the wish to go somewhere, and the *bodhicitta of application*, which is like actually making the journey. In both cases, bodhicitta is generated through formal practice, and so it is known as "coarse bodhicitta arising from signs."
>
> Ultimate bodhicitta only arises through the power of meditating on the path, and is therefore known as "subtle bodhicitta, which is gained through reality itself."
>
> Relative bodhicitta has two points or aspects: compassion, which is focused on sentient beings, and wisdom, which is directed towards perfect enlightenment. If either of these two aspects is lacking, then it will not be the bodhicitta of the Mahāyāna, so it is important that they are both complete.[70]

In this chapter, we mostly focus on the compassionate aspect of relative bodhicitta; we will explore the element of wisdom in the following chapters. If these terms sound complicated, please enjoy the following story.

My dear spiritual friend Samuel Bercholz once shared a wonderfully eloquent anecdote about Kyabje Dilgo Khyentse Rinpoche (1910–1991), one of the great masters of the twentieth century. Khyentse Rinpoche was physically imposing yet incredibly loving, with unfathomable erudition, wisdom, and realisation. He taught many eminent teachers, including His Holiness the 14th Dalai Lama.

One day, as disciples were gathered around him, someone asked him to name the most important teaching. I suppose everyone paid close attention, hoping to hear something profound, perhaps something complex, a secret "high-level" teaching. Khyentse Rinpoche leaned over and murmured, just loud enough for others to hear: "Be kind."

This, I believe, is how to find spiritual clarity and ensure we stay on the right track. When we are lost, we could ask ourselves: am I becoming kinder? In other words, am I becoming more open, genuine, caring? That is the essence of practice. Despite the complexity and ruggedness of life as we know it, despite neuroses and habits that keep returning, are we being kind?

Compassion, Courage, and Complexity

In the lineages I follow, Tulku Thondup Rinpoche, Dilgo Khyentse Rinpoche, Dzigar Kongtrul Rinpoche, Chögyam Trungpa Rinpoche, and others have written amazing books on loving-kindness and compassion. For example, Tulku Thondup's gem *The Heart of Unconditional Love* makes it abundantly clear—through reasoning, numerous scriptural quotes, and actual meditation exercises—that love has tremendous power and benefits. It's extraordinary. Specifically, bodhicitta, or the compassionate heart of awakening, has been praised by generations of enlightened masters as an inexhaustible well of virtue and happiness for oneself and others.

The benefits of loving-kindness for our physical, emotional, mental, social, environmental, and spiritual health could fill a whole book. However, in the context of our reflection on how to find sanity in the age of information overload—how to live with clarity, tenderness, and integrity in a fast and noisy world—I would like to explore more specifically the relationship between compassion, courage, and complexity.

We live in a complex world, and our minds are currently complicated. By adopting healthy habits in our day-to-day lives, and especially through the practice of meditation, we can learn to simplify our minds—slowly clearing them of useless conceptual intricacies, painful emotional patterns, and veils of wrong beliefs. When our minds become simpler—not dumb (quite the contrary), just less chatty and less prone to unfounded judgements and spiralling scenarios—our relationship with all phenomena becomes more direct. We are then able to apply our natural intelligence more accurately. We may not have all the answers, but we are much better equipped to face the inevitable complexities of life. To do that, we need compassion and courage.

Compassion for ourselves: this whole process takes time, and we need to be kind and patient when obstacles arise and old habits resurface.

Compassion for others: we are all in the same boat. We all want to avoid suffering, and all beings deserve happiness—perhaps all the more urgently if they are stuck in a hellish state of hatred and utter confusion. In any case, it is only thanks to others that we can develop spiritual qualities.

Courage to work on ourselves honestly: it's not always easy, and it's not always pretty. It takes courage to acknowledge our own neuroses and fixations, to overcome laziness and negative self-talk, and to persevere in our meditation practice despite the agitation, boredom, and fogginess.

Courage to work for the sake of others: it's certainly not easy to contemplate others' suffering—let alone act to relieve it—and to suspend our judgemental aggression when we disagree with others.

Courage to face complexity: our desire for a simpler, more direct, more coherent life won't be satisfied by merely retreating from the world's profuseness. We need to face our predicament. Complications can be intimidating, but we can approach them with an open mind, a heart full of vigour, and a willingness to engage.

The bad news is we often confuse courage with rashness, stubbornness, neurotic heroism, worldly ambition, illusions of grandeur, and lack of humility. The wonderful news is that love and compassion do fuel authentic courage and strength.

In this context, the word "tenderness" is interesting because it brings some of our preconceptions to the surface. For example, we may think that being tender means being a softie. But it is courageous to be willing to be real, to be vulnerable. It is courageous to be willing to be cracked open in the face of our fellow beings' suffering. It is courageous to show up naked, so to speak, unafraid of the vividness and ruggedness of life. That's not recklessness or adrenaline-seeking, but genuine bravery.

To learn to really *show up* like this, we need to take the time to sit and contemplate the nature of suffering, and to cultivate a warm and tender heart.

There is also a positive feedback loop: as we saw earlier, clarity fosters compassion and compassion fosters clarity. In the same way, clarity fosters courage, which in turn supports compassion. How can clarity lead to bravery? One of the main elements of seeing clearly is the lessening of our self-referential distortions, and this is what naturally makes us less afraid. Why? Ego-clinging is like a target: the smaller it is, the less we have to fear being hit and poisoned by arrows.

Years of hypochondria and anxiety earlier in my life taught me that lack of courage stems from only thinking about ourselves—which may actually be the very opposite of courage. Conversely, by thinking about others, we shed our childish obsession with personal comfort, which naturally frees up space and energy for more meaningful and altruistic deeds (which can be as simple as a five-minute shamatha meditation dedicated to the benefit of others). Truly heroic people (including "ordinary heroes") are often selfless or at least less preoccupied with their own appearance, their own matters, and their own reputation. The most accomplished spiritual masters of the past were incredibly inspiring in their dedication, courage, resilience, and strength of character. They also had great love for all living beings, including all humans and animals.

So let's make no mistake: it's not that compassion is the new strength. It has always been that way.

General Advice for Meditating on Suffering and Compassion

In chapters 3 and 4, we contemplated three of the four thoughts that turn the mind away from the neuroses of samsara: 1) the extreme rarity and tremendous potential of a precious human life; 2) impermanence; and 3) causality. In the following pages, we will contemplate the fourth one: suffering.[71] From the Mahayana perspective, the point of these contemplations is to steer us on the path to enlightenment, with the ultimate goal being to reach buddhahood. In the meantime, they can also help us function better in the world.

Contemplating suffering can be intense, and we may come up with all sorts of defence mechanisms, thinking, "Is this really necessary?"

"It can't be that bad!" or "Wow, that's depressing." But the goal is not to make us feel bleak or morose. Rather, contemplating suffering is aimed at helping us see things more clearly, with less bias and confusion. It also aims to foster a more welcoming attitude in the face of life's challenges. Strangely, disillusionment is often thought of as a negative experience, but the lessening of our illusions ultimately leads to joy. The four contemplations break the spell of superficial pursuits and unreliable objects of attachment. They eventually provide the impetus to set our priorities straight and reinforce our motivation for an authentic and consistent spiritual practice.

As such, the four thoughts that turn the mind towards the Dharma are key allies on our path to clarity, integrity, and unconditional happiness. They also lay the foundation for practicing the "four immeasurables," or the "four boundless attitudes," namely, impartiality, love, compassion, and empathetic joy, which we will also explore later in this chapter.

But first, here are three pieces of advice that I have found helpful, regardless of whether we meditate on suffering or on the four boundless attitudes.

1. *Make it relatable.* If we want our contemplation to be inspiring and powerful, rather than vague and conceptual, we must make it vivid and personal. Metaphors are useful, but we should also draw on our own experiences—any memories, images, or events that move us. In some cases, especially at the beginning, it is advisable to start with ourselves. This may sound egotistical, but truly feeling the textures of our own pain and life situations will allow us to connect with others on a deeper level. Of course, sometimes we can directly meditate on others' travails without contemplating our own predicament. Sometimes, circumstances force us to face other people's suffering directly. In those situations, even though we might not be experiencing what they are going through, we

can still relate to their experience to a significant degree through the power of *empathy,* which works to close the conceptual divide between our immediate experience and that of others.

2. *Don't be afraid of it being unsettling.* It's supposed to be—at least from the ego's point of view. Whatever you feel, try not to shy away from the rawness of your experience. That being said, it should not be aggressive asceticism either. Be kind and patient with yourself, especially when you catch yourself not wanting to contemplate suffering, whether your own or that of others.

3. *Proceed step by step.* This sounds simple, but it has many applications. First, as Tulku Thondup Rinpoche points out in *The Heart of Unconditional Love,* some people are completely overwhelmed by meditation on others' suffering, and it would be unfortunate if that prevented them from pursuing spiritual training. In those situations, focusing on love instead of compassion can be a wonderful solution: it is less intimidating, and as we cultivate love, we will naturally cultivate compassion as well.

The second reason to proceed step by step is that, as with any training, we should aim for the long term and not hope for magnificent improvements overnight. Truly familiarising ourselves with the four thoughts that turn the mind away from samsara and with the four boundless attitudes, and going beyond intellectual understanding and initial emotional reactions, is a lifelong journey.

Thirdly, we should still work on tranquillity combined with mindfulness of feelings to recognise the differences between renunciation and defeatism, between love and attachment, and between genuine compassion and emotional contagion.

Lastly, our goal should be to make our meditation sessions universal or impartial. First, we think about ourselves; then we contemplate our loved ones; then we include people with whom we have a neutral relationship; then we start to include our so-called enemies; and eventually, we embrace all beings in all directions. Beginners like ourselves can use this sequence to enhance our loving feelings, which could otherwise seem feeble, biased, or unnatural.

Contemplation: Suffering (A)

Sit with your back straight in a comfortable posture. If you are Buddhist, you can take refuge and generate bodhicitta. Relax your mind, focus on your breathing for a minute or two, then contemplate the following seven types of suffering.

Birth. Though celebrated as a tremendous source of joy from the family's point of view, for the child and mother, birth is an incredibly painful and traumatic experience. The baby, after spending months in a warm womb, is forced through a small opening. Think of the sheer pressure exerted on the baby's tiny body and fragile skull, sometimes for hours, which is extremely painful for the mother as well. From the familiar darkness, the baby finds herself thrown into blinding light, in an area packed with tall, agitated creatures she's never seen before. There are all sorts of terrifying sights and sounds. Her skin is so sensitive that even a soft towel feels like sandpaper. Even if all goes well for the mother and even if there are no medical complications, birth is still considered the support for other types of suffering.

Ageing. Our body degrades over time. Think of how each one of our senses dwindles. Our physical strength, balance, coordination, concentration, memory, and intellectual capacity all decrease. If we are lucky enough to reach an old age, even the things that we enjoyed in our youth—sweet, spicy, fatty, or salty food, alcohol, sports, sex—are either forbidden due to medical conditions or become a source of pain. We can't work as much, we tire easily, we have fewer friends, social gatherings make us dizzy, and perhaps fewer people enjoy our company. We become more and more limited geographically, and unless we took the time to develop a stable spiritual practice when we had the opportunity, we are likely to experience a growing fear of death and all sorts of anxieties.

Sickness. Everything compounded is impermanent; elements dance and change. When our elements become unbalanced, which can happen to anyone at any time, we experience suffering in the form of illness or disease. Think about how varied the symptoms of illness are and of how many types of illness exist. Think about how intense some of those illnesses can become, and how all of them are unwanted. No one wants to suffer, but like birth, ageing, and death, sickness is part of the human predicament.

Death. Birth inevitably implies death. Our ratio of happiness and suffering in this life can vary from that of our neighbours, depending on our karma, our spiritual practice, and so on, but one thing is certain: a day will come when we draw our last breath. While life can be the basis for much suffering, it also provides us with an unimaginably precious opportunity to tread the path to joy, unconditional love, and true wisdom. Unfortunately, death can come sooner rather than later—there is no telling when—and this very uncertainty is also a source of suffering. The only thing we know for sure is that birth will lead to death. It is like an arrow shot in the air: it *will* land somewhere at some point.

Encountering what is unpleasant. Everything is in flux, and we are bound to occasionally meet what we deem unpleasant. As a human being, there is no life scenario in which we can continually avoid this: even the richest people have to regularly face things they dislike.

Parting from what is pleasant. All relative phenomena are impermanent. Change is in the nature of things. Anything that comes together—such as when we meet enjoyable circumstances—is bound to separate at some point. Think about how, when two friends meet, anything can happen, but only one effect is certain: they will eventually part.

Not getting what we want. All human beings—children and adults, the poorest people and the wealthiest few—have desires. Some of these desires are bound to remain unfulfilled. And the nature of our craving is such that when we finally get something we want, soon thereafter we set our fickle minds on something else. This exhausting dance between hopes and fears, expectations, and frustrations, is a form of suffering we can see at different levels almost every day.

Slowly go through these seven types of suffering and contemplate how they universally apply to both yourself and others. At some point, simply remain with any newborn feelings (be they of determination to find freedom and meaning or of solidarity with all beings). Just remain with these feelings, without commenting on them, so that they become a part of you. You can end your session by making heartfelt prayers of dedication for the welfare of all beings.

The Turbulence That Arises from the Aggregates

In Buddhist teachings, the previous list of seven types of suffering often includes an eighth type: the *turbulence related to our basic psychophysical components* (also known as "aggregates," or *skandhas* in Sanskrit).

Essentially, the five aggregates are the building blocks of all our experiences. They come into play every time we relate to a visual form, a sound, a smell, a taste, or a texture (all of which are collectively referred to as "forms," the first aggregate).

Forms come together with our sense faculties, giving rise to painful, pleasant, and neutral *sensations* (the second aggregate).

These sensations lead to *conceptions*—notions about our experiences. At the level of the third aggregate, we are no longer simply experiencing raw sensations; we label phenomena, conceptualising them as attractive, unattractive, or neutral, and perceiving them as fixed and independent "things."

The fourth aggregate includes all *conditioning forces*, sometimes called "mental formations"—mental states that build up our individual karmic vision and push our mind towards certain actions.

All this information is linked together by *consciousness* (which in Buddhism is a polysemous word that can be interpreted on different levels that work together, hence the regular use of the plural form, *consciousnesses*).[72]

These five basic psychophysical components—forms, sensations, conceptions, conditioning forces, and consciousnesses—are what are called "the five aggregates" in Buddhist teachings.

Until we can dissolve all distortions and clinging, this system of aggregates is bound to cause suffering. The aggregates are so closely linked that any sense experience—everything we see, hear, smell, and so on—can reinforce our gross and subtle mind habits and karmic tendencies, keeping us trapped in the cycle of samsaric existence. According to Buddhist psychology, it is onto these five constituents of our experience that we project the notion of a distinct, autonomous, inherent "I" which we habitually cling to, and as such they are considered the basis for the suffering of samsara.[73]

The wonderful news is that meditation can help us slow down this chain reaction that reinforces karma, and eventually remedy this state of affairs altogether. In Buddhism, when we talk about training the mind, we are not talking about reinforcing or oiling the ordinary machine of the aggregates. We recognise the habitual processes, but by being increasingly aware of them, we let them breathe a bit, instead of mindlessly allowing them ensnare us further into negative patterns and illusions.

Contemplating this eighth type of suffering should make us realise that our ordinary way of apprehending things is unreliable. We should ask ourselves, "What is it that I want to rely on? What is it that I should truly cultivate? Do I want to rely on an egotistic triumvirate of attraction, aggression, and indifference? Do I want to keep cultivating the illusion that I can confine dynamic and ultimately open phenomena into little boxes?" In this way, examining the system of the aggregates can illuminate our spiritual path.

Contemplation: Suffering (B)

Before we begin this contemplation, it is important to understand that traditionally, there are said to be six major modes of existence within samsara, referred to as the six realms or six classes of beings. Nirvana and samsara are not geographical locations; instead, these six modes can be viewed as psychological states or as physical realities.[74] However you approach them in this meditation, remember that the habits of mind, karmic perception, and afflicting emotions are so powerful that they taint all our experiences.

Sit in a stable and comfortable manner, and relax for a moment. Align your "three doors," which refer to body, speech, and mind: we want a still but resilient body, silence so as to limit discursive thinking, and a calm, open, and receptive mind.

As you contemplate the following paragraphs, trust your heart and try to come up with vivid images and poignant examples for each of the six classes of beings. Taken together, these six modes of existence represent the main categories of destructive emotions that can enslave us at any given moment or throughout our lives. They form a baseline for our experience. Contemplate how these six realms and the beings within them encompass or symbolise all possible scenarios of unenlightened living.

Hell. Typically, we react to whatever we encounter or think about with either indifference, attraction, or aversion. Aversion leads to anger, which then leads to hatred, violence, and harmful experiences for oneself and others. When anger predominates, we see red and our whole world can seem filled with enemies, resulting in hellish situations—seemingly endless cycles of senseless savagery and escalating violence. War zones and places of extreme suffering are examples of this realm: places where beings are being burned or frozen alive, tortured, repeatedly raped, maimed, and dismembered.

Hungry ghosts. This realm represents miserliness and a poverty mentality. Unable to appreciate the world's beauty and recognise the immeasurable richness of our buddha nature, we constantly feel like we lack something and we become greedy. This greed, like drinking salt water, only increases our craving. Extreme covetousness leads to fewer and fewer friends, loneliness, and a sense that no one understands or even sees us. The "hungry ghosts" are traditionally depicted with long thin throats and big distended bellies, symbolising unfulfilled cravings. In some cases, they live in a world of utter scarcity and constantly roam stark lands hoping to find scraps of edible mould.

Animals. Beyond the aversion and hatred of the hell realm and the attachment and greed of the hungry ghost realm lies the ignorance and stupor of the animal realm. While it's true that animals possess intelligence and that some, such as bees and ants, rely on highly sophisticated systems, their potential for spiritual growth is evidently restricted. They seem to lack the capacity for self-reflection and long-term planning, often repeating the same mistakes. Some animals have particularly ephemeral lifespans. Some are treated like slaves. Others witness the disappearance of their whole species and have to struggle with environmental changes. Many are constantly fighting among themselves. Countless animals are trampled on, crushed, or cut in half as larger species carelessly move about. Many are hunted as trophies, or preyed upon by other animals. Millions are eaten each year, after being bred, farmed, and kept in the most alienating conditions.

Humans. This is the realm of passion or desire. Out of the six modes of existence, it provides the best window of opportunity for spiritual practice and awakening: in the lower realms, the immediate pain is overwhelming, and in the domains of the gods, the pleasant delusions are so strong that it is hard to break their spell and genuinely seek liberation. The human situation provides all the intellectual and emotional capacities required for spiritual growth; at the same time, it produces enough suffering to foster renunciation and act as a wake-up call—a call to awaken. However, our ordinary ambitions can easily draw us away from our true nature. The human realm is one of ceaseless projects and distractions. Even when we develop an interest in spirituality, we constantly oscillate between hope and fear, nihilism and eternalism. Our life passes swiftly, peppered as it is with the eight types of suffering, starting with birth, ageing, sickness, and death.

Demi-gods. When jealousy predominates, no matter how wealthy, powerful, or successful we are, we become entrenched in one-upmanship. Soon, competition in the higher circles occupies all our mental space. Titans are constantly at war with the higher gods, failing to learn from their defeats, and so they keep fighting.

Gods. Generally speaking, in Buddhism, the gods (not to be confused with enlightened deities or buddhas) are still trapped in samsara. Their characteristic emotion is excessive pride. They live in great ease among sensory delights, often for surprisingly long periods. In this sphere, life seems good, but clinging is still involved, and the constant pleasures divert them from practicing authentic spiritual disciplines. If the stars align and the gods manage to extract themselves from all the glorious entertainment and become interested in some form of meditative approach, they often fall prey to spiritual materialism, puffing themselves up with arrogance or developing a type of deluded concentration that seems powerful but does not lead to awakening. When their delightful sojourn ends, as it inevitably must, the gods—since they did not cultivate bodhicitta and true wisdom—are all the more alarmed at their impending death. From this lofty position, the idea of being recycled in the turmoils of samsara is suddenly much more frightening.

As you contemplate, you can go back and forth between the six modes of existence. Investigate whether any unenlightened situation provides truly lasting peace. When you conclude that a deluded life brings only suffering, stay with that feeling for a moment. Then, reaffirm your intention to cultivate loving-kindness and wisdom for your sake and that of all sentient beings, and relax in openness.

Contemplation: Suffering (C)

Contemplating suffering fuels our journey on the spiritual path. It is crucial if we wish to develop stable clarity, true serenity, and genuine compassion. So, let us be courageous and engage in a third meditation, using another traditional set of categories called the "three types of suffering."

Sit in a stable and comfortable manner, relax your mind, and focus on your breathing for a minute or so. You can take refuge in the Buddha, Dharma, and Sangha and generate an altruistic attitude oriented towards awakening for the sake of all beings. Then slowly contemplate the following:

Blatant suffering. This includes the more obvious types of suffering, such as old age, sickness, death, grief, pain, and sorrow—everything from small discomforts to serious accidents and illnesses.

The suffering of change. This relates to impermanence. Regardless of our current situation, relative phenomena are bound to change. The suffering of change is experienced when something that felt safe or pleasant becomes painful—like a greasy supper that keeps us awake with nausea, a friend who turns into an enemy, a beautiful car that gets into an accident, a reverse of personal fortune, a beloved house or district that falls into decay, a sudden public health crisis, or a spike in anxiety attributable to political instability. Additionally, sensory enjoyments are fleeting and cannot last forever.

The all-pervasive suffering implied in everything conditioned. This type of suffering is typically unperceived and relates to the suffering latent in all unenlightened experiences. It involves the five aggregates mentioned earlier. Whenever we perceive a phenomenon, we cling to it and (often unconsciously) apply mental elaborations that support future suffering. In other words, our systemic deluded reactions—egotistic attraction, repulsion, or indifference—reinforce our karmic vision, fostering our emotional turmoil and all manner of future pain and distress. As long as there is clinging, this subtle chain reaction will continue.

Contemplate how these three types of suffering are part of the unenlightened predicament. Investigate to see if there's *any* life scenario, based on our ordinary, confused way of operating—with even the most subtle clinging and delusion—that provides lasting comfort. Is it possible to find lasting happiness if one's life is based on the assumption of a static, independent ego? Is it possible to find lasting happiness if one keeps reifying things as permanent, fixed, and autonomous? Approach these notions from different angles; use your critical intelligence to examine and analyse them. Don't feel pressured to come up with clear-cut answers to all these existential questions immediately. Instead, befriend your inner wisdom and trust the power of repeated examination. Look, and look again, to see whether there is any unenlightened situation that is devoid of both suffering and the potential for future sorrow.

When you conclude that a deluded life only brings suffering, cultivate the understanding that the chain *can* be broken, and stay with this feeling for a moment. Then joyfully reaffirm your intention to make the most of your precious time, deciding that from now on, you will take any opportunity to cultivate tranquillity, clarity, warmth, and wisdom to lessen your own suffering and, especially, that of others.

A Welcoming Attitude in the Face of Suffering

No matter how much we take care of ourselves and our life situations, suffering is always latent. It is bound to manifest every now and then. When it does—whether it takes the form of sickness, grief, the loss of a job, a difficult situation with a friend, or something else—we can learn to stay present instead of running away, denying, repressing, or violently pushing it away.

Of course, some so-called "problems" are not worth our attention and are resolved by themselves. Conversely, some situations need a quick fix, and some symptoms and health problems obviously need immediate attention. We should not be overly sensitive either. Worrying about every little itch on our body and every little oddity in our life is a path to hypochondria and anxiety (I have personally wandered several years on that path). When we find ourselves being too sensitive, it is important to trust that there are many ways to deal with that brittleness, including raising or grounding our energy (depending on our profile), practicing meditation, cultivating patience, developing strength of character, and even learning to show some humour and nonchalance.

In any case, the suffering I am referring to as being worthy of a welcoming attitude *can* include anxiety or the recurrence of any old habit. It can be painful to notice that something that we dislike about ourselves keeps coming back over the years. Yet, in those situations, judgement tends to add to our suffering.

Being aggressive in wanting to quickly get rid of our pain can aggravate the problem or, at best, delay it. Of course, as we said, some conditions require immediate medical assistance. But in the case of minor ailments and common disruptions, having a welcoming attitude and allowing ourselves to simply stay present with our discomfort without elaborating or commenting on it is a small marvel of loving-kindness towards ourselves. Since we cannot be genuinely compassionate towards others if we are not kind to ourselves, this is a key point.

This does not mean that we should not attempt to remedy our suffering when that is doable; it only means that it is unnecessary to add aggression to the mix.

For example, I have a back issue that has caused me pain on and off for several years, despite my best attempts to permanently fix the problem. One day, the issue may completely dissolve, but for the time being, when it returns, I sometimes feel disappointment. The pain makes me less patient, and I tend to play the victim. Later in this chapter, we will discuss other ways to deal with challenging situations. But one thing that helps me when this back pain reappears is to simply adopt a welcoming attitude. When I feel aggressive towards the pain, the mental tension seems to increase the physical tension and burden my nervous system, intensifying the discomfort. It is important to note, however, that making friends with the pain is not the same as yielding to disheartened resignation. I still do stretching, postural exercises, and whatever can alleviate the problem.

Interestingly, familiarising ourselves with the contemplation on the suffering of samsara can make our rougher experiences a little smoother, because we do not compound them with a sense of injustice. We remember that suffering is part of the deal, so to speak; this makes us more composed and can even induce a touch of humour. For example, I remember the contemporary teacher Orgyen Chowang Rinpoche saying: "People complain, 'Oh, this person doesn't like me anymore, why is that?' *Of course*, things like that are going to happen! Everything is impermanent; there's nothing unnatural about it!"

I thought this was funny, true—and strangely comforting.

The Four Boundless Attitudes

Currently, the Buddhist teachings tell us that our view is askew, and our relationship with our thoughts and emotions is unhealthy. This relationship is based on confusion and clinging, even if it's sometimes so subtle that we don't recognise it at all. This grasping reinforces negative emotions and self-absorption, perpetuating the cycle. Enlightened buddhas, who are completely beyond emotional instability as we know it, show us how to heal our relationships with thoughts and feelings, which are fleeting, conditioned, and thus devoid of any form of solid, inherent, or independent existence. By clearing away this confusion, we can progress towards genuine clarity, unbiased love, and unwavering integrity. This doesn't mean that all thoughts and emotions are bad. In fact, they can be used on the path to fundamental sanity. By cultivating wholesome thoughts and emotions, such as love and compassion, we can reduce our self-absorption, fostering a fundamental openness that eventually helps us cut through all forms of clinging. At the very least, these positive emotions can bring more meaning and joy into our lives and soothe our relationships with others.

Which positive emotions should we cultivate? As mentioned earlier, Buddhist teachings emphasise four boundless attitudes, also called the four immeasurables, which are of paramount importance on the Mahayana journey. They are equanimity (or impartiality), loving-kindness, compassion, and empathetic joy. These attitudes are called boundless because their object is all living beings—humans and non-humans of the past, present, and future, in our immediate vicinity as well as throughout the universe. The notion of boundlessness also evokes the limitless qualities of buddhahood that we wish for all these beings. Simply wishing others well without wishing for their enlightenment could be called a "virtuous attitude." The special variant of the Mahayana is what makes these attitudes "boundless" or "immeasurable." We wish that all beings obtain both temporary and ultimate happiness. In other words, we wish that all beings become buddhas, freeing themselves of all cognitive and emotional obscurations, and that in the meantime, they find peace, relief, health, longevity, joy, and all kinds of positive circumstances.

This may sound ambitious, but there are methods and sequences to train ourselves. In the following pages, we will contemplate the four boundless attitudes, first one by one, then in combination. We will start with impartiality, and it is important to devote some time to it. This is because it will help us stabilise our mind and approach the other attitudes with fewer biases towards our usual objects of attachment and aversion.

Contemplation: Impartiality (A)

Sit in a stable manner and relax your body and mind. You can take refuge in the Buddha, the Dharma, and the Sangha and formulate the wish to train in boundless equanimity for your sake and especially for that of all living beings. Then slowly contemplate the following:

1. *Think of someone you like.* Clearly imagine someone you feel close to, like a friend or partner. Now, think about how this closeness may not always have been there. Perhaps this person was neutral to you in the past, or you were not even aware of each other's existence. Had you met under different circumstances, you might have never experienced positive feelings towards them. Maybe a conflict arose between the two of you at some point, and the other person seemed like an enemy or the relationship caused suffering.

Disputes aside, it would be impossible for your feelings to retain their exact quality and intensity continuously over time. Now, think that in the future, there is no guarantee that your loved one won't become a distant acquaintance, an enemy, or a source of sorrow due to various reasons such as growing apart, misunderstandings, moving away, disease, or death. All conditioned phenomena are impermanent, and it is in the nature of everything that comes together to eventually part ways. Even memories fade with the passage of time.

Do not be distracted by the thought that this meditation could lessen your love for the person. If anything, an understanding of impermanence can help you appreciate the moment and all of your relationships. A love with fewer illusions and less self-referential attachment can be even more powerful. For now, do not worry about this.

When you see that your close-knit relationship with this person largely depends on circumstances, contemplate how this has been true in the past, how it is true in the present, and how it will be true in the future. Then relax in this newfound understanding. You may notice a growing sense of openness: you are not becoming indifferent to this person, just less fixated on the relationship as an independent, cemented thing. If you feel this openness, stay with it for a moment.

2. *Think of a neutral person.* Now, think of someone who evokes no strong attachment or aversion in you. Contemplate how this distance and lack of concern are also conditional and impermanent. Every day, all over the world, millions

of relationships evolve: strangers become best friends, lovers become estranged, and so on. Using the example of the person towards whom you feel completely neutral, remind yourself that things can change. Contemplate how this has been true in the past, how it is true in the present, and how it will be true in the future. Then relax in that new understanding.

3. *Think of someone who bothers you.* Now that the ground is a little more stable, think of someone who irks you, someone you consider an enemy. Reflect on how the appearance of an enemy is circumstantial. When we feel strong aversion toward someone, we tend to cling tightly to their perceived identity as an enemy, often freezing our understanding of the situation. However, effects come from the momentary gathering of causes and conditions, and while some causes and conditions are obvious, many are unfathomable and subtle, including perceptions, habits, karma, environmental and social circumstances, and so on. Circumstances can change at any moment. Competitors can become collaborators, adversaries can become allies, and annoyances can suddenly appear as boons, if we see that they offer opportunities to practice patience. Even a cruel person who does not see the harm they have caused can be used to fuel your compassion—the actions they have performed have consequences they may not perceive, and that very state of delusion is a sad situation. Reflect on how someone you find irksome can change, how you can change, and how the relationship can change. "Enemy" is a temporary label. Contemplate how this has been true in the past, how this

is true in the present, and how it will be true in the future. Then relax in openness.

Perform this exercise regularly with these three types of relationships. At the end of the session, express a wish for the welfare of all beings and pray that they overcome obsessive attachment, indifference, and aversion.

Contemplation: Impartiality (B)

Sit with your back straight and your shoulders open and relaxed. Observe your breath for a moment, take refuge in the Three Jewels, and connect with the altruistic heart of awakening. Then start to investigate.

Ask yourself: what are the most common denominators among all races and species? Are there any truly universal denominators, despite differences in shapes, behaviours, beliefs, and other attributes?

You may see that there are two: everyone wishes to find happiness, and everyone wishes to avoid suffering. These are the two most fundamental aspirations we share with all living beings.

Test this statement thoroughly and be creative in your investigation. Challenge yourself to find counterexamples. For instance, think of someone who commits suicide, someone who seemingly enjoys pain, or someone who pretends they are not interested in happiness. Through the power of empathy and wisdom, in your heart of hearts, try to understand the fundamental aspirations that motivate their actions, no matter how confused, erratic, contradictory, sad, cruel, indifferent, proud, oblivious, or unaware they may seem. Consider beings that do not seem to have a centralised brain or the type of consciousness with which we are familiar. Think about how even plants, in their own way, seek comfort and proper conditions and naturally try to avoid adverse conditions.

If you wish, use the three types of relationships we contemplated in the previous exercise: slowly think of a loved one, a stranger, and an irksome person, and see how they all desire to be happy and how they all try to avoid suffering.

Alternatively, you can refer to the six classes of beings we discussed in our second contemplation on suffering: beings living in hot and cold hells, hungry ghosts, animals, humans, demi-gods, and gods. Slowly go through these classes one by one, remembering that this classification represents all possible scenarios of unenlightened living.

You can also proceed geographically. First, think of your own household, with all the animals, insects, and even plants it may include. Then think of your street, your city, your region or state, and so on. Imagine that you scan the whole universe, asking yourself if it is likely that there are any beings who do not share these two fundamental aspirations, deep down.

When you feel that these truly are universal tendencies, stay with this insight for a moment. Then, imagine that you let go of your judgements, fixations, obsessive attachment, disdain, indifference, and misplaced anger—and relax in openness. In this way, you can alternate between investigation and contemplation.

Contemplation: Love

Sit in a stable and comfortable manner, relax your mind, and focus on your breathing for a minute or so. You can take refuge in the Buddha, the Dharma, and the Sangha and formulate the wish to meditate on love for your benefit and that of all living beings. Then slowly contemplate the following:

First, stabilise your mind by taking a moment to contemplate equanimity: think of a person you like, a person towards whom you feel neutral, and a person you dislike, and see how relationships and perceptions are impermanent and circumstantial. "Friend" and "enemy" depend on countless conditions that are transitory. Relax in this understanding, and decide to let go of any excessive desire or anger.

From this more impartial foundation, take a moment to consider how all living beings desire happiness. Focus on that, recognising that this fundamental wish is not different from yours.

Now, think of a loved one. Ask yourself what would make this person happy—anything that would make them feel safe, joyful, and inspired in the moment, including material necessities, encouragement, physical health, fun projects, and so on, as well as anything that would completely fulfill them on a spiritual level. Think, "How wonderful it would be if that person found comfort and ultimate happiness! May it be so, without delay!" Imagine this person receives all fortunate circumstances and develops all good qualities, and rejoice from the bottom of your heart.

Then, in the same way, slowly proceed in sequence, including more friends, then distant acquaintances, strangers, so-called enemies, and finally all myriad living beings, including yourself and all the subgroups just mentioned.

You can be as precise and methodical as you want, or proceed in a more intuitive or creative way. Just make sure that you move from the intimate to the universal, and avoid falling into pure abstraction.

When you strongly feel the wish that all beings find happiness, let go of conceptual thinking and let this loving-kindness permeate you. At the end of the session, return to equanimity for a moment, relax, and dedicate any positive energies generated by your meditation to the welfare of all beings.

Contemplation: Compassion

Start with the usual preliminaries: proper posture, gentle presence, spiritual refuge, and altruistic intention. Do a brief meditation on equanimity, then proceed with the following meditation.

If you have a specific memory or image that immediately makes you feel pure compassion—the strong wish, unpolluted by self-referential attachment, that another being is relieved of their suffering—you can start by contemplating it for a moment to kindle the fire of compassion. If nothing comes to mind, simply proceed with the following.

Imagine that a loved one finds themselves in utter pain and distress. They are lying alone in a pool of blood by the side of a road after a hit-and-run accident in the middle of the night. Or they are trapped in a burning house in a remote area with no neighbours or first responders in sight. Or they lose their footing at the edge of a precipice, desperately clutching to a few blades of grass for survival.

Imagine your loved one's unbearable torment until you feel an urge to help them; and being too far away, it breaks your heart that the only thing you can do is hope and pray: "May they be saved! May they find comfort and assistance! May they be immediately relieved of their suffering!" Beyond timely relief, think, "May the cause of their wandering in samsara be extinguished forever!"

Proceed in the same way with a neutral person, then with a foe. Contemplate how they are all suffering equally, and how wonderful it would be if they could find immediate relief and ultimate enlightenment.

Relax in this compassionate feeling for a moment; let it permeate you without trying to conceptualise it. To conclude the session, dedicate any positive energy generated through this meditation to the welfare of all beings.

Expanding the Scope of Our Compassion

When you feel ready, you can try another contemplation on compassion. Follow the same sequence as above, contemplating how wonderful it would be if your loved one, a neutral person, or even a foe could find relief from their suffering.

Then slowly expand the scope of your compassion. With an altruistic mindset, refer to any of the three contemplations on suffering we did earlier (the eight types of suffering, the six classes of beings, or the three types of suffering), and see how pervasive suffering is. Contemplate how all unenlightened beings, at any given time, are either suffering in one way or another or harbouring causes of future suffering. It doesn't matter if our friends are not currently experiencing the exact scenario we imagined to ignite our compassion. All of us, considering impermanence, the turbulence that arises from the psychophysical aggregates, our subtle nihilistic and materialistic tendencies, and our willingness to obey our ordinary, restless minds, suffer from confusion and afflictive emotions. Until we reach enlightenment, we all wander, repeating samsaric patterns. Contemplate how samsara is but an overwhelming heap of suffering. When tears come to your eyes, pray that all beings find swift and lasting relief, and decide to keep doing your part, no matter what.

Be as precise and methodical as you want, or proceed in a more intuitive or creative way, but always move from the intimate to the universal, ensuring your meditation doesn't fall into abstraction. Before you end the session, return to equanimity and rest. Conclude by mentally dedicating any merits or positive energies produced by this meditation to the welfare of all beings. Pray that all beings be free of suffering and the causes of suffering. While we often wish that people are relieved of their immediate pain, the Buddhist way is to wish that all beings extirpate the deeper *causes* of suffering as well.

Compassion has an element of sadness, and initially, these meditations can make us feel uneasy. Our ego has plenty of defence mechanisms, and we need to learn to see through them. However, if meditating on compassion is too difficult for you at this time—whether you feel dread, unbearable anguish, intense agitation, indifferent stupor, or cold denial—focus on love instead. It is also important to keep up with foundational exercises such as tranquillity meditation and contemplation on impartiality. Don't be afraid to get out of your comfort zone, but do so wisely: be kind to yourself, be patient, and if you feel overly depressed, contemplate the rarity and potential of a precious human life. You can also do the following meditation on empathetic joy.

Contemplation: Empathetic Joy

Sit in a stable position and settle your mind. As always, you can take refuge in the Triple Gems and generate an altruistic motivation.

Take a moment to cultivate equanimity, either through the lens of *impermanence* (people change, relationships are circumstantial, everything is in flux, friends become foes and vice versa) or through that of the *universal denominator*, the understanding that all beings share the wish to find happiness and avoid suffering. When the tightness of your attachment loosens and the fire of your aversion diminishes, contemplate the following:

Think of a loved one who seems happy and fulfilled. Rejoice over their particular talents and personal accomplishments, such as being a good parent or thriving professionally. Especially, marvel at their positive qualities, whether it be generosity, patience, integrity, wisdom, or anything else that comes to mind. Completely forget about your own wants and needs for a moment. Rejoice again and again at your friend's success and happiness. Let your heart fill with joy, and think, "How wonderful it is! How wondrous it would be if they were never separated from this happiness, if all their qualities kept increasing, and if they continuously travelled on the path of wisdom and compassion!"

Then, proceed in the same way with an acquaintance. Imagine that they are happy and fulfilled, and wholeheartedly rejoice without any trace of jealousy. Take your time to truly experience joy.

Likewise, contemplate a so-called foe, and train yourself to appreciate their own success and happiness. This does not mean condoning scandalous behaviour or anything of the sort; it means imagining that this person experiences positive inner and outer circumstances and training yourself to appreciate this with no envy or perplexity. If this person has proved highly unethical in the past, imagine they have stumbled upon a genuine tradition of wisdom and that they delight in it. They have found a way to repent, and they begin earnestly meditating on love, compassion, impartiality, and joy. How wonderful!

Relax in this empathetic joy. Let it fully permeate you, then return to meditating on equanimity for a moment. To conclude the session, dedicate any positive energy generated through this meditation to the welfare and enlightenment of all beings.

Rejoicing over Spiritual Qualities

The contemplation above, like many others, uses the power of our imagination. This helps us develop good habits. In particular, sympathetic joy acts as an antidote to jealousy. It also energises us.

We could rejoice over anything that produces an experience of joy and fulfilment, such as pleasant material conditions—a wealthy person living in a beautiful mansion, for example, or a poor child enjoying their favourite candy. We can also rejoice in any form of relief, like someone hearing great news from their doctor or finding something of value that had been lost for a long time. Both real and imaginary things, as well as positive deeds and experiences from the past, present, and future, can all be objects of our empathetic joy. All these methods and approaches are important, but it is especially powerful to rejoice in spiritual qualities and realisations.

Over the centuries, millions of people have earnestly dedicated themselves to living ethical lives, cultivating love, and caring for fellow humans and animals. Countless people have strived to meditate on the union of wisdom and compassion, and many have reached enlightenment. It is said that if we see someone giving alms to the destitute or making an offering to representations of the Buddha, and we genuinely rejoice in this positive action, we find ourselves in a situation akin to that of the giver. In other words, we also acquire merit or positive energy. Empathetic joy is so powerful that if we read the biographies of the enlightened masters and fully appreciate them, we are likely to connect with their energy—this is closer to what we would ordinarily call devotion, but regardless, it's as if their own positive deeds and extraordinary qualities uplift us.

Rejoicing in positive qualities somehow makes them part of us, or at least inspires us to move in a positive direction. It's not a matter of envy, but simply of cause and effect. This is also why we should be careful not to rejoice in negative deeds.

Combining the Four Boundless Attitudes

We can cultivate the four boundless attitudes both formally and informally—while sitting on our meditation cushion and spontaneously in between sessions. Additionally, we can work with all four immeasurables within a single session.

As always, we begin by sitting in a stable posture and settling our mind. In Mahayana Buddhism, we also take refuge and generate bodhicitta, formulating the wish to bring all beings to enlightenment. Then, we can meditate on impartiality. If impartiality turns into indifference, we can shift our focus to meditate on compassion. If compassion makes us overly depressed, we can meditate on love or joy. If joy shifts to elation, or if love veers towards attachment, we can return to equanimity. We aim to gradually make all four attitudes universal and familiarise our mind with them again and again. In this way, we can be creative and resilient, adapting our meditation as needed. The four attitudes balance each other, and each one can serve as an antidote if our meditation gets diverted. I speak of "diversion" here because while I believe there can never be too much of the four boundless attitudes in their pure aspects, we often experience a rerouting or some kind of alteration: just as pure chocolate can be adulterated with additives, a little bit of confusion can seep into our meditation. That is perfectly okay: we are beginners, and our meditation is still conceptual. We are simply training to replace bad habits with good habits—gradually, we shift from thinking mostly of ourselves to thinking mostly of others. It's important to remember that this transition is not exactly linear.

Once we've covered all four immeasurables and allowed time

to fully experience them and let them permeate us, we relax in equanimity. We then conclude the session by dedicating any positive energy generated during our meditation to the welfare and enlightenment of all beings.

A Simple Prayer

Anyone who contemplates the workings of the mind can't help but recognise the power of habits, and anyone who contemplates the power of habits comes to recognise the power of speech. Using positive words and expressing positive aspirations does have an impact, at the very least on ourselves. The more we pray with an open heart for the welfare of all beings, and the more we develop compassion, the more we can radiate warmth and help others in direct and indirect ways. The process of cause and effect can be both very simple and extremely complex, but one thing is sure: filling our days with altruistic thoughts, words, and deeds leads to a more meaningful life.

One way to combine the four boundless attitudes is to recite and contemplate this popular prayer found in all schools of Tibetan Buddhism:

May all beings enjoy happiness and the causes of happiness.
May they be free from suffering and the causes of suffering.
May they never be separated from the supreme happiness that is free from suffering.
May they remain in the mind of boundless equanimity free from both attachment to kin and hatred of foes.[75]

It is important to remember that being "free from both attachment to kin and hatred of foes" also involves being free from indifference. In other words, we don't wish that all beings lack heart; quite the contrary, our wish is that they be free of partiality, agitation, confusion, and any kind of energy or afflictive emotion that troubles them.

Also, note that *we* are included in "all beings." There is nothing wrong with wishing to be free of emotional pollution, cognitive obscurations, and the causes of suffering. To cultivate genuine altruism and loving-kindness, we have to start with ourselves—that is, we should recognise the truth of suffering in our own situation. But the beauty of this prayer is that it keeps things in perspective: on the one hand, it is perfectly legitimate to want to be free of suffering and confusion, but on the other hand, other beings, who fundamentally share the same aspiration, are truly countless. We are but a grain of sand, a drop in the ocean. So we could pray openly, without fixating on specific results. We can pray with a tender, sad heart, or with sheer joy—our basic sanity can accommodate both. And we can pray in our formal practice as well as in between sessions. It is especially good to connect with the four immeasurables as we start a meditation session, regardless of the topic or method. As Tulku Thondup advises in *The Heart of Unconditional Love*:

> [W]hatever Dharma practice we do, we should do with the four boundless attitudes—with the aspiration for all beings to attain happiness *and* enlightenment.[76]

Myriad Benefits

Tulku Thondup's book, which we just quoted, beautifully addresses the countless benefits of loving-kindness. It has been an inexhaustible source of inspiration to me.

In the context of discovering clarity, tenderness, and integrity in a busy and conflicted world, we can simply say this: meditating on the four boundless attitudes can simplify our lives, bring meaning to our days, pacify our unstable emotions, benefit both ourselves and others, and provide perspective on all our problems. That may sound like a big promise, and it is. Look at it this way: lack of clarity, lack of integrity, lack of confidence, and lack of tenderness are all linked in one way or another to deluded self-cherishing. The four immeasurables help to reduce this. In fact, since samsara is based on clinging, and since the four boundless attitudes cultivate openness and loosen our grasping at a supposedly fixed or independent self, they address the very cause of our suffering.

In particular, meditating on the four boundless attitudes is the cause for developing bodhicitta.[77] When we sincerely wish that all beings enjoy not just temporary happiness but also supreme enlightenment, we reach a point where we feel compelled to do our part. It's not about becoming missionaries or being on a religious trip; it's that impartial love leads to a sense of universal responsibility. We start to wonder: what's the best way to help fellow living beings? We realise that the best way is to achieve spiritual awakening ourselves, to see reality as it is, and to help others do that too. Of course, we can provide material means, temporary solace, and all sorts of positive circumstances. We should make an effort to give money to charity if we can, heal others if we have the required qualifications, take care of the environment, and so on. But truly lasting happiness comes from dissolving the very cause of sorrow. The Buddha and all the great masters say that this is perfectly achievable.

Slowly, as we cultivate the four boundless attitudes, we start to connect the dots: *full awakening . . . for the sake of all beings.* At some point it becomes very clear. It doesn't really matter *who* achieves enlightenment first; it's not a contest, and in fact, we focus less and less on our own desires and concepts. We take refuge, and as we refine our understanding, we have more and more devotion for the undeceiving Triple Gems. The more insight we gain into the workings of samsara, the more we see that defilements and painful emotions are temporary and adventitious—they are not inherent to one's true nature—and this leads us to recognise everyone's potential for utter clarity, wisdom, and compassion. To acknowledge this potential is to acknowledge everyone's fundamental dignity; and the more we do that, the more we can embody that dignity ourselves. As we tread this path, as we contemplate the four thoughts that turn the mind away from samsara and train in the four boundless attitudes, we naturally develop an urge to benefit others, and this aspiration leads to taking the bodhisattva vow.

This vow builds on the refuge vow and can be taken with a qualified preceptor or lineage holder. If you haven't had a chance to meet one, don't worry: expressing heartfelt and sustained aspirations to meet such a person will bring results. In any case, there are wonderful books that we can study, especially Shantideva's *The Way of the Bodhisattva*. Many modern teachers, including Pema Chödrön and His Holiness the Dalai Lama, have written excellent commentaries on this classic text. I also highly recommend Dilgo Khyentse Rinpoche's teachings on *The Thirty-Seven Practices of All the Bodhisattvas*, published under the title *The Heart of Compassion*.

The Sixfold Training of a Bodhisattva

As mentioned earlier in a quote from the great master Patrul Rinpoche:

> Generally there are said to be two levels to bodhicitta, the relative and the ultimate. *Relative bodhicitta* is the mind that is intent upon attaining perfect enlightenment for the sake of others, and *ultimate bodhicitta* is the wisdom that directly realizes emptiness.

The notion of "emptiness" is frequently misunderstood; we'll get to that later. First, let's focus on relative bodhicitta, which itself has two aspects. As Shantideva writes:

> Bodhicitta, the awakened mind,
> Is known in brief to have two aspects:
> First, aspiring, or *bodhicitta in intention*;
> Then *active bodhicitta*, or practical engagement.
>
> They correspond to the wish to go on a journey
> And then to setting out.
> The wise should understand respectively
> The difference between these two.[78]

So, while bodhicitta in intention entails the altruistic wish to attain enlightenment for the benefit of all beings, bodhicitta in action involves training in the methods to actually achieve that aim. More specifically, the training of a bodhisattva is geared towards the "six transcendental actions," more commonly known as the "six perfections," or the six *paramitas* in Sanskrit.

In this context, the word "perfection" may seem a bit vague. Some people may get the wrong impression that they need to be perfect in order to practice these. However, the point is that these are trainings geared towards perfection. The way I see it, the term does not necessarily refer to the end of the path, but provides a general sense of direction. In other words, there's an apprenticeship involved.

In any event, these six practices are interrelated and they are extremely profound. They encompass all the main topics of Mahayana practice and aim towards what is called "the union of skilful means and wisdom." These paramitas can be studied in more detail in classic works such as Shantideva's *The Way of the Bodhisattva* (as mentioned earlier) and Patrul Rinpoche's *The Words of My Perfect Teacher.* For now, I thought it would be auspicious and inspiring to list them. The six paramitas are:

Generosity: This includes sharing our resources, time, and talents, with an unselfish attitude.

Discipline: Refraining from harmful thoughts, words, and deeds, and undertaking positive actions to benefit others. Rather than a fixed system of "moral righteousness" that thrives on guilt and fosters tightness, true discipline relates to humility, openness, understanding, and a good heart. It is a matter of dignity and respect.

Patience: This means patience when wronged or in the face of adversity. Bodhisattvas also train to be patient in their Dharma study and practice, and they develop the patience to face truths that may challenge all their preconceived notions.

Diligence: Joyful perseverance to avoid becoming discouraged or satisfied with mere intellectual understanding, and to take delight in meditation, study, and positive actions. We strive to avoid laziness and keep up with actual practice.

Concentration: Giving up distractions and actually developing different levels of meditative concentration, such as "one-pointedness." This involves tranquillity and evenness, but not in a blissed-out or disconnected kind of way. Buddhist meditation takes root in one's experience, and concentration ideally goes hand in hand with openness and vivid awareness.

Wisdom: This comes through three related ways: hearing, contemplating, and meditating. We need to understand the words spoken by a spiritual teacher, internalise their meaning through reflection, and become one with that meaning through meditation.

The six paramitas are often translated as the six "transcendent perfections." You may remember that the four boundless attitudes, to be called "boundless" and not merely "virtuous," must encompass the wish for all beings to achieve enlightenment. Similarly, for the perfections to be *transcendent* and carry oneself and others beyond the habitual mechanisms of deluded living, they must be imbued with wisdom.

"Wisdom" can have many different meanings. For example, in Buddhism, there is a distinction between what is called *sherab* and *yeshe* in Tibetan (or *prajna* and *jnana* in Sanskrit, respectively). *Yeshe* is often translated as "primordial wisdom," and it refers to the natural state of our awareness. *Sherab* is the sixth paramita that helps us recognise that natural state and allows us to precisely discern phenomena. In other words, we train in *sherab* to befriend *yeshe*. They are not separate.

This may sound a bit technical, so for now we will simply use "wisdom" to refer to an understanding of emptiness and interdependence. But then again, what does that mean?

In Buddhism, emptiness is not mere nothingness or some kind of nihilistic void. In fact, some teachers explain that the Sanskrit term *shunyata* could just as well be translated as "fullness" or "openness." Essentially, emptiness means that, no matter how much we believe that phenomena are unitary, permanent, independent, and autonomous, these imputed characteristics are illusory and not at all inherent. Our contemplations on impermanence and karma gradually foster this understanding, and our tranquillity meditation also prepares the ground for the wisdom that sees things as they are. In what follows, we will use the perfection of generosity to understand how the six perfections are interrelated and how any perfection can be combined with wisdom.

Imagine giving a healthy meal to a hungry person. If the meal is given in an ordinary way and with no particular selfish motives, it can be a positive action. If it is given with the inner wish that, in addition to being freed of hunger, this person could rapidly find joy and ultimately enlightenment, it would be imbued with a motivation akin to bodhicitta. But if this act of generosity is to be transcendent in the Mahayana sense—if it is to be truly part of the bodhisattva's sixfold training—it also needs an element of wisdom. Typically, and unknowingly, we give with an element of ignorance: we subtly grasp at the concepts of *giver* (in this case, ourselves), *gift* (the meal), *receiver*, and *giving*, as being somewhat independent, inherently existing entities. However, if we recognise that object, subject, and action are interrelated and inseparable, and if we proceed with genuine openness and with no—or with less—conceptual grasping, then wisdom comes into play.

This may sound challenging, or perhaps too intellectual. On a practical level, the basic advice is to give generously, unselfishly, with a good heart—we give simply, wholeheartedly, without over-conceptualising, and without any hope for results. As we give, a subtle experience of tightness or agitation may appear within our mind: for example, we may succumb to hope or fear, or perhaps some kind of desire for recognition. Long-term investment in sitting meditation will help us notice these mental events on the spot; when they happen, we can just recognise them for what they are—mental events—and let go.

I cannot stress enough how important the actual practice of sitting meditation is to this process and training. Experience in mindfulness and meditative clarity will help us notice the shifts and movements of our mind, and will slowly teach us how to reconnect with basic sanity, simplicity, and openness at any time and place.

"My Job Is to Love"

Now that we have explored the paramitas, the four immeasurables, and some of the benefits of loving-kindness, I would like to share something with you that I have found quite inspiring. At this point, we may start to admire how vast and profound the Buddhist teachings are—this book only scratches the surface through the ramblings of an ordinary practitioner. Personally, when I find this richness overwhelming, I like to think of the following nugget of wisdom a friend once shared; it helps me simplify my life and bring my practice back to what matters.

That friend is Rémi Tremblay, who founded La Maison des Leaders in Quebec, a meeting place for entrepreneurs, administrators, and business leaders from all walks of life, united by a willingness to become more humble, mindful, courageous, and compassionate. Rémi has written several books in French. Once, I heard him say this:

"For so many years, I was trying to be loved. It was a constant struggle. But one day, everything changed: I realised that my job wasn't to *be* loved—it was to love, period. From that moment on, my life changed for the better."

We may have been told that wanting to be loved is a natural yearning. Some might even argue that it is the most fundamental and legitimate of all desires. We certainly need love, and a baby who doesn't receive any care wouldn't survive. But as we grow older, embarking on a never-ending quest to find external nods of approval is tiresome and alienating. It can be subtle. Maybe we don't need our boss to give us a bonus every other quarter. Maybe we're not the "hugging type." Maybe we sigh when our friends mention our birthday or panic when we find ourselves receiving more attention than we think we deserve. Maybe we're timid, downright antisocial, or lack training in tenderness. It doesn't make any difference: given the choice between social recognition and a bad reputation, most of us would pick the former. We like it when someone says that we're brilliant or beautiful—or if we don't like *hearing* it, we'd still appreciate knowing that people think it. We may itch when our good deeds or spiritual qualities go unnoticed, or feel that our talents and skills are underestimated. Maybe our products and services don't sell much, and we take it personally. Or something like that.

But *loving* is so much simpler.

Shantideva said:

> To cover all the earth with sheets of leather—
> Where could such amounts of skin be found?
> But with the leather soles of just my shoes
> It is as though I cover all the earth![79]

Looking for love all over the place is like that: every person we try to please is different; every outer nod of acceptance has only a fleeting effect. This doesn't mean we should stubbornly ignore feedback; it just means that when it comes to love, sending it out is so much more powerful—and even realistic—than craving it. Though kindness should not be a mere strategy, it happens to be more effective than the vampire approach: if you want people to love you as you are, love them as they are. See what they *could* be, but don't cling to it; don't lock anyone into any preconceived notion you may have about them. Just see the potential and remember that buddha nature is everyone's birthright. Open your heart to their suffering, or if it's too hard for now, at least connect with a common denominator—there's always one.

Albert Schweitzer, the Alsatian-German theologian, philosopher, writer, and physician, reportedly said, "Happiness is the only thing that doubles when shared." Equally, we could say, "love doubles when shared." Or maybe love and happiness are basically the same thing. Either way, it's the experience of it that elevates us. It's about that feeling of tenderness-openness that hints at nonduality. Maybe whether we are giving or receiving love doesn't matter that much; what matters is the *sharing*. It's not about caring for or being cared for, but more about *care* itself—some generic, simple yet powerful, basic human feeling that echoes the interdependent nature of all.

So let us try to be like my friend Rémi. "My job is to love." Philosophical musings aside, this is eminently practical. And if you have trouble with authority, don't see it as an obligation, something you *have* to do. Consider changing your perspective and see how it drastically simplifies your life. We don't have to do a thousand things anymore, trying to please this person and that person; there is but one thing to do. Love. That involves paying attention. That involves caring. Though this one thing will unfold in countless ways, both simple and complex, our heart and mind may become surprisingly uncluttered. We will find a tremendous amount of inner space and a sense of freedom that continues to expand until, one day, all boundaries dissolve.

In the meantime, let's remember Shantideva's advice and wear good shoes: no matter how complex our itinerary or how spontaneous our approach to traveling, we'll still be walking, simply and safely.

The Bodhisattva's Privacy?

Nowadays, there is a lot of talk about the right to privacy and confidentiality. So much data is being collected on each of us that it has become a widespread concern. Many half-jokingly evoke Orwell's Big Brother; there are chilling stories of hacks, leaks, and identity thefts; consumer groups advocate for proper data handling by corporations; and legislators split hairs trying to protect individuals. We're increasingly concerned about the protection of our privacy, and educators develop programs to raise awareness of this issue amongst the youth, starting at a very young age.

Of course, privacy is important and should be taken seriously. But while this fascinating—and worrying—issue is often looked at through a legal, social, or global lens, it is worthwhile to investigate the value of our personal privacy from a Mahayana point of view. I realize this is a bit of a bold segue, as there is a huge difference between the legal context regarding the mining of personal data, often without people's knowledge or consent, and the bodhisattva's relationship to "privacy" in a broader sense, which we will explore below. I am simply pointing out that since the term "protecting our privacy" is on everyone's lips, this could serve as an interesting reminder for spiritual practitioners who may want to look within and explore what privacy really means in their own lives from a different angle.

A bodhisattva vows to bring benefit to all sentient beings. Regardless of how long it will take to reach full capacity, i.e., buddhahood, she trains in the paramitas—practices that aid in transcending the ego. As we have seen, these paramitas are traditionally listed in a specific order, but they do not necessarily represent a chronological sequence; they are often intertwined. For instance, generosity is generally listed as the first paramita, but the other paramitas can all include an element of generosity. Additionally, all practices, if they are to be transcendent, have a dimension of wisdom, which is often listed as the sixth paramita in textbooks.

In any case, as Chögyam Trungpa Rinpoche says:

> Taking the bodhisattva vow implies that instead of holding on to our individual territory and defending it tooth and nail, we become open to the world that we are living in. [...] We are no longer intent on creating comfort for ourselves; we work with others.[80]

Our capacity to give ourselves to others is often discussed through the lens of generosity, but whatever angle we choose, it can boil down to this: *a bodhisattva gives up privacy.* As Reginald A. Ray writes in his engaging and thorough handbook, *Indestructible Truth*:

> This means privacy in the physical sense—we do not regard our personal "space" and resources as belonging to us alone but are willing to invite others in to share them. It also means privacy in the psychological sense—that we do not "hide out" and pretend to be other than we are, but that we are willing to share ourselves, as we actually are, with others. Further, it means privacy in terms of our ambitions and projects. We no longer simply work for our own selves or our own ideas of what should be done, but we are responsive to the larger world, to the suffering beings that appear before us. And finally, the bodhisattva vow means giving up the privacy of the human world; we are willing to include all sentient life—not only of the seen but of the unseen worlds—in our commitment, as well as the animate and the inanimate worlds in the largest sense.[81]

This idea is radical but also eminently practical. It is quite freeing when we stop fighting all the time to defend a territory, and we can experience this every single day. It is not asceticism either: the aspiring bodhisattva will occasionally take time to rest, but only with the motivation that his body may be a vehicle that serves others—a compassionate pit stop, if you will.

Our digression about data privacy was more than just a clever, contemporary comparison. There's a kind of semantic vagueness about the insistence on privacy that can be detrimental to one's spiritual ease and freedom. As fundamental as privacy is in terms of rights and justice, when we become overly concerned about our own little privacy in a more subjective sense—our own little bubble, our own comfort—we can develop a tendency to shut down and indifferently withdraw from the world. Let us not be naïve online or oblivious to the way our personal data is handled; that's not the type of privacy we're talking about here. But every time the opportunity arises, let us keep in perspective our strongly ingrained desire to maintain our sense of identity and defend "our space." Without judging it, let's acknowledge this tendency with loving-kindness and understanding.

This territorial inclination can be prevalent when we embark on a spiritual path and yearn for more clarity: we start to see how scattered we can be, and in an attempt to find some focus and see through our hopes and fears and fantasies, we feel the need for more "alone time." While it is true that a conducive environment is important in the initial stages of meditation, generally speaking, the Buddhist approach is to see the so-called "interruptions" as very much part of the practice.

It is good to notice how disdainful we can be: the world seems sticky; we don't want to get our hands dirty, having more than enough of our own dishes to clean. But to paraphrase Shantideva, the bodhisattva ceaselessly invites all beings to a banquet. I've read the *Bodhicharyavatara* many times, and I don't recall the author complaining about the dishes that pile up in the kitchen while he entertains his guests in the living room!

At the time of writing these lines, I still value any opportunity I have to read alone in a quiet environment with a good cup of tea. Whenever someone invades this "sacred" space and I catch myself tensing up, I find it's a good antidote to imagine myself as a grumpy cat and laugh at my own irritation. Nothing is sacred that reinforces ego—in fact, that is perhaps the very opposite of sacredness. So, instead of reacting with aggression, why not share that store of peaceful energy with the intruder? Alternatively, when we notice our tendency to defend our territory like a crazy person, we can pray to our teacher or to the bodhisattvas for inspiration so that we keep opening our heart.

Abandoning Expectations

As we read and think about the benefits of meditation and bodhicitta, we may become inspired to actually practice, which is wonderful. However, inspiration often gets derailed, sometimes ever so subtly, and turns into expectations. We hope for some kind of fruition, or a palpable result. According to Buddhist teachings, constantly oscillating between hope and fear is not conducive to genuine happiness—at least not if these hopes and fears are based on petty, illusory, or self-referential attachments. As we have seen in chapter 4, it is often much healthier to simply focus on the process and let the results take care of themselves. This applies to both worldly affairs and spiritual ones. Of course, some situations require careful planning, but we should not let our muddy thinking and materialistic habits transform the spiritual life into mere project management. Expectations typically provoke a tightness that is counterproductive in meditation. As we familiarise ourselves with immaterial wisdom and qualities, it is best to proceed with openness—and with energy, of course, but in a way that allows us to stay at ease in the present moment.

One of the keys to meditation is simplicity. To understand how we can simplify our practice—shedding expectations of results or rewards—let us take the example of a sentence that may sum up our usual approach to spirituality:

"I will meditate, *and then* this will happen." Every time we tightly grasp at the "and then" part, we clutter our mind and our meditation. If we want to simplify our lives, we should simplify our relationship to spiritual practice. We could simplify this phrase down to "I will meditate," period.

But then again, why should it be in the future tense? "I meditate" suffices: it even connotes natural elegance, freedom, and dignity. Now we're down to two words.

As we keep practicing, we realise that most of the junk lingering in our mind comes from our attachment to the self—a supposedly autonomous, permanent, most-important entity. Over time, our rigid concept of "I" starts to melt. There's no need to focus too much on the "I" part in "I meditate." So maybe we're down to just one word.

As we further familiarise ourselves with shunyata and the wisdom that sees emptiness, we start to notice subtler forms of confusion and grasping. It's like owning a house with an attic, going up there after a time, and noticing cobwebs, foul air, and too much humidity. It's only a matter of time before mushrooms set in and bigger problems arise. These inconspicuous causes of further problems are akin to a subtler grasping to concepts, which, though barely noticeable, will still lead to suffering. Going back to our little sentence, "I meditate," at this stage we make less of a fuss about "I," but we are still clinging to the "meditate" part. With the wisdom of emptiness, we start to see that even that last word is just a word, a label on which we project our own experiences. It's an assemblage of letters that could be further divided into lines and dots and so on. Like all labels, it can be useful, but it is relative. Another way to experience this is to feel that subject, object, and action (our mind, the object of our meditation, and our meditating) are not at all separate; they have never been distinct, autonomous entities. Knowing that we're not dealing with mere nothingness either, we can finally start to relax and familiarise ourselves with a more genuine openness. We're not "spaced out"—in fact, we are still very much present and aware—but this awareness is much vaster, freer.

Analysing this sentence—"I will meditate, and then *this* will happen"—was just a facetious example. Of course, meditation and untightening the mind are not exactly like cleaning up an attic, and immaterial wisdom does not come about through mere rhetoric or mental gymnastics. But the idea is that on the meditative path, and in the practice of any of the paramitas, expectations can get in the way.

Dzigar Kongtrul Rinpoche gives the example of a garden, which blooms if the proper conditions—seeds, soil, weather, hard work—are gathered and fails if these conditions are absent, *regardless of anyone's hopes and fears*. He adds:

> The [mind training] practices, when done with the proper motivation, generate merit, which naturally brings us favorable results, such as a goo tion and increased comfort. Our hopes and expectations for these types of fruition don't contribute at all to a positive outcome. In fact, because these hopes are focused on the small self, they undermine our practice and actually prevent us from receiving its benefits.[82]

Courage and Uneasiness

The path to simplicity can be filled with awkwardness and complications. Although love is, in essence, utterly simple, as we learn to open our hearts, we may go through stages in which everything feels sticky, odd, complex, or extremely uncomfortable. At times, we may find ourselves feeling disdainful, cold, incapable, or downright horrible. But working with these feelings is also part of our training. We should develop the courage to open up to all forms of uneasiness.

Let's take an example. At the time of writing these lines, there are protests all over America, and in fact in many countries, ignited in part by the dreadful murder of yet another African American, Mr. George Floyd, by a police officer. That specific event was just the tip of the iceberg—a gruesome occurrence that shook up the masses. Every day for the past 450 years or so, countless other Black Americans have been suffering daily due to repression, prejudice, ignorance, fear, and hatred. Thankfully, we are finally starting to shed light on systemic forms of racism, and we can only hope that this is a pivotal moment in our collective history. But as we watch the news and scroll through social media, our attention goes from one thing to the next, and we shift from anger to fear to bewilderment—through a whole array of painful emotions. When it gets too intense, we may feel like we need a break.

Or maybe we have a tendency to oversimplify things. While racism can be boiled down to ignorance, the global situation is extremely complex when we take into account the interrelated domains of politics, economics, public health, civil rights, and education. When we feel overwhelmed by this complexity, we risk falling prey to muddy thinking. In an attempt to deal with the unfathomable vastness of the problem, our minds cling to a narrow view and tries to come up with a "quick fix." For example, we may find ourselves channelling all our anger towards one specific person. At other times, we may cry rivers and feel powerless, or blame ourselves for being unable to feel or cry.

It's all human. We may resort to any or all of these mechanisms—avoidance, oversimplification, desensitisation, polarisation, and so on—and some may last seconds while others last weeks or even years. But oftentimes, as we go through these mechanisms, we do so with little or no self-awareness. We're well aware that we are ill-at-ease, but we desperately want to escape the discomfort.

Courage and the path of meditation require us to fully open up to our feelings, no matter how unpleasant they may seem. Kindness and honesty go hand in hand, and thus we must be fully present: we acknowledge what's going on within us, without judging. "Not judging" doesn't mean tolerating the intolerable or that we should flush our discernment down the drain; it's just for the time being, in the context of our meditation. This is how we familiarise ourselves with our thoughts and feelings. Systemic racism does not stem from any single person; it is rooted in ignorance, hatred, and attachment. Unless we are fully enlightened beings, we all have these three poisons within us. It is important to get to know these poisons, see how they feel, how they manifest, evolve, appear, and dissolve. Our inner turmoil might pull us in different directions, but as we meditate, we try to refrain from commenting on our feelings. We acknowledge the thought without compounding, amplifying, or solidifying it. We take a step back, open up, and witness the whole process. If we never learn through repeated experience how one thought leads to the next and how we continuously get carried away by our concepts and emotional responses, we will never be able to cut the roots of bewilderment and anger within ourselves.

We also need to take action in the world and do our part with whatever talents, skills, or resources we have. But without meditation, awareness, genuine openness, wisdom, understanding, and loving-kindness toward ourselves, enlightened action and true healing are simply not possible. So if we ever put a knee on the ground in remembrance of the murder of George Floyd, we should think of a man who died and of a man who killed—but we should also look within.

Whatever the turmoil, we need to be able to look within and assess ourselves. We need to really see what's going on. We need to acknowledge our own disdain, our own biases, our own hatred, our own confusion, our own covetousness—whatever the case may be. Having deluded thoughts or poisonous emotions does not necessarily make us a bad person—that's partly what we mean by "not judging." We also need to see that even though we have negative thoughts, we have beautiful thoughts and emotions as well, and that it is always within our power to deliberately cultivate them. But we need an honest self-assessment. In doing so we are developing courage, because we may notice things within us that are not so great—horrible, even. However, we cannot overcome obstacles unless we first take the time to recognise them.

The same principle applies to any part of our training, and even to our reading this very book. As we read and meditate, we may feel overwhelmed by the task ahead, or strangely numb when we're supposed to feel compassion, or foggy when trying to learn new concepts and terminology. Welcoming all these experiences, with an attitude of loving-kindness and impartiality, is an integral part of our training. In fact, it is one of the most important aspects on the path of meditation.

Rejoicing, Abundance, and Simplicity

For several years, I lived in an apartment in a white and blue building that was about 150 years old, located in a small, quiet neighbourhood that stretched out along a hill. My apartment was midway up the hill: half a mile up were commercial streets and busy roads that led downtown, and half a mile down were the St. Lawrence River and Champlain Boulevard with its neat bicycle paths. The neighbourhood, known as the *faubourg ouvrier,* was historically home to workers and craftspeople. Some of the original doors were slightly shorter than today's standards, presumably because the people were shorter due to different eating habits. When I lived there, cats roamed the streets nonchalantly, and I knew a dozen of them by name. It was a lovely neighbourhood, not particularly affluent, but still retaining its working-class vibe.

I've always enjoyed walking. When I walked up the hill and headed west, I often ended up in another residential neighbourhood, one of the wealthiest in the city. Its streets were lined with luxurious houses. The crossroads were nearly always empty, save for the occasional upmarket four-by-four or electric car, which was surprisingly noiseless at low speeds, or an elderly lady walking her fluffy little companion. Joggers, dressed in sophisticated attire, would silently pass by, sending a friendly smile my way. The courtyards were large, with splendid landscaping—delightful groves, delicate flowers, freshly cut grass, perhaps a little stone path leading to the garage (or often, multiple garages). Some homes had artisanal lamp posts in their private parking areas, and through the large windows, one would occasionally catch glimpses of lush interior plants, massive kitchens, or even larger windows on the other side of an open-space extravaganza. The varied architecture was fascinating, often featuring exquisite dark wood, carefully chosen stones, old bricks, brilliant new steel, and shining shingles. It wasn't Beverly Hills, and many houses were more modest, but there was a definite feeling of abundance and professional success.

Now, let me be brutally honest.

For a long time, I walked through that neighbourhood with mixed feelings.

Sometimes, I felt perplexed: "How can there be so many big houses? Just how many rich people are there in this town?"

Sometimes, I felt a form of disdain: "Debt, that's what it is. Nine out of ten, I'm sure, have contracted crazy debt out of materialistic aspirations. Besides, I'm so glad I don't have to take care of that house—there's always something to fix, and it must take forever just to vacuum."

Sometimes, I even felt a subtle anger, making completely random and gratuitous judgements about how the owners might have made their money.

I know, it's not pretty. I told you I'd be forthright. The disdain and anger were never really blatant; I've got friends from all walks of life, and thankfully I rarely allow my mind to linger too long on such prejudices. But I can now admit that as I walked through that neighbourhood, there was often background noise in my mind.

The worst feeling, and the most prevalent, was some kind of envy. "How great would it be to live in one of those mansions; I could set up a proper library, instead of having hundreds of books scattered all over the apartment. I could design plenty of inspiring spots to read, write, and meditate; I could add a nice greenhouse, set up a proper guestroom, and enjoy a heating system that doesn't predate the Cold War."

I may have been wealthy in a past life, and financial wealth may manifest again sooner or later, but for the past twenty years or so, making a living out of my love of books has not been easy. I have put my heart into writing, had some great gigs, and achieved some *succès d'estime*, but I haven't experienced any "big break" (thankfully, I now realise that many extraordinary life paths don't rely on any such thing as a Hollywoodesque "big break"). In any case, for a long time, as I walked through that neighbourhood, I couldn't help but feel envy or covetousness—not the kind that doesn't want others to enjoy what they have, just a strongly self-referential desire to access the same kind of circumstances. It was clear to me that this was silly: I knew that all circumstances can fuel both the writing life and the spiritual path, I knew well that one's happiness does not depend on the cubic footage of one's property (heck, more often than not I fantasised about living in a tiny house in the wild—we all have our contradictions), and I was wary of such mundane desires that are very much akin to salt water, which never quenches thirst but only aggravates it. However, it became clear that intellectual understanding was not enough, as envy still lingered about like a shadow.

I regularly practiced contemplations on rejoicing—on my meditation cushion. For example, I could happily think of and celebrate other people's spiritual qualities and professional successes while sitting in front of my home altar. It felt nice and natural. I could experience my heart opening up and feel empathetic joy. But then I decided to try this meditation while walking through the wealthy neighbourhood. Not just for a few seconds here and there, but continuously and deliberately, cultivating empathetic joy as I marvelled at the architectural beauty.

It changed everything.

The swiftness with which envy was transformed into joy was astonishing. It required some initial effort, but the investment was minimal: it was simply a change of perspective, like adjusting a camera angle or lens. Instead of focusing on myself, I began focusing on those enjoying these positive circumstances. It was delightful.

Connecting with other people's fundamental aspiration for happiness and well-being allowed me to open my heart and let positive perceptions flow freely. It all came down to being constricted versus being open: we can either cultivate a vast, inclusive view or cling to narrow, self-referential thinking. Through the lens of empathetic joy, a lush garden brought joy, a renovated façade brought joy, freshly repainted wooden shutters brought joy, and a gigantic Victorian house brought joy.

It was extremely simple. Not euphoria, just warmth, openness, and playful energy. Thanks to my basic training in the four immeasurables, I could get a taste of that abundance. Perhaps the most wondrous part of it all was that I didn't have to go through years of hard work and suffering to afford a particular house; through the power of empathy, I could enjoy a whole neighbourhood.

Whenever my mind clung to my own experience of enjoyment, I felt something was off. At those times, I simply reoriented my focus towards others, much as we do on the meditation cushion, kindly bringing the attention back to the breath when we notice our mind has wandered.

Feel free to experiment with the meditation on empathetic joy and come to your own conclusions. For me, I discovered that the joy that filled my heart at the thought of other people enjoying pleasant circumstances was always available. That was, in itself, a richness I could always reconnect with. I didn't have to own everything.

Learning to Disown

So, empathetic joy can teach us that we don't have to own everything. This brings us to a key point: meditation teaches us to disown.

Once, I listened to an interview given by Michael Carroll,

a teacher in the Kagyu-Nyingma lineage of Tibetan Buddhism, on the subject of Dharma art. Something he said really resonated with me. "The non-aggression of Dharma art is the ability to express your creativity and *also disown it*." As I thought about this expression over the following days, I realised that it was very much linked to sitting meditation. We follow the breath, observe it, but we don't cling to it; we let it go; we disown it. We observe thoughts but don't compound them; we disown them.

Now, I don't know exactly how Mr. Carroll saw the term "disown," but my understanding of it, in our context, is not that we should refuse to acknowledge any connection whatsoever with our work, or somehow push our art, our projects, or our lives away; it is not at all about rejection, aversion, or denial; simply, we fully accept that we ultimately don't have ownership over them. It is not so much the object that we relinquish as our grasping.

We never really own anything anyway—if *owner*, *object*, and *owning* are all impermanent and interdependent, there's no lasting, autonomous, indivisible owner. So we might as well relax a bit. We can start to have a healthier relationship with the world, one that is not based on territoriality, which almost inevitably leads to one form or another of aggression. We follow the breath, not too loosely but not too tightly. We watch the first thought arise and dissolve. Typically, we live in the second and third and hundredth thought—the comment on the comment on the perception—and this too carries some form of aggression. We don't have to cling to anything or force any kind of ownership. This may sound abstract, and to some people, it is likely to sound crazy, but over time, experience on the cushion will show the middle path.

If life's complications come from clinging tightly to objects, subjects, and actions, and if empathetic joy and the other boundless attitudes allow us to release some of that grasping, then learning to disown and cultivating these virtuous attitudes will have tremendous power on the journey to simplicity and clarity.

Sending and Receiving: A Training in Openness

I would now like to discuss one of my favourite practices: a meditation called *tonglen* in Tibetan, which means "giving and taking." In this powerful practice, we give happiness and well-being and receive discomfort, fear, and suffering. Tonglen radically counters our self-centred habits and develops a genuinely brave heart.

In the Mahayana context, it is typically taught alongside the practice of "equalising and exchanging oneself with others." This approach helps us start to value others just as much as we currently cherish ourselves and learn not to make a big deal out of our personal comfort and hang-ups. Compassion is at the heart of the Buddhist path. All living beings, just like ourselves, aspire to be happy and free of suffering. Also, it is only by relying on others that we can cultivate qualities that bring joy and dignity to our lives, such as patience, generosity, and loving-kindness. These qualities propel us along the path to enlightenment.

As we have seen earlier in our contemplation on interdependence, every single thing we enjoy—an apple, a pen, anything—depends on countless other beings. At the same time, our suffering comes from negative emotions such as hatred, obsession, jealousy, pride, and fear. These emotions stem from a basic confusion, or ignorance, related to viewing our "self" as independent, autonomous, indivisible, and permanent. Our suffering is closely linked to clinging and self-absorption. To combat this habitual focus on ourselves, it is not necessary (nor beneficial) to mistreat or belittle ourselves. Instead, we must learn to adjust our view, which is currently askew. As Shantideva wrote in *The Way of the Bodhisattva*:

All the joy the world contains
Has come through wishing happiness for others.
All the misery the world contains
Has come through wanting pleasure for oneself.

Is there need for lengthy explanation?
Childish beings look out for themselves;
Buddhas labour for the good of others:
See the difference that divides them![83]

The practice of sending and receiving, or tonglen, helps us gradually close the gap between self and others, transitioning from a childish, self-centred way of living to a more enlightened way of being. This practice can be done anytime and anywhere, both formally and informally.

In the following pages, we will cover the basics of tonglen. If you wish to explore this powerful and beautiful practice further, consider the teachings of the Kagyu nun, Ani Pema Chödrön. Her advice on tonglen is clear, inspiring, and pragmatic. In any event, it is important to learn tonglen within the broader context of a structured meditation practice: we should begin from a place of stability and openness.

What follows is a concise introduction, but remember to continue working with the shamatha principles discussed earlier and the vipashyana principles that will follow. Everything is connected.

Meditation: Sending and Receiving

Find a stable posture. As always, you can start your meditation by taking refuge in the Triple Gems and generating an altruistic motivation. Then let your thoughts and concepts fall away like a brick wall collapsing, and relax into openness.

When thoughts resurface, pay attention to your breathing. In . . . And out . . . In . . . And out . . .

Now, slowly start to work with *textures*, or feelings. Associate breathing in with the rawness of life: accept—without judging—narrowness, ruggedness, pain, fear, and discomfort. Associate breathing out with comfort, confidence, openness, and well-being. You don't have to work with specific scenarios at this point; just familiarise yourself with these textures for the time being.

Next, as you breathe in, take in your own pain, fears, and sorrows. Proceed gradually, starting from simple discomfort, like stiffness in your knees, and then move to your larger worries. This is bravery: openly and honestly facing your suffering. Let your pain and fear gather in the centre of your body and dissolve. Don't rush to cure your suffering or discomfort; instead, feel its texture and give it space. As you breathe out, mentally and kindly give yourself relief, confidence, strength, and a sense of openness.

Work with your own life situation in this manner for a while. You can be as specific as you want, but avoid overconceptualising. Regularly return to focusing on the breath and feel its textures. This is a healing practice, but don't cling to any expectation of results. Just breathe in the suffering and breathe out happiness and comfort. Breathing in is compassion; breathing out is love. They are two sides of the same coin.

After a while, bring to mind someone you appreciate. Remember that they share the same fundamental aspirations as you. They want happiness, and they want to avoid suffering. Slowly start to take on their physical pain, financial problems, emotional wounds, or whatever difficulty they may be experiencing now and in the future. As you breathe in, imagine that their suffering and the cause of their suffering enter your own body and heart, and dissolve there. As you breathe out, mentally send happiness, health, trust, joy, and wisdom. Again, you can be as specific as you want—you can send them a new job, great doctors and remedies if they are sick, loving friends if they are lonely, inspiring books, anything—but keep *feeling*. A traditional and powerful approach is to imagine light emanating from your body or nectar filling their body. Think and feel that your friend receives your healing energies, that they are happy and safe, and then rejoice. Continue sending, receiving, and rejoicing for a while.

As you take on others' pain, you can visualise dark smoke or soot entering you—don't fear it, and know that it completely dissolves in your heart of loving-kindness until there's not the slightest trace left. This will not make you sick; again, this is both a healing practice and a practice of courage.

Then, as we did with our meditations on the four boundless attitudes, gradually open up and proceed in stages, practicing tonglen with loved ones, then acquaintances, people you are usually unconcerned about, so-called enemies, and finally all beings equally.

Make sure you balance both aspects of the practice: giving and taking. If fear arises, you can go back to the first step, welcome that very fear and let it dissolve, then offer yourself comfort and relief. At every stage, take the time to rejoice.

After a while, let go of the visualisation and simply relax in openness, silence, or equanimity. To conclude the session, dedicate any positive energy generated through this meditation to the welfare and enlightenment of all beings.

— —

This practice can be done for a few minutes or an hour on your meditation cushion, or for a few seconds here and there as you walk on the street or ride the train. You can be creative in how you approach it, as long as you keep a spacious mind and focus on the feelings rather than mental elaborations. Also, ensure that you practice loving-kindness towards yourself, too, and regularly reconnect with the energy of joy and a sense of fundamental peace and confidence.

Ceaseless Opportunities

Before we conclude this chapter, I want to mention some additional resources that can help cultivate bodhicitta. I have already mentioned a few texts and authors, including Shantideva's *The Way of the Bodhisattva*. While there are many books available, the point here is not necessarily to become scholars. Instead, take your time, choose wisely, follow your intuition, and really take the time to appreciate whatever teaching you choose to study and whatever practice you choose to do. My teacher Tulku Thondup Rinpoche often uses the image of a child savouring the flavour of a candy to illustrate how the teachings and one's mind can eventually blend.

One of the most amazing things that we start to realise as we study Dharma is that our whole life can nourish our spiritual practice. Every single day presents countless opportunities to catch our little games on the spot, bravely open up, and connect with a source of love and serenity. Training does not only happen on the cushion; it permeates all aspects of our daily life.

A particularly inspiring body of literature on this subject is referred to as the *lojong* teachings, of which tonglen practice is an important part. "Lojong" is a Tibetan term often translated as "mind training," and it typically refers to training the mind in relative and absolute bodhicitta. This involves methods and exercises to familiarise ourselves with the four boundless attitudes and openness-emptiness, cultivating compassion and becoming increasingly caring and grateful towards all beings.

The core of these exercises and teachings has been summarised by Atisha (982–1054) and Geshe Chekawa (1101–1175) in what are known as the *Seven Points of Mind Training*. These points contain pithy slogans and extremely useful advice on tonglen and other complementary practices. Personally, although (or perhaps because) they constantly challenge me, I have immense devotion towards these precious teachings, and I strongly encourage you to study them by reading the excellent contemporary commentaries, such as those by Dilgo Khyentse Rinpoche, Chögyam Trungpa, Dzigar Kongtrul, and Traleg Kyabgon.[84] Additionally, the short text *Transforming Suffering and Happiness into Enlightenment* by the Third Dodrupchen Rinpoche (1865–1926) is an excellent resource that shows how any situation can be used on the path to freedom, clarity, and loving-kindness.

Trusting that all circumstances can be put to good use is incredibly uplifting and comforting. This confidence propels us on the path to clarity, tenderness, and integrity, no matter how chaotic the world seems to become. Whether facing pandemics, economic crises, or personal problems, we begin to see that every situation is fertile. Despite how we sometimes feel, our life is never barren—as long as we irrigate it with the blessed waters of love and compassion.

Studying and practicing the lojong teachings significantly simplifies our lives. We become less prone to blaming external conditions and start to see that self-centredness is the main source of the obstacles and complications we face. Simplicity brings clarity, clarity fosters confidence, and confidence combined with love brings strength. From this foundation, we can devote ourselves more effectively to any endeavour or cause, whether it's an artistic project, defending civil rights, protecting the environment, public education, or anything else, at any scale.

Training the mind is a lifelong journey. There will be times when we forget or feel like we're not up to the task. But we return to the teachings, and they illuminate our path. This is how we train: we keep coming back to the practice. Like physical exercise, maintaining spiritual health requires consistent effort throughout our life, not just a few workouts in our youth. The good news is that the more we study the lojong teachings, the more we realise how vast, rich, and helpful they are. This, in turn, brings further joy and wonder, propelling us further on the path.

How Noise Can Actually Help Us Cultivate Bodhicitta

We often associate contemplation with silence. While we may have heard stories of people meditating in busy places like Central Park or on a train, we generally believe that noise and intensity are obstacles to authentic spirituality. In some respects, this is true. To learn meditation, it is beneficial to have a quiet and inspiring environment because, until we become stable in our practice, our attention is easily derailed, and our energetic system is heavily impacted by our surroundings. Creating a proper environment is common sense, and less agitation in one's demeanour is generally considered a characteristic of a dharmic person. Constant busyness can be a subtle form of laziness or an unspoken nihilistic fear that if we stop for a few minutes, our sense of a coherent self might vanish. It is essential to learn to slow down, enjoy doing less, and taste the freedom that comes from not constantly relying on outer and inner stimuli to reaffirm ourselves. That being said, the mind training teachings tell us that *every* situation can be put to good use, including noisy and chaotic ones.

Here, take "noise" in both its literal and metaphorical senses, from information overload to cognitive and spiritual distortions to the frequent notifications on our phones and the traffic down the street.

In the following contemplation, we will pay attention to the constant samsaric rumbling and see how it can serve as a reminder for us to reconnect with sanity and cultivate loving-kindness. This exercise is somewhat unusual, but I encourage you to return to it every now and then, and to be creative in how you approach it. It can help turn stressful situations into fuel for bodhicitta. To make the most of this contemplation, you may want to revisit chapter 2 and review the section titled "The Difficulties Associated with the Current Overload."

Contemplation: The Impact of the Current Overload on our Brothers and Sisters

Take a moment to relax, then slowly contemplate the following.

Think about how difficult it seems for us to slow down. Contemplate the human predicament in the twenty-first century. To avoid mere abstraction, reflect on your own life, and if you want, think of some particularly busy people you know; also use the power of your imagination to create vivid images and examples that show how widespread our addiction to excessive content and busyness is. For example, you can imagine millions of us glued to our phones, or thousands of news outlets broadcasting content 24/7, or countless cars inching their way to work every single day—as far as the eye can see, disposable vehicles polluting the environment and disturbing animals, not to mention the stress, pain, and mental exhaustion that the drivers endure and the risks they face.

In your mind's eye, consider what happens on a typical day when we get back from work. Some of us immediately grab a drink, while others run around fulfilling family obligations. Some of us go to the gym in an attempt to feel good, which sometimes works, but our grasping at our fitness goals can somehow end up contributing to the very stress we're trying to sweat off! Some, supposedly relieved that their workday is finally over, turn on their computer as soon as they get home in order to do some more work. Consider how years of materialistic habits have made it seemingly impossible to stand still for more than a few seconds. We lack contentment and satisfaction, we barely know our own minds, we feel like we don't know what to do with ourselves, and we are so afraid of boredom that we fill every minute with some "thing"—a project, a flavour, an idea, a fantasy, anger, a pop tune, a fun video, checking our email, whatever.

Yes, some of these activities are useful. But take a moment to reflect on how fearful, addicted, and directionless we actually are.

Reflect on and consider how seriously we take our discursive thoughts, our emotions, concepts, and belief systems. Look at how we are constantly "doing" and how rarely we are simply aware of the present moment, enjoying it in all its richness.

Every once in a while, we slow down and truly savour the aroma of a cup of freshly ground coffee or the beauty of breathtaking natural scenery. When that happens, we feel joy, gratitude, openness, simplicity—a natural sense of abundance and even awe. This empowers us, and then if we relax even more and let the experience happen simply without grasping at it, we can discover some clarity within, an unshakable confidence, and a sense of being interconnected.

But we rarely do that.

Even if we're lucky enough to taste these experiences, they are mere glimpses—a few seconds in the course of a day, just minutes over the course of a month. Even for the happy-go-lucky or jovial type, how many of these fun times and serene moments are actually imbued with bodhicitta—an altruistic intention to benefit all beings, a truly open heart, and less grasping at "this" and "that"? We spend the majority of our time with little or no awareness, awkwardly trying to reconcile the past and the future, thinking of ourselves, looking for entertainment, and clutching at hopes and fears.

That's not to judge. It's all very human, and we are all in the same boat. The point is to see how easy it is to be distracted from our true nature.

Now, consider all that noise, all these distractions and distortions that can so easily add to our stress and make us veer off course and forget about fundamental ease and dignity. Formulate the wish that from now on, you will not add to the chaos and confusion. Commit to being kind, as much as you can. Formulate the wish to cultivate clarity and wisdom for your welfare and that of all beings.

You may start to notice a deep coherence across all the exercises and themes that we have explored so far. We contemplate the preciousness of human life and make the contemplation on impermanence our constant companion. We also reflect on cause and effect, and on the suffering that self-centredness and ignorance inevitably produce. These four contemplations weaken the seductive power that samsaric patterns hold over us—patterns that prevent us from experiencing true clarity, tenderness, and integrity.

Additionally, we contemplate how all beings, just like ourselves, desire happiness and want to avoid suffering. From this understanding, we cultivate equanimity, love, compassion, and empathetic joy, and we value bodhicitta above everything else. Bodhicitta simplifies our lives, brings meaning, and fosters power, resilience, and confidence, for our benefit and that of all living beings. And in parallel to all these contemplations, we keep practicing tranquillity meditation, and begin to see that we can always reconnect with basic sanity, whoever and wherever we are. All these practices reinforce each other.

Yet, we still need a crucial ingredient: wisdom. In the following chapter, we will explore this notion further and start to truly befriend our mind.

— VI —

Clear Seeing

MOST SPIRITUAL TRADITIONS OFFER tools and methods to develop some sense of inner peace. Calmness of mind is not limited to Buddhists; many people achieve some form of tranquillity or meditative stability. Nowadays, "meditation" is taught in all sorts of contexts, including non-spiritual ones. Even those who do not meditate can achieve good concentration through dedication: high-level athletes, seasoned craftspeople, and business people often demonstrate laser-like focus and an ability to deal with their scattered thoughts. Modern psychology also provides techniques to reduce agitation and find balance. How these experiences compare to the different levels of shamatha as they are practiced and understood in the different schools of Buddhism is open to interpretation, but the point here is that there are numerous methods to cultivate some form of tranquillity.

However, from the Buddhist point of view, tranquillity alone is insufficient for full awakening. What truly distinguishes the Buddhist meditative systems is *vipashyana* in Sanskrit, or *lhagtong* in Tibetan, often translated as "insight."

We could also use the terms "clear seeing," or "true seeing." I appreciate those alternative translations, because nowadays, the word "insight" is regularly thrown around in all sorts of materialistic contexts—referring to business intel and whatnot. Here, it especially refers to insight into the empty or open nature of thoughts and of reality. The Buddhist practice of meditative insight cultivates a special form of intelligence, allowing one to reconnect with an atemporal wisdom. It often involves using analytical skills and alternating between thorough investigation and resting. So vipashyana is very much connected to the wisdom aspect of the path, which is fundamental.

As we have seen, loving-kindness is another fundamental aspect of the Buddhist path. It is important to acknowledge that most religions and spiritual traditions also have teachings pertaining to love. However, the view of bodhicitta and the methods of lojong, or mind training, are very special, and they are unique to Buddhism. Rarely do we find such methods which teach us to put others before ourselves, using practical techniques like tonglen. They help us see that the problem lies not in others nor in ourselves as inherently flawed beings, but in our clinging to things, including our sense of identity, as if they were permanent, independent, and unitary. Regardless, countless people are loving, and we should rejoice in that.

It is a great comfort to remember that. However, it is questionable how one can reach truly unconditional love, if one doesn't also cultivate the wisdom that sees the nature of conditions. In other words, if we don't develop fundamental openness and deep insight, our love will always be conditioned and limited by personal preferences, emotional hang-ups, and conceptual categories. Furthermore, we often feel compassion, but lack the insight necessary to discern the best course of action. We want to help but don't know how. This is why the bodhisattva path includes both compassion and wisdom. In fact, "bodhicitta," or the heart of awakening, has two aspects: the relative and the absolute. They work together and are never really separate.

A common image used to explain this is that of the two wings of a bird. The wings are those of wisdom and compassion. With just one wing, a bird can't go far. We need both to reach our destination. Although it is never good to overstretch a metaphor, we could also say that in addition to allowing us to reach the other shore, having two strong wings could even allow us to gather food for the fledging, guide lost mariners, and quite simply, freely enjoy the sky.

The Point of Insight Meditation

Often, one first acquires some experience of tranquillity meditation before moving on to clear seeing exercises. However, for some people, flashes of insight will occur first, or quite early on. In any case, a practitioner needs both; otherwise, calmness brings limited results, or insight lacks stability. Furthermore, it is said that shamatha pacifies the afflictive emotions, but that we need vipashyana to truly uproot these afflictions and deep mental fog. Focusing only on the former would be like preparing a meal with great care but never actually eating it, thus never really nourishing oneself. We need insight to see through the veils of our confused habits and uncover our buddha nature.

Generally speaking, all Buddhist schools engage in shamatha and vipashyana practices. The practices themselves, however, vary widely depending on context. Sometimes, there's a clear-cut distinction between conceptual and non-conceptual meditations, or between analysis and resting. In some other contexts, the distinction is not so obvious. For example, Chögyam Trungpa Rinpoche sometimes gave vipashyana instructions that seemed strangely similar to shamatha instructions. The contemporary teacher Dza Kilung Rinpoche also presents vipashyana as a natural extension of shamatha, instead of insisting on specific lines of investigation. This seems to be a more organic approach to vipashyana meditation with insight unfolding naturally as opposed to deliberately cultivated. But all these approaches lead to an experience of non-duality and spaciousness.

In the present context, we'll refer to vipashyana exercises as meditations that involve analytical skills. It is a widespread misunderstanding that meditators should not engage with thoughts and concepts. However, in Buddhism, we can employ our critical mind to dismantle confusion. This is key. It involves a paradigm shift, at least as far as our studying Dharma and meditating are concerned. Ultimately, the point of our practice is not to add new conceptions, but to remove false ones. One can still learn languages and study science and acquire knowledge in other fields. Any pursuit that contributes to happiness, well-being, understanding, harmony, and prosperity is perfectly allowed and is sometimes even encouraged. However, as far as Buddhist spirituality is concerned, the core of the path is not to accumulate new ideas and random facts, but to hack away at delusion. This is so that we can learn to see the way things are, untainted by our biases and habits (as they inevitably are until awakening).

Mahayana Buddhism speaks of two types of obscurations: emotional and cognitive. To make genuine progress in removing these two veils, we need the stability provided by shamatha, but we also need analytical skills. We hone those with vipashyana exercises. We ask specific questions—we inquire into the nature of certain phenomena, or the nature of our thoughts and emotions—we investigate, again and again, until we reach a clear conclusion; then we can relax and let that newfound insight penetrate us fully; and then we start again, until we further eliminate doubts and wrong beliefs.

In essence, we're learning to see things clearly. To say that we're looking into the nature of reality might sound ambitious, to say the least. But that's still what we're slowly starting to do. We're questioning our assumptions about reality, about our outer and inner world, and seeing what happens when we give it some space.

In this chapter, we'll approach meditative insight from different angles. We'll examine so-called external phenomena as well as our own thoughts and emotions, shifting between them. Some approaches emphasise a particular sequence, such as analysing external phenomena and then looking at our sense of self, or focusing on the mind which will naturally alter our perspective of phenomena that are perceived as external. Here, we'll adopt the view that examining things from different angles can be beneficial. We'll also include follow-ups on tranquillity meditations to provide a more experiential approach to vipashyana, interspersed with information to support our analytical meditations.

Precision Alone Does Not Suffice

As we have discussed, shamatha, or tranquillity meditation, helps develop focus and accuracy. It cultivates a sense of precision, allowing us to focus on one thing at a time without getting lost in discursive thinking. Often, we use an object—such as the breath—as an anchor to help us stay focused despite occasional emotional surges, and to notice when our mind has wandered. Over time, we become calmer. However, the peace and accuracy gained through tranquillity meditation alone are likely to be conditional: they depend upon circumstances. The Buddhist path implies that we progressively travel towards unconditional peace and wisdom, and for this, we need the practice of insight.

For example, if we recognise distractions such as thoughts and emotions as they arise, we may remain impervious to distraction for a while. But if we learn to see and familiarise ourselves with the *nature* of thoughts and emotions, there will come a point when they will no longer be distracting, even when they naturally arise. As a result, we'll be able to enjoy a more expansive view and even use thoughts and emotions to enhance our meditation, adding clarity and energy to it. This has a profound effect on our inner freedom and on our ability to handle the complexities of life when we're not sitting on the cushion.

However, if insight is not stabilised, its benefits will be limited, hence the need for shamatha. So, whatever practice you do, generally speaking, it is best to take a moment to settle your mind. Additionally, you can and should invest more time in shamatha exercises whenever you feel that your capacity to abide peacefully on a chosen object declines due to agitation, stress, worries, and so on.

Contemplation: Looking at Thoughts

Adopt a good posture: sit with your back straight, aligned, and at ease. Take a moment to relax your body. If you consider yourself Buddhist, you can take refuge in the Triple Gems and rekindle bodhicitta. Otherwise, you can still feel gratitude for the Buddha, his teachings, and the lineage holders. Appreciate the opportunity to practice meditation and cultivate an altruistic intention.

Take a few minutes to settle your mind, using any familiar shamatha technique, such as counting the breath up to 21 cycles.

Now, you may still notice the arising of thoughts, memories, emotions, concepts, expectations, and fantasies. Don't worry too much about their presence. If their intensity diminishes, that's good, but the key is to stay aware. If you notice your mind frequently wanders or you constantly lose your focus, spend more time with shamatha to encourage your awareness and to find a proper balance between being too loose or too tight.

Eventually, you will reach a calmer, clearer state. Initially, your mind might feel like a thundering waterfall of thoughts. Later, it may feel more like a quiet lake. Enjoy this peace without contriving it—just be mindful, remain fresh and at ease.

When a thought or any kind of mental event arises, look at it and ask:

Where did it come from?

Where does it go?

Does it stay anywhere between coming and going?

Does the thought have a particular colour, weight, or form?

Is the thought permanent?

If it has a duration, it must have a beginning, a middle, and an end.

But can you pinpoint any lasting middle, any fraction of time that cannot be further divided into a beginning, middle, and end?

If there's no lasting fraction of time, could there be any inherent identity to the thought? Can you find any inherent essence, any independent "thingness" to the thought?

Can you pin it down with clear-cut delimitations?

If it's fleeting, how can we say it lasts?

If it's made of parts, why do we feel it has an inherent "thingness"?

If it depends on causes, circumstances, and conditions, how can it be seen as an independent entity existing "from its own side"?

— —

Take your time with this investigation. You may find that you can befriend the thought—all thoughts and emotions. When you reach such a conclusion, relax your analysis and rest in openness. Then, repeat with another mental event or even a sense perception.

End the practice with some non-analytical resting and a dedication of any positive energy generated through the meditation to the welfare and enlightenment of all beings.

The Practice of Not Finding

Some of the questioning that we engage in during vipashyana exercises can be upsetting at first. We hope for clear-cut answers, but they often seem elusive. This uncertainty is very much part of the process. In fact, if we immediately come up with some kind of certainty, some kind of automatic response, it might be worth examining it more deeply. "Looking deeply," I suppose, is another way to translate "vipashyana." However, the *vi* in *vipashyana* more precisely connotes a "special" or "superior" way of looking at things. Instead of relying on our same old, egotistic, deluded patterns, we proceed with an open mind so as to familiarise ourselves with a wiser, more accurate perspective.

If some inquiries frustrate you because you can't immediately find a concrete answer, don't worry. You can relax in the knowledge that while insight meditation utilises and hones analytical skills, it also affects a subtler, non-conceptual level. In other words, something's cooking in the background. This is similar to shamatha practice. We don't do these meditation exercises just once, but again and again. True insight comes through repeated investigation, and that's important to remember. We value intellectual understanding above all, but our habits are so deeply ingrained, and the mind can be so subtle, that a mere conceptual glimpse is not enough. We need to investigate, again and again. That's how we develop certainty.

Even frustration with, or attachment to, this process can be used as an object of investigation. We can dismantle our aversion or attachment, examine it from different angles, and see if it has any permanent, unitary, or independent existence.

In any event, my advice is to take heart and approach this process with a joyful and curious mind.

For inspiration, contemplate the words of the great enlightened Tibetan yogi Milarepa (1040–1123):

> When we do not realise the inner workings of mind,
> We wander in samsara.
> When we realise the nature of thoughts and concepts,
> We realise wisdom.
> This is how we become fully developed.[85]

Like Noise Heard from a Window

In the next exercise, you will be encouraged to view your thoughts as you would consider noise heard through a window. This exercise is largely inspired by the following excerpt from a meditation instruction given by Chögyam Trungpa Rinpoche:

> While you're meditating, all kinds of thoughts arise: thoughts about your life, your future plans, conversations with your friends and your relatives. All kinds of things come through the mind. Let them come through. Let them just come through. Don't try to say whether they are bad or for that matter whether

> they are particularly good. Just let them come through, as simply as you can. By letting them come through, you find that there's a sense of openness. You don't find your thoughts threatening or particularly helpful. They just become the general gossip, the traffic of your thoughts. If you live in a city, you hear the traffic coming through your windows: there goes a motorcycle, there goes a truck. There goes a car, and then there's somebody shouting. At the beginning, you might get involved in or distracted by the noise, but then you begin to think, so what? Similarly, the traffic of your thoughts and the verbosity of your mind are just part of the basic chatter that goes on in the universe. Just let it go through.[86]

We will slightly adapt this to our specific context. In the following exercise, the point is not to *forget* about the thoughts or to stop noticing them altogether, like background noise that you end up tuning out. We need to stay aware and cultivate presence of mind. As we progress along the path of meditation, it is beneficial to learn to see the subtler thoughts that usually go unnoticed, like a bit of unseen water in the underbrush, says a text,[87] that can insidiously dampen and addle our meditation.

The point here is not to phase out all thoughts and pretend there's nothing going on in our minds. The aim, to paraphrase Trungpa Rinpoche, is to learn to see that thoughts are neither threatening nor particularly helpful. The way you relate to thoughts becomes more flexible. You don't blindly follow your thoughts, but you don't need to forcefully reject them either. You also don't fall into an indifferent stupor; on the contrary, you maintain awareness and freshness of mind. You simply allow some space, and learn to be present and relaxed even when thoughts are active.

Exercise: Relaxed Openness

Relax your body. Relax your mind. Remember the Three Jewels, feel gratitude for the opportunity to practice, and reconnect with the heart of awakening.

For a few minutes, practice shamatha focused on the breath. Count your breaths up to 21 cycles, starting back at 1 whenever you lose track. When you reach 21, let go of the counting but continue focusing on the breath for a few more minutes.

Then, gradually broaden your focus. Treat mental chatter like street noise heard from a window. Remain aware without getting side-tracked by daydreaming. Relax any clinging to thoughts, without rejecting them—the meditation can include them. Relax your mind and allow external stimuli to come through: don't deliberately look for external stimuli, just open yourself up to a more panoramic experience. Take your time.

Recognise that there's a quality of presence to your meditation. There's sheer cognisance, simple presence of mind. Notice how it's unnecessary to grasp at a specific object to stay focused. What's important is that you can reconnect with awareness each time you become lost in discursive thinking, personal storylines, or emotional complications. Instead of worrying about the past or the future, or commenting on the present, just remain aware. Slowly expand the scope of your awareness to include your inner and outer environment.

Remain relaxed, fully open, yet fully present. Rest in that state for a while.

If you fall into a stupor or "space out," readjust your posture, shake yourself up, and start again. To counter lethargy, reconnect with the vibrancy of the present moment—the universe and your own body are full of life—or simply raise your gaze or remove extra layers of clothes if it's warm. If you feel good and cling to that experience, take it with a bit of humour, and recognise that this desire too is like a thought or emotional rambling heard through a window. Just stay present and aware, with no particular expectations.

Spend some time in all-accommodating, relaxed openness.

To conclude the session, dedicate any positive energy generated through this meditation to the welfare and enlightenment of all beings.

Exercise: Combining Relaxed Openness and Vipashyana Investigation

Before diving into this exercise, I recommend familiarising yourself with the two previous ones. You can practice them in separate sessions or with a short break in between.

Sit with your back straight and in a comfortable posture; take refuge and generate bodhicitta. Next, imagine that light emanating from the Buddha and lineage masters clears away mental fog, tightness, laziness, pride, and any obstacles to meditation.

Now, return to the previous exercise and spend the majority of your session in relaxed openness. Recognise your capacity to simply remain present and all-accommodating, without commenting on your experience or fixating your attention on any specific object. Remain in that panoramic awareness for a while.

Occasionally, if a thought feels particularly intense or aggressive, or if it seems to carry a particular weight or clarity, you can try to "grab" it and analyse it, as we did earlier in the "looking at thoughts" exercise. If needed, use the same lines of inquiry. Investigate and really try to see if the thought has any solid reality, any self-existence, any lasting "thingness" that you can pinpoint.

At some point, you may see that the thought is empty of inherent identity, and yet it arises. Once again, there's no contradiction. When you reach this conclusion, relax your analysis and rest again in openness. Then you can repeat this with another mental event or even a sense perception, such as a sound.

Always end with some non-analytical resting and a dedication for the benefit of all beings.

Nihilism, Eternalism, and the Middle Way

The teachings of the Buddha lead us to discover our true nature. This is the refrain throughout the texts, and over time, we learn to understand its implications. The Dharma also allows us to reconnect with a "fundamental right." All beings have this right, even if they often forget about it. It is the right to find and enjoy true inner freedom. We all have the right to develop a healthier and more open relationship with our own thoughts and emotions.

Nowadays, Buddhism is often referred to in the context of feel-good techniques, which can be problematic. The real purpose of Dharma is not the pursuit of comfort in the usual sense of the term; rather, it aims to go beyond dualism. Nevertheless, there is a kind of fundamental ease to which everyone is entitled from the moment one has a mind—it is a bit like being born into a royal family, except that everyone else is blue-blooded too. No one can grant or take away your right to experience inner freedom. However, to regain this freedom, there might be a long journey ahead. Hence the need for study, reflection, and meditation. Practicing Dharma allows us to gain more flexibility and wisdom in the way we interact with the world. Sometimes we react rashly, or catapult ourselves into extreme positions, but if we practice, we begin to see that there is a different way to live.

Generally speaking, the path we are embarking on provides us with the means to cultivate more openness, compassion, and humour. We sometimes find ourselves getting uptight about a situation or a character trait we thought we had corrected years ago, causing us to crystallise the situation. However, the Buddha and the masters who followed him provided ways to see our predicament with more humour, which can be another form of kindness.

This is all linked to what is called "The Middle Way," a fundamental concept for Buddhists. (To be clear, "Middle Way" is also a translation of "Madhyamaka," a philosophical school of Mahayana Buddhism; here, we will use the term in a broader sense, without going into the particularities of different philosophical tenets.) It is an incredibly vast and profound topic that scholars within the Tibetan tradition study for many years. That doesn't prevent us from addressing this topic, starting with the question: "Middle in relation to what?" This question is important because the term "middle way" implies that there are two extremes. What are they?

The two extremes have significant implications for our lives and in our approach to meditation. For about fifteen years I read, travelled, met with masters, and dabbled in all sorts of practices without understanding how fundamental this subject was, until one of my teachers, Sam Bercholz, emphasised the importance of recognising these two extremes again and again and again, in keeping with the teachings of one of his own root teachers, Thinley Norbu Rinpoche. Thinley Norbu Rinpoche wrote extensively about this in *A Cascading Waterfall of Nectar*, which is also in keeping with the teachings of the noble Buddhist sages of the past.

These two extremes are eternalism and nihilism.

Eternalism

"Eternalism" is a broad term that refers to all sorts of philosophical views, and to different approaches to spirituality. In Western philosophy, it might be used differently, but here it particularly refers to the illusion that compounded phenomena are permanent. "Compounded phenomena" means things that are made of parts and depend on causes and conditions. Take a tree, for example. It's easy to see that a tree is compounded: at the macro level, it has distinct parts such as roots, branches, leaves, and a trunk. At the micro level it has cells and vascular tissue, xylem, phloem, and so on. All of this depends on causes and conditions, such as a seed, water, sunlight, nutrients. Therefore, it's clear that a tree is not a singular, autonomous entity. The same applies to furniture, the human body, buildings, social events, schools, political institutions, and so on.

The eternalists believe that compounded phenomena, or at least some compounded phenomena, are permanent. Eternalism is also linked to the belief in a soul that always remains somewhere within us until it travels to another place or body at some point.

(Incidentally, Buddhism does speak of rebirth, but it is not the same as the concept of reincarnation found in other Indian religions.)

A related eternalistic notion is that of a self that is unitary, autonomous, independent, and lasting. For example, let's say I have faced many difficulties in my life, constantly searching for myself in my career, studies, relationships, and so on. At some point, I may want to try various methods to help see within myself more clearly, hoping to finally find a definitive biographical note that will perfectly define who I really am. I proclaim, "This is my personality," and I crystallise that eureka moment by repeating to myself, "Yes! This is me! This is exactly who I am! I've been looking for so long!" We get attached to this kind of narrative as if it were describing something lasting, totally objective, and independent of causes and conditions.

Another variant of eternalism is the belief that there is something outside of us that is independent, autonomous, and separate from our mind that will save us. In Buddhism, this is often considered a form of magical thinking. In addition to the idea of a saviour, eternalism can also be associated with the concept of an autonomous Creator. Logically, it is difficult to defend the notion of an autonomous and independent agent that can create impermanent things while remaining unchanged. But let's set logic aside for now and instead look at our own experience. When we buy into the hope that something entirely external will save us, we risk losing our sense of responsibility. Buddhism takes these views with a grain of salt. I don't want to attack your beliefs, but simply to invite you to consider what the philosophical positions that we hold imply, psychologically and spiritually.[88] Do we expect all our problems to be solved by some external power? This is a question worth asking.

In Buddhist teachings, there are many colourful and inspiring stories of buddhas, bodhisattvas, and manifestations of enlightened figures saving people. This is wonderful and I personally feel tremendous support from the buddhas, bodhisattvas, and lineage masters. No one is saying that we cannot relate to enlightened manifestations, or to special embodiments of wisdom and compassion. All we are saying is that there is an interaction—that there are causal principles in this world, and that the line between inner and outer is not always as clear-cut as we think. Furthermore, it is incumbent upon us to make efforts on the path.

Nihilism

The other extreme, nihilism, is associated with the illusion that there is nothing—*nil* as in "nothingness"—beyond matter. In other words, it denies anything beyond phenomena that can be directly observed and measured by the senses. One of the most frequent manifestations of nihilism is to disregard the fact that our actions have consequences beyond those that are immediately apparent. For example, a friend told me about a nature park managed by her husband. He found that some people regularly dumped waste near a beautiful lake situated in the park. Recently, someone had discarded a kitchen oven on the bank of the lake, instead of taking it to a recycling facility. Such actions show an underdeveloped ability to perceive the broader consequences of one's actions—on oneself, others, the planet, and other organisms, both big and small. Acts like this are symptomatic of a nihilistic attitude, which is clearly a dangerous view.

Nihilism also comes with the idea that everything ends at death. If this is our philosophy, we might live without bothering to improve spiritually, since nothing matters once we draw our last breath. With this belief, we don't have to worry about anything beyond our own immediate comfort or, at best, that of our family. This view can easily lead to narrow-minded individualism and a counterproductive form of cynicism. It's a slippery slope! (A healthy dose of cynicism can sometimes turn out to be helpful on the path, but that's not the form of cynicism we're talking about here.)

To simplify, we can say that nihilism is a rejection of spirituality. A common example is the belief that prayer has no effect whatsoever. Yet isn't it obvious that if one prays—regardless of one's religious tradition—it will at least have an effect on one's own mind? If a person prays with an open heart and in a positive way, it will undeniably impact their inner life. From there, it will likely affect their surroundings as well: people's disposition influences the type of interactions they have with others, and to some extent, it can inform other people's experiences of the world. We cannot predict the extent of this "environmental" impact, which may be too subtle to notice, but we must agree that there is a chain of causes and effects. There is some interdependence at play. It is a nihilistic perspective to reject the possibility of immaterial phenomena and to affirm that prayer is useless because we cannot perceive its effects directly through our ordinary senses.

Another widespread idea today—connected to scientific materialism (which is associated with nihilism)—is the belief that the mind is limited to the brain. Wanting to explain everything by the action of neurons is a narrow view that implies a rejection of intangible and subtle spirituality. Whenever we fall prey to such a view—and it is extremely tempting these days—we should be brave enough to look at it directly and question its value and implications.

So, on the one side, there's eternalism, and on the other, nihilism. On the one hand, there's the risk of wishful thinking, and on the other, a form of defeatism. These two extremes are also prominent in our relationship to death. Either we expect to remain fundamentally the same person—that's an eternalist view—or we believe that all forms of consciousness die along with the body, which Buddhism considers a nihilist view.

For Buddhism, most religions, which are theistic, generally lean toward eternalism. This is not a condescending statement for at least two reasons. The first is that Buddhism recognises that we *all* have both nihilistic and eternalistic tendencies. They are very much part of the samsaric predicament. The second is that if we are going to wander away from the middle view, we would do better to wander on the side of eternalism. At least on that side there is hope and the possibility of cultivating positive qualities. Nowadays, extremely harmful forms of nihilism afflict the world and run rampant.

Relating to the Two Extremes

We've mentioned a key point above: it's not just "other people" who hold these extreme views. If we take an honest look at our own experience, we will see that we all regularly cling to various forms of nihilism and eternalism, even though we may not experience them exactly as described. Although we might have a particular propensity towards nihilism or eternalism, Buddhism teaches that we generally oscillate between the two, swinging from hope to fear.

We hope that we will find the key or the secret ingredient that will make us feel good about ourselves forever, allowing us to live happily ever after. Then suddenly, we fall into defeatism, asking ourselves, "What's the point? Why am I still depressed or anxious, even though I've prayed and done some meditation?" Or, "There are so many problems in the world; I'll never be able to do anything really useful!" That kind of thing.

Even when we experience pleasure, it is often tinged with delusion. (As mentioned earlier, this does not mean that joy has no place on the path.)

Buddhism considers that eternalism and nihilism—including all their variants—are extremes. They are "extreme" in that they do not provide a complete or adequate definition of reality; they only represent part of the story, often distorting it completely.

Sometimes, we cling to the notion that our life, our body, our personality, or anything that we enjoy will last forever. Other times, we reject spirituality or its most subtle elements. Regularly, we sway between idealism and defeatism, hope and fear, elation and depression. When we realise that we keep oscillating between these extremes, we seek a path. But even when we find the path, this oscillation continues! The difference is that we learn to recognise, mitigate, and dissolve these extremes; the ups and downs become less abrupt, and we navigate with more and more clarity and discernment. This marks the dawn of fundamental sanity.

To avoid abstraction, I'll provide two examples of how we can personally suffer from these extremes.

The first example is heartbreak. Let's say we've been in a romantic relationship for six months, five years, thirty years, whatever, and we break up with our partner. Different scenarios are then possible.

We could become attached to the idea of permanence, hoping the relationship will last forever. We crystallise the relationship, our conception we have of the other person, and our conception of ourselves, as if it were all permanent and unchanging. This is a form of eternalism and it leads to suffering.

Another scenario is losing confidence in our ability to love and be loved, which often happens after a tough breakup. We might fall into a form of scientific materialism that reduces everything to small connections in the brain, as if all of reality were limited to those electrical impulses. "Ah! It's all the play of hormones; it's purely animal; love is bullshit, we just have to meet someone whose hormones are aligned with ours at the right time." We then risk denying our own potential for tenderness, which, when you look at it, is not exactly unlike a rejection of spirituality. This scenario too leads to suffering.

And if we tell ourselves, "Well, enough with the pain!" and start looking for another romantic relationship, but with the idea that the next one will last forever, it's not much better. We will begin a new relationship based on an eternalist concept, setting the stage for future sorrow.

This doesn't mean that everything is doomed and that you shouldn't aspire to build healthy relationships or put effort into your marriage. The problem lies in attachment and delusions. It's like coming to the end of life: whether you're 30 or 110, if you're attached to the idea that you're never going to die, you're going to have a difficult time when death comes.

The second example is a personal one, set in the *faubourg ouvrier*, which I mentioned earlier. As a teenager, I had been going through a period of anxiety when one day my father took me for a walk. We walked through the *faubourg ouvrier* neighbourhood, and at some point in the course of our father–son conversation, I felt a sense of openness.

This shift I felt was likely due to his loving presence combined with the wonders of a long walk, which has the effect of relaxing the conceptual mind, allowing one to reconnect with the basic goodness of the surrounding environment—the ground below and the sky above. It was a somewhat ordinary but fundamentally healthy moment. I let go and I felt lighter, as if some form of insight might arise. That particular moment coincided with, and was positively associated with, my discovery of the *faubourg ouvrier* and its natural spaces. "Wow," I thought, "I'd like to live here some day."

For years after that moment, I dreamed of living in the beautiful Sillery area of Quebec City. Nearly twenty years passed until I was fortunate enough to move into one of the few rental units in that neighbourhood—a beautiful apartment that was a perfect fit for my lifestyle. But after a couple of years of living there, construction sites started popping up all around. No matter which direction I walked, I immediately came across a building site. Natural areas began shrinking, and heritage sites began being used for condos. There were many more cars and a lot more noise. Despite this, it was still a privileged situation, in a safe environment. Yet, for me and my neighbours, these changes instilled a sense of claustrophobia: we felt territorial, as if we were being encroached upon.

Under the circumstances, my thinking could have frozen around an eternalist position. If I had been clinging to the illusion that the house, city, or neighbourhood I had chosen to live in would always remain static, I would have inevitably suffered.

I could also have sunk into defeatism. For example, when I went for walks, I could have given into the energy of frustration. I could have complained about the construction sites, the noise, and the urban densification. If I had indulged in these counterproductive thoughts and emotions, ignoring the ever-present possibility of reconnecting with primordial goodness and with the wisdom of the Dharma—truly open-ended wisdom—this would have been a form of nihilism, and I would have suffered.

Towards a Middle Way

Our goal is to find a path and a practice that leads beyond the two extremes of eternalism and nihilism. As mentioned earlier, this is called the "middle way." We'll explore this concept further as we go along, but first let's clarify a few things.

Genereally speaking, Buddhists are wary of conflicting emotions; but they are not saying we should repress or suppress our thoughts and emotions and pretend that everything is fine all the time; practicing Buddhism is also not about becoming robotic, indifferent, or passive to the point where we never say or feel anything. That is—of course—*not* the goal. The same principle applies when discussing the middle way: avoiding the extremes of hope and fear doesn't mean that we become stuck in some kind of boring psychological flatland. Buddhism also does not encourage inertia. In fact, apathy and indifference belong to ignorance; in other words, never wanting to get involved is not seen as a positive thing. On the contrary, Buddhism encourages us to cultivate a strong sense of fellowship and universal responsibility. Even if this manifests as a desire to go into long-term solitary retreat (which would be wonderful), such a desire would still be accompanied by a heartfelt compassion and a sense of enthusiasm. The point is that the middle way approach, however it manifests, is not leading us to become indifferent. It is not as if the only option beyond eternalism and nihilism is I-don't-care-ism—elation, depression, or inconsideration, "pick your poison!" There are other ways to relate with situations.

Beyond philosophical considerations and terminology, the simple and regular practice of sitting meditation helps us understand the two extremes. It helps us see them in ourselves and to consider other possibilities.[89] In other words, meditation helps us heal our relationship with the world. It makes us more flexible. At the moment, we live in the world as we *imagine* it, constantly putting layers and layers of concepts on phenomena. But eventually, we can have a fresher, more direct relationship with whatever arises. We find ourselves in a better position to appreciate this world. And when things go wrong, we are better able to discern whether we need to act or not. When we do need to act, we have a better chance of discerning the most appropriate course of action given the circumstances.

As we use words ending in "ism"—such as eternalism and nihilism—let's not fall into abstraction or settle for a purely intellectual understanding. Throughout the history of Buddhism, there have been some great masters who were also great scholars, spending much of their lives in monastic universities. On the other hand, there have also been great masters who had no formal education yet achieved high levels of spiritual realisation. So, you don't necessarily need to express yourself like a dictionary. The important thing is to practice.

Daily Investigation

The last section was pretty juicy, so let me give you a little homework. This may help you integrate the content, relate it to your meditation practice, and assist you in your quest for simplicity, clarity, and integrity in this fast and noisy world.

When we suffer—and we might notice this happens often!—let's ask ourselves some questions. As you now realise, this is also part of the path. Investigate. Sure enough, we are all used to cogitating: we think and think, intensely, wishing to break away from our problems. But try a different approach. Next time you encounter a problem, don't try to find a solution right away, which might be considered a bit aggressive. The goal is not to shy away from discomfort, but to use your natural wisdom that is quietly emerging—thanks, among other things, to tranquillity meditation—to sharpen your powers of discernment. Ask, "Why am I suffering? I'm getting angry at some guy who gave me the finger on the road, but is that really the *cause* of my suffering?" We may find some very interesting answers along the way. So rather than pushing away what you assume is the cause of your discomfort, investigate. It's not about beating yourself up and blaming yourself—"It's all my fault!"—it's about keeping an open mind.

Ask yourself, "If I am suffering today, or this week, or in my life, is there a connection to eternalism? Am I clinging to the idea of the permanence of a phenomenon that by nature cannot be permanent? Or is my sorrow due to a nihilistic tendency? Am I rejecting possibilities because I cannot see them with my eyes?" For example, if you lose confidence in your ability as a meditator, you may be flirting with nihilism, or a form of materialism: only tangible, quantifiable results may seem valuable to you. These tendencies must be recognised and brought to light.

The Buddhist view that overcomes extremes harmoniously integrates impermanence, interdependence, and *shunyata*. In the next section, we'll explore the meaning of that term more specifically.

Emptiness, Openness

If you think that the previous section was a little hard to digest, or if you're struggling with some of its implications, consider the following.

One of the most widely studied sutras in the world is the *Prajnaparamita hridaya*, or "The Heart of the Perfection of Wisdom Sutra," more commonly known as "The Heart Sutra." It is recited aloud daily in temples and centres around the Mahayana world, especially amongst Chan and Zen Buddhists. It is "akin in importance to the *Shema Yisrael* for Jews or the *Lord's Prayer* for Christians."[90] The sutra is a condensation of the Mahayana teachings on so-called "emptiness," and as such, contemplating this brief text and its paradoxical language loosens our grasping at things as fixed entities.

The Heart Sutra was taught when the Buddha was residing at Vulture Peak in Rajagriha. On that occasion, something interesting is said to have happened as some adepts first heard of the fundamental groundlessness of life. Here's how the erudite Karl Brunnhölzl sums it up:

> There are accounts in several of the larger prajñāpāramitā sūtras about people being present in the audience who had already attained certain advanced levels of spiritual development

> or insight that liberated them from saṃsāric existence and suffering. These people, who are called "arhats" in Buddhism, were listening to the Buddha speaking about emptiness and then had different reactions. Some thought, "This is crazy, let's go" and left. Others stayed, but some of them had heart attacks, vomited blood, and died. It seems they didn't leave in time. These arhats were so shocked by what they were hearing that they died on the spot. That's why somebody suggested recently that we could call the *Heart Sūtra* the *Heart Attack Sūtra*. Another meaning of that could be that this sūtra goes right for the heart of the matter, while mercilessly attacking all ego trips that prevent us from waking up to our true heart. In any case, so far nobody has had a heart attack here, which is good news. But the bad news is that probably nobody understood it either.[91]

I also don't know of anyone dying from a heart attack while studying this sutra! However, one thing is certain: when we discuss emptiness, there's often a kind of malaise. It's okay; after all, the teachings on emptiness are meant to challenge our false assumptions about the nature of things. They are designed to dismantle the ramshackle complex of our ordinary conceptions, which is bound to provoke all sorts of reactions. Generally speaking, we can classify the malaise we might feel into two types: one that comes from our egos being upset, which is quite normal, and one that comes from misunderstanding what is referred to as emptiness. To some extent both can be related.

The problem, when we translate *shunyata* as "emptiness," is that many people project nihilistic assumptions onto the term. In some rare cases, it has even been translated as "voidness," which is quite misleading. We interpret it to mean some kind of total blank or poetically as some "thing." But shunyata is neither mere nothingness (which would be nihilistic), nor is it an abstract-yet-palpable cosmic energy (which would veer toward materialism). In other words, it is not referring to a mere absence, like a black hole devoid of any qualities whatsoever, and it is also not particularly esoteric.

In Buddhist teachings, *shunyata* can also be translated as "openness," which is already more eloquent. It refers to the idea that, in their true nature, things are open, not fixed or constricted. Things inter-are, to reuse Thich Nhat Hanh's expression. Sometimes, "emptiness" could just as well mean "fullness," or "boundlessness." Things are ultimately boundless in the sense that we cannot define their identity by pointing to strict borders that isolate them from the rest of the world. In any case, we're not saying that things have no existence whatsoever on the relative level, just that they're not existing *inherently*, "from their own side." That's a crucial distinction.

Now, there are different schools of Indian Buddhist philosophy, each with a slightly more refined—or perhaps we could say, more inclusive—understanding of shunyata. Serious students often explore the main philosophical tenets in sequence: they study the views and practices of the Vaibhashika, Sautrantika, Cittamatra, Madhyamaka Svatantrika, Madhyamaka Prasangika, and Shentong schools, each having its own uses, context, and profundity.[92] This takes a long time, and although it is well worth it, it is beyond the scope of this book. However, we need to understand that none of these schools say, "Nothing exists, period. Do whatever you want—it doesn't matter, as it is all just nothing."

The great seventh-century master Chandrakirti gave the example of a chariot to establish how the "self" is merely a designation. We will come back to this, but for now, understand that if I say, "The car is empty" (in the sense of shunyata), the implication is, "The car is empty of any unitary, lasting, autonomous, inherent identity. Ultimately, we cannot pinpoint such a thing as a car that is permanent and independent from its parts and from the mind that considers it. It is a transitory collection, arising due to ever-changing causes and conditions, and devoid of any real self-identity; and yet it appears and it can be driven."

So, things are empty yet appearing. Not only that, they can only appear *because* they are empty. This is a key point. If things had inherent, autonomous existence, they would be independent of other factors and could not change because nothing would affect them. No one could ever assemble a table because a "table" would be independent of its parts; it would have had to exist all along, which is absurd. A seed could not turn into a sprout if a sprout was a self-sufficient thing. We could not claim that a baby can grow into an adult because the "adult," according to this understanding of the world, would be a self-existent thing and thus would not have any relationship whatsoever with an entity called "baby." If phenomena were independent, there would be no connection between cause and effect, which makes no sense.

In the same way, things are empty *because* they are dependently arisen from causes and conditions; they depend on parts, circumstances, and a multitude of factors, thus they have no autonomous identity. This does not prevent them from functioning on a relative level.

Understanding that emptiness and dependent arising are not separate is fundamental, as it avoids the two extremes. Emptiness avoids eternalism: conditioned phenomena have no inherent, lasting essence. Causality and dependent arising avoid nihilism: things can and do appear and function when the circumstances are gathered. This is true for outer phenomena—a table, a car, a building, the seasons—and this is also true for our thoughts, emotions, and conceptual hang-ups.

Understanding this intellectually is not enough. We have to study, reflect, investigate, meditate, receive teachings, request clarifications, and practice accordingly, until there's a definite transformation in our outlook and our relationship with the world. If we think we understand emptiness but continually get lost in discursive thinking, destructive patterns, emotional upheavals, and all sorts of symptoms of an egocentric, unenlightened lifestyle, we are deluding ourselves. Of course, this is not an all-or-nothing situation, as there's a progression involved in treading the path.

We have to work hard to understand emptiness, and to do so, we must constantly renew our enthusiasm. Therefore, it would be beneficial to contemplate how the concept of emptiness relates to our main subject matter: clarity, tenderness, and integrity in a fast and noisy world.

With insight into the nature of phenomena, we can see things clearly. We understand their impermanence and their dependence on causes and conditions. This clarity fosters our discernment and unburdens us from the complexities of our life.

When we stop falling prey to the illusion of permanence and independence, we become naturally less egocentric. This reduction in egocentrism in turn fosters integrity as well as tenderness. Loving-kindness is further reinforced when we realise that much of the suffering in the world depends on a view that can be corrected by, and transformed into, the wisdom of openness.

This transformation takes time, and a step-by-step approach. I also believe that the actual practice of taking refuge makes all the difference, since it is the gateway to the Buddhist path. My advice is to keep it simple and review the material on emptiness periodically, chewing on it with an open heart and a sense of humour.

If you want to enjoy the paradox, next time someone tells you, "My car got stolen!" just tell them, "Relax, mate, it's all empty!" and see what happens.

No—please don't.

Open-dimensionality and the Dreamlike Quality of Experience

Presenting emptiness too soon and out of context is risky. People who don't have sufficient understanding may misinterpret it. They might shut down, think they are not up to the task, or dismiss the teaching altogether based on an incorrect interpretation. They could study it intellectually for their own egotistic gratification—a particularly nasty twist on our goal-oriented refrain, compounded by the common error of mistaking intellectual understanding for spiritual realisation. Worse, they might construe emptiness as a nihilistic doctrine. If one claims that they can do anything because ultimately, nothing is real and thus nothing matters, it completely contradicts the teachings of the Buddha and leads nowhere but to more suffering for oneself and others. If one thinks, "I'll just meditate and use my understanding of emptiness to see that subject, object, and action have no inherent existence and reach a place of no-guilt," that's completely mistaken.

We would be much better off following in the footsteps of the great enlightened masters of the past, such as Guru Rinpoche, the Lotus-Born, who famously said: "My view is higher than the sky, but my attention to actions and results is finer than flour."[93]

Misinterpretation is one of the reasons why it is so important to contemplate how emptiness and causality work together. Causes have effects because they are interdependent, lacking any fixed, lasting, independent identity. In other words, things happen because they are empty; things are empty because they happen.

We can develop a more open relationship with the world, reducing our tendency to congeal our discursive thinking and belief systems, while being more conscientious in our daily lives.

There's no contradiction there. That's the way of freedom and harmony.

In most cases, this quality of freedom is first experienced on the cushion. Regardless, it may be helpful to consider yet another term that can be used to interpret *shunyata*: "open-dimensionality." I believe this term is inspired by the German Buddhist philosopher and translator Herbert Günther. It is unusual, but I find it eloquent and relatable. Things are open, not enclosed or fixed. Labels are useful, but entities are never static—they always evolve. Situations have some degree of workability.

Claiming that all phenomena are empty implies that all phenomena are subjective. It is important to realise that this does not deny the suffering in the world, nor the complexities and harsh realities of war, pandemics, and so on. When we approach the world with the view of shunyata, we become simpler and clearer in our thinking and more sophisticated, sensible, and sensitive. It does not diminish our discernment and analytical skills; quite the contrary. That's the difference between quixotism and what I like to call "sensible optimism."

But let's go further and dig into our own experience. During a recent teaching, author Elizabeth Mattis Namgyel offered an interesting exercise.[94] She asked, "What is 'the world' to you?" Go ahead: read the word "world," and close your eyes, and ask yourself what you see in your mind.

Notice the first image that comes to mind. Perhaps, a blue marble seen from space. Or perhaps you see a busy city, an open sky, or a particular detail that signifies life, such as a baby crying or a flower blooming.

Now, let's ask again: what is "the world" to you? Look within once more.

The result is likely to be different the second time. Even if you come up with a similar image, the details you focus on will be different. And if you try again and again, you may notice that your idea of the world keeps changing.

Interesting, isn't it?

Our own concepts are fleeting and conditional, and deep down, we know it.

Now, there's no problem with the fact that concepts are conditioned. The problem is that we assume that subjective phenomena are objective. This assumption is closely tied to the samsaric life, the whole process of delusion, and as such, it affects our capacity—or lack thereof—to reclaim sanity in an overloaded era.

When we cultivate a proper view of emptiness, our world slowly opens up. There's more space within and without. We can move more freely, and we can be relaxed but responsive, at once positive and lucid, fearless and conscientious. To evoke this sense of freedom and boundlessness, the teachings give the analogy of a dreamer who knows she is dreaming and can thus fully enjoy the dream. If she is stuck in a terrifying nightmare, she can even wake up and help fellow sleepers do just the same, or at least provide them with some comfort.

Once again, when the Buddhist teachings evoke the dreamlike quality of phenomena, they are not encouraging a nihilistic way of life. They are not saying that everything is *literally* a dream, but that it is dreamlike. In other words, images and experiences manifest through the play of causes and conditions but are taken to be inherent and objective by the mind that is subject to deep mental fog—the deluded mind that has made a habit of fixating on identities, thoughts, emotions, concepts, and belief systems. This beautiful, resourceful mind that has everything it requires to be fully free!

The point of all this? To stop congealing our experience.

As Elizabeth Mattis Namgyel brilliantly says, if you think that open-dimensionality is odd, ask yourself, what's the opposite of seeing things as open? What does it do to your mind to see things as open-dimensional? Doesn't it help you navigate more clearly? These questions are worth investigating.

Creative Investigation

It is worthwhile to integrate philosophy and meditation. Many of us are inclined towards one and somewhat reluctant to take up the other. In the West, although the purpose of philosophy for the great Greco-Roman sages was to change one's life, nowadays it often remains largely a conceptual exercise. Regularly practicing some kind of mental gymnastics to stretch and reinforce one's intellectual capacities can be wonderful—Buddhists would agree, and philosophical debate is a key part of the traditional curriculum for monks and nuns. However, if it stays confined to the realm of the intellect, without improving our capacity to access our fundamental wisdom mind and positively changing the way we interact with the world, then something is missing. Unfortunately, many brilliant people are fascinated by philosophical ideas but are reluctant to take up the practice of meditation. All too often this kind of attitude results in ideological materialism, which can be considered a form of nihilism.

At the other end of the spectrum, there are people who take to meditation like a duck to water, but are disinclined to engage in intellectual study. Among Buddhist practitioners, some base their approach mostly on reason while others rely primarily on faith. Interestingly, though both styles are accommodated and encouraged, those who rely on faith often end up attaining results more quickly. However, this is not the distinction we are focusing on here. We are talking about people who enjoy meditation but don't want to invest time in actual study, for various reasons—lack of inspiration, lack of guidance, lack of access to proper materials, lack of confidence in their capacities, disdain for the overly intellectual, romantic notions about spirituality, laziness, sheer habit, or any combination of the above.

The problem is that these meditators can rapidly reach a ceiling. Obstacles surface, and they don't know how to deal with them. Seemingly positive experiences arise, and they misinterpret them. They may subtly cling to their own view, with no way of identifying their blind spots, challenging their understanding, or digging deeper into the wisdom offered by an age-old tradition.

Generally speaking, it is best to balance study and practice, integrating both meditation and philosophy (if by philosophy we mean something of actual value for one's life and pursuit of liberation). If you need to prioritise one on any given day—due to unexpected circumstances taking up much of your schedule—choose practice over study. However, putting some effort into both areas will pay off in the long run. For some people, philosophy is more challenging; for others, the main challenge is to actually sit down and meditate. It doesn't matter; Dharma is challenging and that's part of its beauty.

To stay inspired, I encourage you to find creative ways to study, reflect, and apply the different reasonings and lines of inquiry you find in this book. For example, you could revisit chapter 4 and go over the contemplation on karma again, then try to see how karma relates to insight. Another suggestion would be to rest your mind for a moment, then pick two interrelated topics—such as clinging and suffering, or insight and compassion, or karma and integrity, or clarity and complexity—and explore how they relate. You could also spend time chewing over a quotation that you find particularly inspiring, testing how well you understand the author's intent, probing deeper into its meaning, and considering its subtle implications. Occasionally, step back and consider how your own assumptions play out.

Alternatively, you could carry around a small notepad as you go about your daily affairs, jotting down any flashes of insight, inspiring quotes, or interesting lines of inquiry you'd like to pursue when you have time to sit on the cushion. You could draw mind maps or humorous sketches if that's your thing. Or you could start a study group or a small book club to discuss these ideas with friends. It might also be helpful to experiment with switching mediums to keep the mind fresh—reading written material, attending live teachings, posing questions to qualified people, listening to audio archives from great lamas, and so on. Whatever works for you.

Contemplation: "It's All Relative!"

Take a few moments to settle your body and mind. Then, take refuge and generate bodhicitta. Approach the following exercise from a state of quietude and clarity.

— —

I'm being a bit mischievous with the title of this contemplation. In basic debate, "it's all relative" is not considered a strong argument. Still, it is worthwhile to spend some time to see that even the things that seem the most universally accepted also have a relative or subjective aspect.

Remember the six classes of beings from the traditional teachings? The great seventh-century master Chandrakirti noted that these six types of beings perceive a simple body of water differently. Beings in hell see and experience it as a source of torment—as burning, freezing, and life-threatening. Humans see it as something to drink. Fish see it as a home. Hungry ghosts perceive it as a disgusting, undrinkable liquid—as pus and blood. God-like beings see it as having nectar-like qualities, and so on.

Now, consider the very book you are holding. Contemplate it for a moment. How would you describe it? Is it different from what you thought it would be like? How might someone who has never heard of it perceive it? Someone who has been studying Buddhism their whole life? Someone who despises Buddhism or spirituality?

Think about how a child who doesn't read yet would see it, or an adult who can't read. What about an adult who can read but never does? How would a fast reader versus a slow reader perceive it? How might it be perceived by someone who's read only a few lines out of context? Or by someone who lives or lived in an area where spiritual books are prohibited or burned? By someone who doesn't read English, or is used to reading from right to left? By a bookworm? By an *actual* bookworm—larvae eating their way through paper and ink? By a spider? A cat?

Even among human readers who have roughly the same level of investment in their reading of this book, don't they all come from different backgrounds? Aren't their worldviews and understanding of what they read shaped by their diverse life experiences? Are there two beings in the world who would have the exact *same* experience of this one book? Look deeply—don't take answers for granted.

When you reach a conclusion, rest for a bit. Then, if you want, choose another object, which could be either specific or abstract, material or mental, and start again. To conclude the session, rest for a moment and dedicate the merit generated to the welfare and enlightenment of all beings.

After doing this exercise, we might agree that everyone has a different experience of, say, New York. There isn't just one fixed New York, not even one Brooklyn, nor one definitive Brooklyn Bridge. This highlights that "the world" is a subjective concept. Yet, in our samsaric predicament, we often conflate subjective experiences with objective reality, mistaking abstract notions for facts. For example, when we hear "the world" (or "our nation," or similar terms), a simplistic, abstract image comes to our minds, along with a subjective appreciation of it, which we then take to be an accurate depiction of reality.

If, out of sheer habit—or after reading a depressing article—when you think of "the world," your mind goes to a very specific, dark place and lingers there, odds are that it will get glued to a partial perspective, one that prevents actual wisdom from blossoming. To be clear, this isn't about denying science or minimising issues like the climate emergency (which should definitely be acknowledged as part of practicing bodhicitta and cultivating universal responsibility). Instead, it points out that over the course of our lives, we are deeply invested in subjective abstractions.

We can all understand that our appreciation of "the world" is subjective. Yet, in the way we act, suffer, and stick to our viewpoints, it's clear that deep down, we cling to *our* understanding of the world as being true and inherently established.

But what happens when we let everything breathe a bit? How does your mind change when you see things as open?

Thoughts Seem Infinitely Complex and Diverse, and Yet . . .

As mentioned earlier, in this chapter we alternate between analysis and contemplation, aiming for a balanced mix of study, reflection, and meditation. It is still important to regularly contemplate the four thoughts that turn the mind away from samsara, which help us establish our priorities in life. We also practice shamatha meditation to reinforce our stability, accuracy, and tranquillity of mind. We continue to nourish the altruistic heart of awakening, bodhicitta, with the moisture of loving-kindness, compassion, equanimity, and empathetic joy. This intention, to fully awaken for the benefit of all beings, gives direction to our lives and brings meaning to all our activities. Additionally, we begin to work with the wisdom aspect of the path through vipashyana exercises, which help us to become familiar with the way things truly are and see through our assumptions and delusions. All this forms a coherent approach that is relevant to our contemporary predicament while remaining true to the timeless path taught by the great Buddhist sages of India, Tibet, and beyond.

There are many kinds of wisdom. There are temporal and atemporal wisdoms, acquired and innate wisdoms, and so on. Generally speaking, on the Buddhist path, we skilfully use the conditioned to reach the unconditioned. Through study, we slowly acquire knowledge, which is conditioned, but only with the purpose of unveiling boundless, unconditioned enlightened qualities.[95] In the same way, we cultivate temporal wisdom to unveil innate, atemporal wisdom. There are also various ways to classify the different types of wisdom. One classification considers that one type of wisdom allows us to see the subtle differences between phenomena, while another allows us to see their commonalities.

To some extent, we all use these two abilities—perceiving both differences and similarities. For example, when cooking a meal, we deliberately select different ingredients, even discriminating between ingredients that look alike, such as picking a fresh broccoli over a not-so-fresh one at the produce stand. At the same time, we intuitively recognise their common edibility: we know that all the distinct ingredients, despite their different textures and flavours, are nourishing for the body. We can change the recipe and proportions to achieve different results, playing around with certain factors and emphasising specific qualities. However, we never put non-edible items in the pot, just like we never start chewing on our plate when we eat. While this may seem like common sense, it actually reveals some remarkable qualities of the mind—fascinating stuff, when you think about it.

However, most of our capacities are underdeveloped. For example, although we see the obvious differences between broad categories of phenomena, we fail to see the subtle differences between phenomena that look alike. Experienced and dedicated painters and photographers know that there are *countless* blues and greens and yellows; they know how to appreciate the way sunlight dances and affects our perception of the different hues, and so forth. They see some of the richness of the world, at least at a visual level. Meditation can help us in that regard, and not just for the sense of sight. Ordinarily, we use discriminating wisdom and equanimity at a very crude level and sometimes mix them up inadequately. We overemphasise differences when it suits our beliefs, and we fail to consider all beings equally based on universal denominators. We also fail to recognise the basic sameness of our own counterproductive patterns, and we end up like a snake biting its tail. Our deluded habits make us confuse everything, leading us to conflate particulars and universals. We fall into abstraction or obsess over so-called concrete details when it is uncalled for.

Daily life brings frequent examples of such confusion. For instance, we might see someone acting a certain way and assume they are always like that. Underlying such generalisations is the assumption of a fixed, lasting, autonomous identity. Sometimes, we believe things are the same when they are not, thinking, "This is the same situation all over again," or "I've failed at this ten years ago, why would it be different now?" At other times, we overemphasise negligible differences, like someone continually ending up in harmful relationships and claiming, "This one's different, I swear!" Often, we try roughly the same thing expecting a different result. Regardless of our basic patterns, we rarely see things clearly.

The Buddhist teachings provide exercises to hone our ability to discern, and to perfect both types of wisdom: the kind that helps us assess different situations given their unique characteristics and the kind that helps us see the universality of samsaric situations.

In the following exercise, we will focus on our own thoughts. This exercise aims to help us see their commonality. As a result of this meditation, we will slowly start to see that although things appear in infinitely diverse ways, they share a universal nature. Seeing this first-hand and familiarising ourselves with this insight over time is an important element on the path to simplicity and boundless wisdom.

Meditation: Befriending Our Thoughts

Sit comfortably, with a straight spine and shoulders relaxed. Take a few deep breaths. As you fully exhale, imagine all immediate worries dissolving, allowing you to focus on your meditation for the time being.

Take refuge in the Three Jewels, recalling the boundless

qualities of the Buddha and the enlightened masters for inspiration.

Then, take a moment to remind yourself that in all directions—north, south, east, west, as well as all intermediate directions—there are countless beings, both human and nonhuman. Consider that all these beings, regardless of what they say and how they behave, wish for happiness and hope to avoid suffering. This universal desire is evident in the way tiny insects react to sudden obstacles, in the way birds and squirrels are constantly on the lookout, and in the way people constantly attempt to reify their world, oscillating between hope and fear. Reflect on the idea that all beings have been our dear parents at some point in the past; that we rely on others in the present to function; and that it is thanks to others that we can reach enlightenment. All beings have the potential to fully awaken and find boundless freedom and unconditional happiness, and yet all suffer due to clinging, delusion, and confused actions. Contemplate this for a moment, generating a deep sense of fellowship and a strong determination to awaken for the benefit of all beings without exception.

Once your intention is clear and well-established, spend a few minutes practicing tranquillity meditation, focusing on the breath.

As strong emotions subside and the mind becomes less discursive, allow yourself to become more relaxed, yet fully present. Let go of any particular object of focus and rest in open awareness.

Enjoy the sheer lucidity of the mind for a moment. Notice

its capacity for bare cognisance, which makes you aware of whatever arises, whether it be sound, feeling, thought, or concept. Don't comment on, follow, encourage, or compound these thoughts and concepts. Simply remain aware of their coming and going.

After a while, you may see that thoughts are not particularly helpful nor threatening. They just play out due to causes and conditions. They're not fixed, autonomous entities; rather, they are momentary, superficial events dependent on ever-changing circumstances.

Occasionally, you may "pick" a thought and examine it to see whether it has any inherent self-identity—an enduring essence that you can pinpoint.

Recognise that all thoughts, diverse as they may seem—whether they relate to attachment or aversion—share a common trait: they are all devoid of any inherent nature. They are all empty, and yet they arise.

Befriend the common flavour of all thoughts for a moment, including thoughts related to your meditation, and even thoughts about the lack of self-identity of thoughts and concepts.

At the end of the session, let go of analysis and simply rest for a moment. Then dedicate the merit.

Although some of these exercises are framed in a non-traditional manner, this book is largely informed by the Nyingma tradition of Indo-Tibetan Buddhism. The next exercise, however, is inspired by Shunryu Suzuki's modern Zen classic, *Zen Mind, Beginner's Mind*, published in 1970. While the context and the approach differ, the exercise nonetheless echoes Suzuki's insight: "In the beginner's mind there are many possibilities, but in the expert's there are few."

We hold many assumptions about our inner and so-called outer worlds, which hinder our ability to experience life fully. It is worthwhile to take a moment to candidly look at how we consider thoughts. The point of the following meditation is to reconnect with a freshness and playfulness of mind, which is extremely useful for vipashyana.

Meditation: "Beginner's Mind"

Sit with your back straight, shoulders open, and hands resting either in your lap or on your knees. Take a moment to feel grounded and enjoy the stability of your posture—feel the weight under your buttocks. If you're sitting on a chair, notice the peaceful and complete contact of the soles of your feet resting on the ground. Scan your body, notice any accumulated tension, and take a moment to settle your mind. Rekindle your appreciation for the Triple Gems and generate bodhicitta.

If you are agitated, take a moment to practice shamatha with an object. When you feel receptive, at ease, and fully present, look within—observe your mind. As thoughts arise, examine how you approach them. With an open and inquisitive mind, kindly consider your habits and automatisms for a moment.

Are you typically aware of your discursive thoughts and how one thought leads to another? Do you have a tendency to see them as burdensome? Intimidating? Seducing? Do they seem concrete? Of no consequence? Do you follow them blindly and automatically, like a moth driven to the flame, constantly deceived and misinterpreting the brightness of conceptuality, and ending up suffering?

Don't judge yourself. Very gently and openly, just consider your usual relationship to your thoughts. Is this relationship itself even always the same? For example, how do you relate to your thoughts when you are having fun with friends versus when you're feeling lonely and despairing? When you need to make an important decision versus when you're day-dreaming? What about when you are maintaining awareness versus when you're not?

Again, don't judge; simply observe how you typically approach thoughts, ideas, and fantasies.

After a while, just rest for a moment without focusing on anything in particular; or, if it helps refresh your session, return to shamatha, focusing on the breath.

Then start again: look within, but this time, try to approach thoughts with a fresh mind, with no assumptions whatsoever—no assumptions about meditation, and no assumptions about the importance (or lack thereof) of thoughts. Be playful and kind, with an inquiring attitude, like a child using a magnifying glass for the first time, discovering the hidden wonders of the natural world. Enjoy the beginner's mind for a moment.

Isn't it marvellous that thoughts can manifest without threatening your basic sanity? All the while, you never lose your freedom to use concepts if and when necessary. You know that you always have your analytical skills at hand, and they become even more powerful when you don't get carried away by discursiveness.

Keep exploring your inner world with a beginner's mind. Is there a freshness, a lightness, some humour to the experience? If so, enjoy it without clinging. And if you notice a tendency to cling to the experience, approach it with the same freshness of mind. Just remain aware, relaxed and free.

To conclude, dedicate the merit to the welfare and enlightenment of all beings.

The "beginner's mind" can also be applied to the way we approach Dharma. Many of us harbour expectations and assumptions that get in the way. We might think that Dharma is this or that, or we may expect enlightenment to come as a grand spectacle, like fireworks. Recognising these conjectures for what they are and approaching the teachings with humility help us remain on track.

The Gap Between Sensation and Conception

Slowing down, letting go of assumptions, fine tuning our attention, and expanding the scope of our awareness help us distinguish between sensation and conception, and between contact and craving. Learning to make these distinctions is a crucial aspect of Buddhist practice.

Typically, when we experience a sensation, we immediately label it as good, bad, or neutral, and then react with strategies based on attachment, aversion, or ignorance, in an attempt to preserve the sensation or keep it at bay. Of course, this is sometimes necessary for survival. Even if you have fully realised emptiness, you still operate within the realm of relative phenomena—you should still move if a truck is coming towards you while you are crossing the road! Likewise, a person who is wise and who has learned to distinguish between sensation and conception would not leave their hand on a hot stove. However, egocentric mechanisms based on attraction, aversion, or ignorance are always at play, including within our own minds when different thoughts and ideas come up. Consequently, we often follow unwholesome habits, entertain hopes and fears, and fall prey to agitation, delusion, and muddled thinking. Foundational training in mindfulness-awareness shows that we are ceaselessly craving for something new, always thirsting for something *else*. This is a primal form of suffering, as we are never fully content.

As we practice shamatha and vipashyana, we start to notice how, when a thought or a sensation arises, we immediately tend to conceptualise. Through meditation, we can allow the conceptual mind to breathe, instead of blindly following our confused storylines as we have been doing again and again throughout our lives, often without positive results. In fact, the Sanskrit word *samsara* connotes a "wandering" (or a vicious circle, in its Tibetan equivalent). This painful wandering continues as long as we "thirst," according to early Buddhism. There are different ways to address this painful predicament. In the Hinayana approach, we might try to interrupt the cycle before craving arises, whereas in the Mahayana, we emphasise dispelling the ignorance that is at the very root of it all. All schools of Buddhism tackle both ignorance and craving, but the emphasis and the methods vary. In this chapter, we focus less on our immediate reactions to specific stimuli—as useful as it is to consider—and more on the way we can gradually replace basic confusion with a soft, open, discerning, clear, and all-encompassing wisdom.

The Dawn of Clarity

Through the previous meditation exercise ("Beginner's Mind"), we reconnect with a sense of lightness, freshness, and playfulness, and our minds become more supple. Through cultivating a simple, inquiring mind, the light of our innate wisdom starts to shine forth.

However, cultivating the beginner's mind does not mean becoming naïve. It's about maintaining freshness and openness while being frank, honest, and direct. This relates to a paradox on the spiritual path: we realise that thoughts can be extremely problematic, yet they don't need to be. They can be worked with. In a previous meditation, we examined the unique flavour common to all thoughts—that they are all empty yet manifest. We began to see that they are not necessarily problematic. At the same time, Buddhism recognises that mind is the forerunner of all. Thoughts have a tremendous effect on our actions, habits of perception, the way we experience the world, and our relationship with others. They have a central impact on our happiness and suffering. Our mind can be our worst enemy or our greatest ally; it is the mind, above all, that experiences life. Since thoughts are both unceasing and a natural function of the mind, they do matter quite a lot.

Is there a contradiction between saying that thoughts are extremely important and that they are empty and not particularly threatening? There isn't. It's a matter of context. Simply put, what matters is awareness. As the great ninth Traleg Kyabgon wrote:

> We have essentially two options: we can relinquish our awareness and chase after thoughts or we can maintain an awareness of thoughts while they are occurring.[96]

While meditating, we notice thoughts as they appear and dissolve, without falling prey to them, encouraging them, or forcefully rejecting them. We also avoid falling into a state of indifferent stupor. By doing this, we gradually untangle deeply ingrained habits of unawareness and diminish their power to lead us astray and create further suffering. This practice is essential for achieving true freedom and reclaiming fundamental dignity. This is also linked to other elements of the path, as Traleg Rinpoche points out:

> When we remain aware of our thoughts, we are in our natural state of being, which is the state of absolute bodhicitta.[97]

The subtle differences between various states of mind and the relationship between different aspects of the path become clearer over time. For now, let's appreciate how all the work we've done so far leads to greater clarity.[98] Earlier, we used the image of inadvertently dropping a key in a pond. If we stir the water with a stick in an attempt to find the key, the water becomes muddy, making it nearly impossible to see the key. For us to be able to see clearly, the mud must first settle to the bottom. That much we've understood. Now we need to recognize that this quality of clearness is not something we *add* to the water. It is the same with our mind. It is important to appreciate that clarity is not something we have to import from elsewhere (like installing software on our computer), but a natural ability of the mind.

Meditation: Allowing Clarity to Emerge

Take a few minutes to begin with the usual preliminaries: tuning into your posture, relaxing your body and mind, reconnecting with the Triple Gems, and committing to practice for the benefit of all beings. Then spend a few minutes practicing shamatha using any method that suits you, such as counting your breath or visualising the Buddha in front of you, allowing your mind to rest on this beautiful mental image.

Let go of expectations and continue practicing calm abiding until you feel a sense of peace and ease.

Then, observe how your mind feels. If you notice any difference in your inner landscape compared to 5 or 20 minutes ago, take the time to acknowledge and enjoy it without grasping.

Now, see how, when your mind becomes calmer, its ability to notice thoughts and mental events increases. That's the aspect of clarity. Notice the sheer cognisance, the natural intelligence of the mind that doesn't rely on concepts.

Observe that as you become more relaxed, present, focused, and comfortable, it becomes easier to recognise whether you are opening up or shutting down, solidifying a thought or letting it naturally dissolve, grasping at a goal or letting it go, and looking at things directly or following your assumptions blindly.

See how inner peace naturally fosters greater clarity and how there is no need to comment on the clarity itself or make it into a "thing." Simply enjoy the clarity that is a natural quality of the mind.

Just rest for a moment. At the end of the session, dedicate any merit generated to all beings, so they can find fundamental health, enjoy positive circumstances, relinquish nihilism and despondency, and ultimately reach buddhahood.

Self-identity Versus Personhood

In the "Processes" chapter, we discussed the concept of *ikigai*, a Japanese term that refers to what makes life fulfilling and gives us a reason to wake up in the morning—our raison d'être—where passion, mission, profession, and vocation intersect. We nuanced the idea of ikigai from a Buddhist perspective: we are encouraged to develop and integrate all aspects of our personhood, while remembering that this personhood is not a solid self, but a constantly changing, dependently arisen "bundle."

From the Buddhist point of view, clinging to the notion of an "I" as though it were inherently real is a significant issue, and one of the hallmarks of unenlightenment. The causes of suffering are said to be negative actions, emotional afflictions, and ignorance, or deep mental fog. If we further analyse these causes, we can see they boil down to clinging to phenomena, especially one's self-identity, as though they were lasting, unitary, and autonomous. One manifestation of this clinging is called "self-cherishing". This term, often mentioned in the mind training teachings, refers not to appreciating one's situation and enjoying a healthy sense of self-worth, but rather to the tendency to make everything about oneself and view the world egocentrically. In the lojong literature, self-absorption or self-centredness is often seen as the enemy. However, even this is a manifestation of a deeper issue: basic delusion. Nobody walks around consciously thinking of themselves as a "permanent, indivisible, independent self" in such terms, but our pains, troubles, and endeavours are symptomatic of such an illusion. If, deep down, we didn't think of ourselves as a singular entity, emotional upheavals would not arise, and we wouldn't engage in behaviours that directly or indirectly harm ourselves and others. As the seventh-century Indian master Dharmakirti said:

When there is self, one believes there is other,
From these images of self and other come attachment and
aversion;
As a result of getting wrapped up in these,
All possible faults arise.[99]

Whenever we encounter anything or anyone, we tend to categorise that object, whether a person or an inanimate object, as a positive thing that can benefit our "self," which leads to attachment; as a threat, which leads to aversion; or as something that leaves us indifferent, often with a trace of confusion. So we have a reaction that falls into one of the three categories of desire, aggression, or ignorance, perpetuating the cycle of suffering. It is exceedingly sad to see that all beings suffer in this way; and the compassion that integrates this realisation is very special. As the great Chandrakirti said:

First, thinking of "me," they cling to self,
Then, thinking "this is mine," attachment to things develops.
Beings are powerless, like buckets rambling in a well—
I bow to compassion for these wanderers.[100]

In Mahayana Buddhism, the notion that the self we cling to is an illusion is crucial. However, this does not mean that we are worthless as individuals. On the contrary, everyone has the potential to fully awaken; every single being is endowed with buddha nature; so no one is ever worthless, quite the contrary.

Despite some of the egocentric and materialistic pitfalls commonly found in the personal development sector, the spiritual path *does* involve a form of development: acquiring knowledge, honing skills, developing qualities, and abandoning certain habits. Buddhist masters advise us to assess our progress and stay true to ourselves, that is, not to try to become someone else. The problem is not in thinking, "Here I am, and here's what I need to do next to improve as a person," or in recognising that each person has unique talents and distinct skills that can and should be used.

This point is worth emphasising, because there seems to be a lot of confusion regarding personhood amongst both non-Buddhists and Buddhist practitioners. For example, Traleg Kyabgon Rinpoche observed that artists and individuals with various interests spent less time with or even renounced their passions once they started to practice Buddhadharma. He encouraged an integral approach to Buddhism.[101] People might think, "I could become a good photographer, but maybe that's just my ego talking, so it would be wrong to pursue it." The point of Buddhist practice is not to deny any form of personality or to remove distinctive traits. No one is asking us to become bland, zombie-like figures. The point is to dissolve delusion and shed self-centredness. The biographies of the great masters show that they made good use of their particular talents. Shantarakshita's service as an abbot was instrumental in the establishment of Buddhism in Tibet, and Vairotsana's contribution as a translator was invaluable. Thangtong Gyalpo built bridges!

It is natural to feel certain "callings" and have certain inclinations. Some will be harmful and delusory at best, but some will represent worthy pursuits. Therefore, we need to distinguish between what is truly beneficial and what isn't. Even temporal benefits can be worth pursuing if they are not our sole focus and if they provide favourable conditions for Dharma practice. It's all about perspective. With proper training and maturity, even so-called negative emotions can sometimes be put to good use, transformed, or at least, viewed differently. For example, in Vajrayana Buddhism, there's the notion of Buddha families, each associated with a predominant mental poison and its transcended counterpart, a particular type of wisdom.

Now, if the distinction between sanity and delusion largely depends on clinging to an "I" as inherently real, it is very important to become clear about the main object of our clinging. An experiential way to notice our attachment to self is through unwanted insults. When someone wrongfully calls us a thief or a liar, or rightfully points out our arrogance, we react strongly, like a cat whose tail has just been stepped on. We feel our precious identity is being attacked and a need to defend it tooth and nail. But is this identity as real and as solid as we believe?

Let's investigate a bit. Attachment to the self ties in with the *skandhas* or psychophysical constituents (also known as the "aggregates"), which we explored earlier in the "Tenderness and Warmth" chapter.[102] When we examine what we typically call "I," we see that it includes many components: physical form, sensations, conceptions, conditioning forces, and consciousnesses. Basically, we believe that there must be a "real me" based on our psychophysical constituents, including our personal storylines. As soon as we form this belief, we want this "real me" to be perpetuated, which inevitably leads to suffering. However, as we said above, "I" is merely a label for a dynamic, ever-changing set of impermanent and interdependent factors. Understanding this concept is important, because this bundle of aggregates or psychophysical constituents is what we typically interpret as being "I." This bundle is dynamic, transient, and compounded, and our person is numerically much less important than "others" (on the one side, there's one, and on the other, billions and billions!). Yet in our distorted view, we see ourselves as stable, lasting, unitary, and more important than all other beings. If we mistake a rope for a poisonous snake, we might spend the whole day in fear of a non-existent snake, when what we truly need is to look at the rope clearly. Likewise, we need to examine what we think of as our self-identity, which is why investigating the skandhas is essential.

All schools of Buddhism examine the psychophysical components. Each school may use different methods, but these methods inevitably lead to the conclusion that there is no such thing as a lasting self. This realisation is something one must discover for oneself through repeated analysis and contemplation.

To explore this, we could examine each of the skandhas one by one, trying to determine if there is a true self somewhere within them. Generally speaking, basic sitting meditation—such as shamatha—helps us recognise the habitual processes of our psychophysical constituents, like how we tend to conceptualise our sensations. By becoming increasingly aware of these processes, we learn to let them breathe, instead of mindlessly letting them ensnare us in negative patterns and delusions. In vipashyana, or clear-seeing meditation, we closely examine each aggregate, as if using a magnifying glass. We look at body parts, sensations, conceptions and labelling, inner forces and conditionings—including all possible volitions, emotions, and states of mind—and consciousnesses, which include the mind's capacity to interact with an object of the senses. My friend Greg Seton, a professor at Dartmouth College and an excellent communicator, uses an interesting analogy: familiarising ourselves with and recognising the skandhas is like arranging puzzle pieces by colours to facilitate the puzzle-making process. Each piece can be further broken down, but while this can be instructive, it is not always necessary. As Traleg Rinpoche explains in *Integral Buddhism*, even if the goal is to go beyond the illusion of independence, we can nonetheless start by isolating things and then looking at their relationships. So, in the case of the skandhas, we could mentally take apart the body, a sensation, the mental consciousness that perceives the sensation, the labelling of the sensation as "positive" or "negative," and so forth. We could then determine if any of these parts is the self, in and of itself, and look at how they interact with and depend upon each other.

In doing so, it is of paramount importance to understand that the five skandhas include *all* possible aspects of one's experience.[103] If we engage in vipashyana investigations in a happy-go-lucky way without a proper understanding of the skandhas, we might end up thinking that there's an inherent entity somewhere else, in some other category.[104] Just as someone convinced there is a robber in their house must check every room to feel secure, so too we must examine all five skandhas in detail in order to reach the conviction that they encompass the totality of our experience. Only then can we develop confidence in selflessness.

In his classic *Introduction to the Middle Way*, Chandrakirti uses the analogy of a chariot and employs a sevenfold reasoning to establish the lack of an inherent self, showing that the "self" is merely a designation. He demonstrates that there is no "chariot" other than its parts, no "chariot" that possesses its parts, and so on. Another, shorter text that is worth spending some time with is *The Wheel of Analytical Meditation*, composed by the great Mipham Rinpoche near the end of the nineteenth century. These texts are useful because the different lines of reasoning tackle the different ways we conceive of and cling to a self. While going into more detail is beyond the scope of this book, I encourage you to keep investigating the self, again and again, like a wheel turning, propelling you towards greater freedom and clarity.

Freedom from Bondage

Reflecting on complexity, mental and spiritual overload, and the quest for sanity in a hectic world highlights that we are bound by our habits and conceptions. To navigate with a mix of clarity and simplicity that does not solely depend on outer conditions, we need to look within and properly train our mind. Yet, the more we do this, the more we recognise subtler forms of bondage to which we are subjected.

The notion of bondage often comes up in Buddhist literature because the whole path is geared towards liberation. It is said that the deluded mind can even turn teachings into a form of bondage. However, hesitant beginners might misinterpret this idea to justify a lack of determination and commitment to a tradition. We need discipline and vigour, and we must be determined to study and practice the teachings all the way, until we achieve complete buddhahood.

We never abandon the practice or the teachings altogether, but there are situations in which a specific method or aspect of the path can become a source of grasping. Is that a problem? Not necessarily. To explain, the great lama Tulku Thondup Rinpoche gives the example of meditation on loving-kindness:

> Even if, when we're meditating on loving-kindness, we have thoughts of clinging to positive deeds and happiness, those are still positive thoughts, and they'll help us and others. Whenever we do anything positive that is inspired by beneficial intentions, it will become a source of peace and joy.[105]

He adds:

> Meditating on loving-kindness will initially be dualistic. But that's what enables us to start because that's where most of us beginners are. Remember, even if it is dual, it is still positive. And positive gradually leads to perfection.[106]

So we progress from negative to positive, then from positive to perfect. Going straight from negative to perfect is unrealistic. Most of the methods we use involve some kind of duality, which is fine, and it is okay if we subtly grasp at positive phenomena for the time being: it is symptomatic of a sense of appreciation and it shows that we are going in a positive direction. As the great master Thinley Norbu and others have taught, we replace bad habits with good habits until there are no more habits. This takes time; this is the path, and it is delightful.

However, if we realise that we are holding on too tightly to our practice, to the point that we're making ourselves tense—stiff during meditation, or even disagreeable during post-meditation—then we need to open up a bit. In shamatha meditation, we are introduced to antidotes that counter obstacles such as agitation and lethargy; but then we are also told that one of the obstacles to shamatha is to keep applying antidotes when it is unnecessary. While it is clear that tranquillity meditation needs to have an element of relaxation, the principle also applies to insight meditation. A reference to this is found in the *Seven Points of Mind Training*, where one of the aphorisms says, "Even the remedy is free to self-liberate." In this case, the remedy refers to analysis, including the investigative process that leads one to some understanding of emptiness. Traleg Rinpoche comments:

> While analysis dismantles the object of fixation, the lojong teachings advise us that analysis has no reality of its own either [...].[107]

In other words, fixating on analysis becomes an obstacle.

The great master Atisha, who was instrumental in the eleventh-century revival of Buddhism in Tibet, also offered similar advice:

Just as wisdom sees no inherent nature
In any phenomena whatsoever,
Let wisdom itself be subject to analysis,
And meditate free from conceptuality.[108]

This is important to consider as we continue to engage in further study and contemplation on emptiness. Focusing too much on the emptiness aspect of phenomena, we risk becoming attached to ideas such as lack of inherent existence, which can be problematic.

It should also be noted that there are different approaches to understanding emptiness among the different schools of Indo-Tibetan Buddhism. For example, practitioners following the Gelug tradition of Tsongkhapa may spend a lot of time studying the philosophical intricacies related to the notion of emptiness, whereas practitioners of the Kagyu and Nyingma traditions might spend more time meditating and engaging in devotional practices after developing an initial understanding of emptiness.

Regardless of the specific tradition, it is helpful to consider the template of the "three turnings of the wheel of Dharma," which classifies the teachings of the Buddha into three groups. A simplified summary would be: the first turning revolves around the four truths of the noble ones and fosters renunciation; the second turning focuses on emptiness; and the third turning emphasises buddha nature and the enlightened qualities that can be found within. The second turning reveals that all objects of grasping are illusory, whereas the third turning frames awakening as a process of *unveiling* buddha within. In other words, the third turning focuses on letting natural qualities shine forth, instead of acquiring external qualities or reaching some distant goal.

Some schools of Buddhism consider that the teachings of the

second turning are the most important and definitive. However, from a Kagyu-Nyingma perspective, all three turnings are precious teachings of the Buddha. It is said that if a practitioner focuses exclusively on emptiness, they risk turning emptiness into a "thing" or falling prey to nihilism. Practically speaking, if a practitioner habitually uses analysis as a weapon to see the lack of existence in everything that arises, they may overuse it, and fail to appreciate the boundless qualities of buddha nature.[109]

This is one of the reasons why the Nyingma and Kagyu teachings often discuss emptiness alongside clarity and other qualities. Although the implications go beyond the scope of this book, we can start to see that while concepts are devoid of inherent identity, the mind that considers them has a natural clarity. There is nothing to hold on to, yet there is boundless life.

At some point, we must learn to let go of techniques, such as constantly analysing thoughts with effort. To understand how and when to do this, it is important to seek guidance from a qualified teacher.

Insight in Daily Life

With practice, our relationship with overload and complexity evolves constantly.

For example, when we first start to meditate, we may be under the impression that we have more thoughts than before. However, a meditation instructor might tell us that we are simply becoming more aware of what used to go unnoticed, marking a step in the right direction as we begin to befriend our mind. Likewise, when we first attempt vipashyana exercises, we might find them overwhelming or wonder why we should even bother with them, seeking instead to take a break from the thinking mind. But as we go along, we find that such exercises are tremendously helpful on the path to sanity.

By now, it should be clear that we are not learning to constantly second-guess ourselves, but rather to examine our grasping, habits, and assumptions. We are also learning the difference between confused, compulsive, discursive thinking that we follow blindly and focused, relaxed, mindful inquiry. We also discover that we can ask proper questions during our daily affairs, not just on the cushion. This, in turn, can help simplify our life considerably. For example, we all like to play the "what if" game—"What if he says this, what if she replies that, what if this or that happens?"—constantly oscillating between hope and fear. Instead of conjuring up countless scenarios, it is sometimes helpful to ask, "What if my view is askew?" Considering whether our way of looking at things is truly objective can open things up, like letting in fresh air through an open window.

Occasionally, it is also worthwhile to examine our reactions. Traleg Kyabgon suggests asking ourselves, "Am I exaggerating, minimizing, or generalizing?" and even, "Who is the person having these experiences?"[110] It is challenging to do this in the heat of the moment, but we can create little pockets of clarity throughout the day. Taking a few seconds to tune in with our breathing to ease tensions and then seeing whether we can look at things in an open-dimensional way is helpful. This self-awareness, in turn, is an essential component of our training in tenderness. We notice our little games, recognise when we shut down, and commit to staying open, slowly replacing biases with equanimity, hatred with warmth, and one-upmanship with empathetic joy and a sense of fellowship.

We should learn to relax and enjoy ourselves, but we should also not be too passive, knowing that it is essential to put effort into training. This can be done creatively. The key point is that the "analysis" referred to in this chapter means looking directly at our experience. Without this direct observation, we will never get true insight, and we will never free ourselves from compulsive reification, misplaced conceptualisation, harmful patterns, and deluded habits.

As the great yogi Milarepa said:

> As long as our minds are clouded by delusion,
> We are bound to external phenomena
> By clinging, grasping and fixation.
> When we realise that appearances are devoid of essence,
> The phenomenal world becomes our friend.[111]

By doing so, we can walk the world freely and simply, remaining caring and responsive.

— VII —

Awakening

By now, it should be clear that the physical, emotional, mental, and spiritual overload that we experience has primary causes. These primary causes can be remedied through focused and ongoing practice. If we are seeking sanity in this day and age, we need to follow a structured path. Proceeding haphazardly will only provide limited, temporal, superficial results at best, and will likely increase our frustration and confusion. The wonderful news is that there is a path, and the only things we need in order to tread it are a mind—which we all possess—as well as receptivity and determination. We can be heirs to the buddhas of the past. It is up to us.

All beings can claim their fundamental heritage through awakening, regardless of gender, age, nationality, and so forth. This heritage also transcends any specific era. There is great power in tradition—and we will explore tradition in this chapter—but true wisdom has nothing to do with a historical perspective; true wisdom is atemporal. True wisdom is timeless, which is excellent news because it means we can fully access it, and we can learn from the great sages of the past. While our problems may seem contemporary and novel on the surface, at a deeper level, suffering is endemic to conditioned existence and has persisted throughout history. The yogis of the past, meditating in caves, may not have had to deal with annoying notifications popping up on their phones, traffic jams, or forms to fill out, but they all had to deal with agitation, laziness, self-absorption, hopes, fears, attachment to likes and dislikes, and countless other inner distractions.

They too had to tame their minds, train their minds, and eventually recognise the nature of their minds, to pacify their suffering and ultimately go beyond sorrow. They committed to a path and did not get carried away by obstacles. It is quite inspiring to read about how they did this.[112]

With the right mindset, our journey towards clarity, tenderness, and integrity is not impeded by noise and constant notifications. So-called obstacles can even be turned into fuel on the path. The turmoil found within and without can serve to foster renunciation and compassion. We begin to relinquish harmful habits, even the most subtle ones, which simplifies our life tremendously. We start to care for all beings who wander endlessly in their own projections, and this love gives our life meaning and integrity. By cultivating wisdom, our love becomes more and more unconditional, as it ceases to rely on illusory appearances and assumptions, allowing us to connect with situations and others on a deeper, fundamentally sane level. With proper guidance and sustained training in shamatha and vipashyana, we become relaxed, focused, and at ease even in the presence of thoughts, emotions, and all sorts of stimuli. In this way, Buddhism offers an integrated path that also includes confidence, appreciation, and devotion, which can be truly powerful.

The notion of devotion makes people cringe in the West. While inspiration is valuable at any level of practice and is seen as a good thing, devotion, a crucial part of the Vajrayana path, is often seen as akin to blind faith and associated with cults, so I will spend some time exploring its general meaning. We will also tackle other concepts that will allow our practice to become boundless, energetic, and effective, and that will help us stay on track and find proper guidance.

The Yearning to Explore

We mentioned that reading the biographies of enlightened masters can be a powerful source of inspiration. However, sometimes we may fantasise about their wondrous lives and accomplishments, hoping for a "big bang" kind of spiritual awakening that will happen in a hypothetical future. This is not unlike any object of hope or fear, where we expect miraculous abilities, or at the very least, an end to our troubles once and for all—the ultimate vacation. It is much better to stay simple, humble, and carry on without any expectations. Our tendency towards spiritual materialism and our contemporary obsession with quantifiable goals and results derail our capacity to enjoy the journey. There is a tremendous difference between having a sense of direction and entertaining expectations. A sense of direction leads to confidence and progress on the path, whereas expectations lead to fixation and a false sense of hope.

If you've made it this far in the book, it may be that you feel a connection with the Buddhist tradition, perhaps especially with Indo-Himalayan schools. You may wonder what's next. In other words, you know that reading a book is only part of the deal, even if you spend time with the exercises that it offers. You may feel a yearning to explore the depth and richness of a particular tradition. If so, that's wonderful. But before tackling how to make the most of that intention, it can be helpful to look at two ways we can deceive ourselves.

The first type of self-deception is to engage with a tradition hyperactively or elatedly. For instance, as soon as we finish reading a book, we start another one; we attend a teaching, and before it's over, we fantasise about the *other* teachings we could attend; we're in the middle of a practice session and we get distracted thinking about other practices we could do in the future. This happens to me sometimes. It might come from a good place, but generally speaking, it's just another form of agitation, another form of discursiveness. We grasp at ideas and chase projections, straying away from the present moment. This tendency to proceed hastily might also come from a lack of humility, thinking that we've "got it" and can move on to something else. Instead, we could slow down, appreciate things fully, and reconcile our enthusiasm with our ability to live in the moment. Tulku Thondup Rinpoche also raises a flag:

> In the past, teachers often had to persuade their students to move to higher levels of meditations, as students were usually humble and cautious. Today, however, even beginners want to practice only the highest meditations, like the loving-kindness free from concepts or emptiness. They dive into ocean-like meditations without any clue of their depths, whether due to arrogance or being unrealistic.
>
> The problem is that, if you try to meditate on high teachings like emptiness without adequate preparation from the ground level, you could very easily fall into the extreme views and experiences of nihilism or eternalism. . . . High realizations will not take place unless you have vigorously trained in the preliminary trainings for a long time. Being smart, prosperous, youthful, or powerful cannot buy true realization.[113]

If we are always searching for the "next thing," we should learn to relax and cultivate appreciation and presence of mind.

Another type of self-deception is believing that outer guidance is unnecessary. Such an attitude is extremely prevalent these days, especially in the West. Most of us have received a decent level of education; we've learned how to read, and have access to tons of information. We like to think we can discern what has value from what doesn't. This belief is partly justified, but also partly delusional. If we really knew what was best for us, we wouldn't be so confused and we wouldn't perpetuate harmful patterns and destructive habits of perception.

Interestingly, we trust educational institutions when we need to learn a profession, accountants and banks with our money, doctors when it comes to our health, and food producers when we go to the supermarket. Even the most brilliant and independent person must learn from and rely on countless others. We all do. Yet, when it comes to spirituality, we often become extremely tense and overly sceptical. This is understandable, especially for those who come from a socio-cultural background that has witnessed abuse from religious institutions. Yet, there is a reason why all the great Buddhist masters had teachers.

It is crucial to emphasise that we should not simply follow any spiritual teacher, however. There are deceitful teachers, and many who are honest but mistaken. Proceeding with caution is recommended. Yet, one thing that often impedes our willingness to engage with an actual tradition—and thus our ability to gain true spiritual accomplishment—is the stubborn desire to create one's "own" path. This often comes from misplaced pride or a deep misunderstanding of what a spiritual path entails.

In some sense, everyone's path is different. Buddhism acknowledges that we all have different karmic backgrounds, different personalities, different histories, and that our neuroses manifest differently according to ever-changing circumstances. Thus, a one-size-fits-all approach to spirituality would be dubious. Buddhism is certainly not saying that everyone should do the exact same thing in the exact same manner at the exact same time. This is why there are so many different teachings. But there are some common elements, and it is important to recognise that some sages have reaped the ultimate fruit of spiritual practice and can serve as reliable guides. They have been there.

For example, Buddha, with his boundless wisdom, has pointed out the pitfalls on the path, ensuring we can make progress toward buddhahood, rather than toward egotistical gratification or some farcical "freedom." That being said, the Buddha himself explained that we should not accept his teachings just because he is the Awakened One, but because we have fully pondered and tested them, "just as a goldsmith tests gold." We are encouraged to test the material using our own analytical skills and our own experience. Some words of truth may not make sense from the ego's point of view, and we may have many defence mechanisms (thinking that we can do it all by ourselves is one example), so this process might take time.

It might also be helpful to study different teachings, philosophies, and religions. But spending our whole life shopping for spirituality won't work. An analogy given is that of trying to dig the earth for water. We could take a shovel and compulsively make little holes all over the place, but to actually find pure and nourishing water, we need to commit to digging deeply in one spot.

Looking for Authenticity

Allow me to extend the metaphor. We're standing there, thirsty, with our little shovel in hand, hoping to find some water. Soon, we start to wonder: "How do I know where to dig?" Of course, we could try here and there at random. In some places, we'll hit a rock right away. In other places, the search will start smoothly, and we'll put a tremendous amount of hope and effort into digging before reaching a dry spot or a vein of contaminated water. Luckily, there are signs that indicate where to dig. Likewise, if we want to find truly nourishing teachings, we need to look for them in the right places. Thankfully, there are ways to determine what is authentic and what isn't.

Now, I cannot speak for other religious, philosophical, or spiritual traditions; I can only share what little knowledge I have accumulated about Buddhism. These days, many people seem to have only a vague idea as to what Buddhism actually is. This vagueness is understandable because Buddhism is not a "religion of the Book," and the sheer volume of its literary corpus is astounding. It includes countless works authored by many people other than the historical Buddha. There are also considerable differences regarding the context and interpretation of these texts. Furthermore, practitioners will often base their practice on advice received directly from a contemporary teacher. This makes it a living, organic tradition, which is crucial. But then, you may wonder: given this plurality of styles, teachings, methods, and approaches, how can you tell whether you are actually Buddhist?

The Four Hallmarks

This is where the "four seals" or "four hallmarks of the Buddhadharma" come into play. Strictly speaking, taking refuge is how one truly enters the Buddhist path, but it is said that whether one is truly a Buddhist also depends on whether they accept these four hallmarks. They are:

> All conditioned phenomena are impermanent.
>
> All that is tainted is unsatisfactory.
>
> All phenomena are empty of self-existence.
>
> Nirvana is true peace.

These concepts are extremely profound, and there are different ways to translate and explain them. For example, the early Pali Canon speaks of "three characteristics of existence," which are similar to the first three seals, seemingly leaving out the fourth. However, the general meaning remains consistent, as the fourth seal is a result of fully realising the first three. In any event, here we will just provide a straightforward summary. If you have read the rest of the book carefully, these concepts should be somewhat familiar, but seeking more detailed explanations would be beneficial.[114]

The first hallmark is that all conditioned, composite, or compounded phenomena are impermanent. This principle relates to the fact that things are made of parts and rely on changing causes and conditions, meaning they cannot last. There are two forms of impermanence: gross and subtle. Gross impermanence is the more obvious type, such as a building collapsing or someone dying. Subtle impermanence generally goes unnoticed and includes the ceaseless movement of atoms, thoughts, and so on. From this perspective, ageing begins immediately after birth. All things, regardless of their level of complexity and their apparent stability, are transient. All conditioned phenomena—from the minutest particle of dust to the largest galaxy in the universe, and from material things such as bananas to more conceptual phenomena such as frontiers between countries—are impermanent.

The second hallmark states that all that is tainted is unsatisfactory. Here, "tainted" doesn't refer to ethical assessments, like saying, "This business was built through unfair and abusive practices." It is not referring to any particular "sins," or original sin, the idea that human beings are fundamentally evil creatures (a notion which is completely foreign to Buddhism). Instead, it refers to something becoming "contaminated" or "polluted" or "tainted" by ignorance, confusion, an askew view, an emotional affliction, or any form of grasping. For now, since we grasp at everything—being under the illusion that interdependent phenomena are lasting and autonomous—our whole experience is ultimately unsatisfactory. This hallmark also means that discursive thinking and conceptual proliferation are ultimately unreliable and that outer conditions are not something to obsess over because they are changing and unstable. We are bound to experience pain and sorrow, as long as a deep mental fog is covering our buddha nature. In this way, the second hallmark relates to the all-pervading suffering of samsara discussed in the "Tenderness and Warmth" chapter.

The third hallmark is that all phenomena are devoid of self-existence or empty of inherent, autonomous self-identity. This means all phenomena have the nature of emptiness. Ultimately, all things are open-dimensional. While only a buddha fully appreciates this, we can gradually learn to see things in this way. The emptiness of phenomena (once again, not in a nihilistic sense) remains unchanged, regardless of whether we recognise it or not. It is their nature, just like the impermanence of conditioned phenomena isn't impeded or accelerated if we deny or acknowledge it. However, recognising emptiness through cultivating wisdom and positive habituation through the actual practice of meditation transforms our experience.

This understanding leads to the fourth hallmark: nirvana is true peace. Nirvana in Buddhism is not a physical place but a state of being. The Mahayana tradition emphasises a "dynamic" nirvana, where, after uprooting personal suffering, one works for the benefit of others without entanglement in delusion. Buddhism does not say "there's *only* suffering," but insists that we also have the opportunity to attain genuine and lasting peace. Here it may be helpful to recall the four truths of the noble ones, which explain that there is not only the possibility of attaining the cessation of suffering, but that there is a path that leads to it.

Someone who comprehends and adheres to these four seals is considered a Buddhist, regardless of their background or their appearance. Conversely, someone who believes that true happiness can be found through egocentric means is not. Most of us still cling to the notion of composed phenomena having lasting self-identity, indicating that most of us have a lot of work to do. The four hallmarks are not meant to make us judge ourselves as being a good girl or a naughty boy; rather they are there to bring clarity and help us distinguish what's truly in harmony with the path.

The Four Reliances

In addition to the four hallmarks, the four reliances are especially useful in maintaining clarity and integrity on the path. As the Nyingma master Khenchen Palden Sherab summarises:

> The four reliances are: rely on the Dharma rather than individuals, rely on the meaning rather than the words, rely on the definitive meaning rather than the provisional meaning, rely on timeless awareness rather than consciousness.[115]

Even though we should respect everyone, we should scrutinise spiritual advice and teachings. Once we determine that they make sense, we should apply them. While the words of the spiritual teachings are important, we should strive to understand their meaning. Furthermore, even though their provisional meaning is useful, we should aim to actualise the definitive meaning. And instead of blindly trusting our ordinary, dualistic consciousness, we should learn to rely on our deeper wisdom.

This is easier said than done. These four reliances need quite a bit of unpacking, and we discover their subtleties as we progress on our journey. But studying the four seals, keeping the four reliances in mind, and occasionally reflecting on the extremes of eternalism and nihilism helps us stay on track towards uncovering deep wisdom and achieving ever-greater clarity.

Taking Refuge

At the end of the fourth chapter, we discussed refuge. If you have mulled over the teachings presented in this book and if they have moved you, you might feel inspired to commit to the Buddhist path. If this is the case, you can find a suitable preceptor and request a refuge ceremony. This decision should not be made hastily. While the person who gives you the refuge vow may not necessarily become your one and only teacher, it's important to ask questions and take time to find a reliable preceptor. However, you don't want to waste your precious time either. In any event, your motivation and your receptivity are the predominant factors—not the size of your teacher's following.

Taking refuge in the Three Jewels, our most precious allies on the path to sanity, provides protection, inspiration, comfort, and a sense of spiritual clarity. It's wonderful if you can take refuge with an altruistic intention, but you don't need to be a great bodhisattva to begin. In fact, the official entrance to the bodhisattva path comes only after taking refuge. No one is asking you to be perfect, or to fully understand the profundity of the teachings right away; you are welcome to take refuge as you are—no big deal. It is normal to struggle with agitation, laziness, egotistic attitudes, and all sorts of odd habits. It is also normal to occasionally feel uncomfortable with the mere idea of taking on the suffering of others, as in the practice of tonglen, or "giving and taking," from the lojong teachings.

These struggles do not prevent us from being candidates for a refuge ceremony. What matters is acknowledging that self-centredness only brings suffering, and that life is extremely precious, impermanent, and yet full of tremendous potential.

During the refuge ceremony, you take refuge in the Buddha as your guide, in the Dharma—representing the union of wisdom and compassion—as your path out of ignorance, and in the Sangha, wise beings who have realized the Dharma, as your companions along the way. By doing so, you stop seeking ultimate spiritual refuge in mundane philosophies, material objects, and self-aggrandising patterns, and instead aim for genuine freedom.

The Subtle and Self-deceiving Art of Seeking Spiritual Badges

If you have been through a refuge ceremony, or are considering attending one, you might find the following reflections helpful. They came to me when one of my closest friends took refuge some years ago. I introduced her to her preceptor and had the joy of attending the ceremony.

My friend was moved to tears. She had been interested in Buddhism for decades but had never officially become a practitioner. Upon meeting her preceptor-to-be, as our little group got together for lunch prior to the ceremony, she was all psyched up—she's always been a determined, even feisty person, and on that particular day she was excited and talkative. I had told her a lot of good things about the teacher she was meeting, and she was eager to connect with him: "I've read this and that book, oh I know what you mean, I so *get* what you mean!"

Don't get me wrong: the desire for a connection with a mature Dharma practitioner, someone who's "been there," is perfectly legitimate, and yearning faith is laudable. Her display of enthusiasm was genuine and quite touching.

I love my friend deeply, and we have so much in common that I often see myself in her—just as she often sees herself in me. The greatest friends are sometimes mirrors, reflecting our own virtues and flaws. Of course, friends don't need to be exactly alike for that mirror quality to manifest. Sometimes, it just takes one to know one, but our own inner state can be reflected everywhere, for our very experience of the world is a reflection of our mind. In any case, over the course of the day, as I observed my friend going through a wide array of emotions, I caught glimpses of my own tendency to grasp at spiritual teachings and materialise spiritual experiences. I could see myself years before, taking refuge, pumped up and ready to add new labels ("Buddhist Refugee and Totally Official Practitioner," or "Buddhist" for short) to the set of characteristics that presumably constituted my identity. I didn't look at my friend with a "been there, done that" feeling or some kind of nostalgia; there was a peculiar presentness to the reflection I contemplated, and to be frank, I could see my spiritual materialism at work that very day. Which made me think.

To be clear, I am not saying that my friend suffers from a particularly rare and intense Achievement Syndrome. She's just like anyone who brims with joy as a result of having finally found their path. And why wouldn't she? To have the freedom and proper circumstances to encounter genuine spiritual teachings, and the willingness and ability to appreciate them, is truly wondrous. But we should be aware of our tendency to seek spiritual badges, medals, and premium memberships. According to Chögyam Trungpa Rinpoche and others, spiritual materialism is a universal tendency—so my friend and I are presumably not alone in this predicament. In fact, grasping is at the root of samsara; materialism is simply there, along with nihilism and eternalism, all the way until enlightenment. Their power and prevalence can diminish as we progress, but old habits die hard.

Soon after the ceremony, my friend asked the teacher, "What should I *do* now? Any particular text I should read?" I ask such questions all the time to my own teachers, and it's good to do the occasional check-up to ensure we're still on the right track; that's why there are teachers. As you walk through an unknown city, it makes sense to ask someone if you're going in the right direction towards the supermarket; it is all the more important to confirm some intuitions and understandings—and not just with any passerby—as we tread a spiritual path. But if I am brutally honest and look within, I must admit that my questions often hide a desire for concrete things—things *to do*. My main teacher could tell me: "Cultivate love and devotion, and relax in openness," which is not just brilliant advice but a profound teaching. It's a deceptively simple statement, more precious indeed than a wish-fulfilling gem; and yet I am so proud and dense that I ask him again and again, "What should I *do*?" And again he finds new ways to tell me, "Cultivate love and devotion, and relax in openness." The truth is that whenever I don't have truly loving and devotional feelings, or whenever I don't relax in openness, I tend to see Dharma as a checklist.

Genuine, complete openness may seem frightening—until it isn't, because why would utter freedom be scary? Some people can fly in the sky, while others prefer the so-called solidity of a good old staircase (while perhaps some others would rather take the elevator). It just so happens that beginners often look for firm ground, which is perfectly understandable.

Yet, we should be wary of trying to collect badges. "After I finish this, then I'll do that, and then after this, I'll . . ." If we practice according to a Tibetan lineage, we may think, "I'll complete the preliminary practices, then receive this or that empowerment, then accomplish an elaborate Vajrayana practice, and then, *then* I'll be the real McCoy, the real yogi." If we follow the Theravada path, perhaps we feel inadequate and incomplete because we haven't yet read the whole Pali Canon; and since the name of that school translates as "The Way of the Elders," maybe we feel that we can only have our say in it once we're, well, elderly. But the Buddha is not some kind of benevolent/admonitory Santa Claus who's hanging up above with a massive legal pad, keeping track of our accomplishments. Of course, there are prerequisites to some vows and practices; of course, there are preliminaries to different paths; and of course, these need to be taken seriously. But one of the main prerequisites is to be ready to let go of our so-called identity. Not that we will dissolve into some nihilistic void or become like a crazy person who's lost his marbles. Rather, we are willing to let go of our clinging to false concepts, including our idea of a fixed "I." We commit to opening our hearts and to stop mindlessly cultivating *kleshas*, which include pride, jealousy, and the desire to protect our territory and to claim that we know everything.

Buddhahood is often said to come about as we perfect the twofold accumulation of merit and wisdom. But the words "accumulation" and "merit" can be misunderstood. To the clinging mind, it may sound like the term "accumulation" refers to savings in a bank account, and the word "merit" may evoke the idea of Scout badges. Often, spiritual materialism is more subtle than we think. We can all spot the obvious issues, but of all isms, spiritual materialism is one of the most insidious. The situation is further aggravated by habits we've developed over the course of our upbringing, at school and at work: the socio-cultural pressures to seek tangible achievements are omnipresent. It can be healthy to withdraw from the turmoil, be it just by offering ourselves a few minutes of silence every now and then, and to contemplate just how we're affected by these influences. Sometimes, these days, it seems everyone is supposed to make an entrepreneur of themselves. Our outer world is so goal-oriented that it is hard not to let it suffuse our inner life.

The point is not that all goals are bad. Buddhism has plenty of goals, one of the most poignant being the one heroically sought after by bodhisattvas—striving to bring all beings to enlightenment without giving up on anyone, ever. Sometimes we're in dire need of a mystical or not-so-metaphorical kick in the butt, so that we stop postponing actual practice, which is a particularly pernicious form of laziness. A little bit of peer pressure helps, too! The idea is to ease up on our obsessive quest for tangible, short-term results.

Personally, when I notice I'm all tense, with the inner achiever all worked up like some ambitious spiritual careerist, I find it helpful to take a step back and laugh. Catching ourselves in the act, spotting ourselves moving like a speedy hamster ceaselessly running in a wheel of its own design—that's hilarious!

It is also important to remember the meaning of taking refuge in the Triple Gems. Buddhists take refuge in the Buddha. Which means taking refuge in the heart of unconditioned awakening and fully trusting in a timeless, changeless, unbounded wisdom. We don't take refuge in some "measurable realisation," nor in some product of our own fabrication. Taking refuge in the Dharma means committing to a path of utter honesty, radical loving-kindness, and understanding that allows us to transcend or cut through whatever masks our wakefulness. Taking refuge in the Sangha means fostering reliable friendships, the rare and precious kind that can help us see through our layers of self-deception and with which we can be completely frank, as one-way relationships only get us so far. To take refuge in the assembly of virtuous companions also means stopping taking refuge in the samsaric rat-race.

Here's a key take-away, and perhaps I could have it tattooed all over my body so that I don't forget it myself: the more we cling to spiritual practice, that much more impermeable to true wisdom we will become. To experience the blessings of the sublime beings and teachings, we need to allow some space. Of course, to do that, some fundamental trust is required, and for some of us, this takes time.

Practicing meditation, studying classic texts, and attending teachings are all necessary and absolutely wonderful activities. We can delight in these activities, as they allow us to extract the essence of our precious life. But if we use the practices and teachings for self-aggrandisement, we miss the point entirely.

To maintain a healthy perspective, we should tune into the openness of the path. In Mahayana texts, bodhisattvas go through many stages, some of which may take eons to traverse. The *Jataka* tales, recounting the former lives of the Buddha, are quite inspiring in this regard. While the notion that reaching enlightenment may take many lives could be disheartening, at the same time, the scale is so vast, so beyond our ability to conceptualise and come up with a neat schedule (with reminders programmed on our phone), that we are forced to let go, relax a bit, and enjoy the path. When we see that the Dharma is absolutely boundless, our idea of "I" becomes insignificant in comparison—no big deal.

On the other hand, there is a Zen teaching in which liberation is found in *nowness*. We may see that Buddha is zazen. Enlightenment can happen either *now*—if we can rest in truly unconditional love or atemporal awareness—or so far in some nebulous future that we should take things simply and earnestly without being too uptight about the ultimate result. A third option might exist somewhere between "now" and "countless lives," but thinking about it is a little awkward and can only lead to unhelpful speculations.

The truth is, we don't know how swiftly we'll reach our ultimate goal of enlightenment. While a "project management" mindset may help us develop new habits and reorganise our schedule to find more time to practice, such a mindset cannot apply to spiritual realisations.

Our tendency to materialise our experience and look for stable bearings is human. We cannot beat ourselves up for being samsaric beings—that's just the way it is. We can, however, smooth out the process with a dash of humour—picturing ourselves as a needy-nerdy kid who collects stickers—and with some compassion for ourselves—as we can't blame the child, recognising that we are unknowingly engrossed in what is, after all, a game, an illusion.

Untangling the Yarn

Some teachings can appear deceptively simple. That's a figure of speech: strictly speaking, the Buddha is undeceiving. But some Buddhist concepts do seem so simple, so logical, so natural, that we think they don't require familiarisation. Assuming that mere intellectual understanding suffices, we don't dig deep enough. Our memory fades over time, and—unless we truly uproot old habits—they will return with a vengeance. This is why it is important to balance study, reflection, and meditation. We receive and read teachings (study), we chew on them and look at them from different angles (reflection), and we spend time on the cushion (meditation). Training ourselves in these three ways is essential.

Sometimes, the "reflection" part, which serves as a bridge between study and meditation, is neglected, or it gets derailed. It may be that we are taking something simple and overanalysing it, due to our habit of doubting or clinging to conceptual proliferations. Maybe we have a hard time letting go and trusting (either a tradition or our own deeper wisdom), or maybe we become infatuated by our own ideas. Alternatively, we may study or contemplate something that is *not* so simple and get intimidated, thinking, "I'll never be able to understand this!" This can lead to a belief that there's no point in trying, or we get hazy and don't know where to start; or perhaps we take the whole thing as some kind of cerebral challenge and grapple with it, becoming really tense.

In such situations, it's good to approach things simply and with humour. If we are the intellectual type, we should distinguish between aspiring to wisdom and relying on conceptual proliferations. We can hone our analytical skills while being wary of over-intellectualising. Striking a balance involves discerning where to put our trust—whether in our own egotist projections or the timeless advice of enlightened sages. If we struggle with low self-esteem, we can shake ourselves up, reminding ourselves that—according to the Nyingma and Kagyu traditions, among others—we possess a fundamentally enlightened nature. Taking things one step at a time is perfectly fine. To paraphrase a Tibetan proverb: there is no arduous project that cannot be divided into small, accomplishable tasks. Besides, we can embrace our beginnerness: it is much better to know we do not know something and to approach it with a fresh, humble mind than to think we know and let our assumptions take over.

We should also consider if our approach to studying is helpful. We tend to consider Dharma as a process of collecting, and in a sense, it is—we accumulate merit and wisdom—but ultimately, the point of our practice is not to add new conceptions, but to remove false conceptions. Seeing things in this way can help us relax, knowing we are not trying to acquire something foreign and remote. Instead, we are gradually removing anything that obscures buddha nature, be it emotional afflictions, cognitive distortions, habits of vagueness, and so on. Any effort we make in this direction is worthwhile, even if we don't immediately see the results.

Recently, I heard the great lama Dzigar Kongtrul Rinpoche speak of a process of reduction (*nam jö*, in Tibetan), which involves eliminating any false assumptions we may have about any particular object.[116] He used the metaphor of untangling a yarn, with many threads of different colours. Practicing Dharma, studying mind and phenomena are often like this. Slowly, we untwist and disentangle, one strand at a time. As we do this, our mind becomes simple and open. As Dzigar Kongtrul points out, this process requires sharpness, but it also *enhances* our mental sharpness. The sharper our mind is, the clearer it gets, and the simpler it becomes—simple, in the most positive sense, like the open sky—all-accommodating.

When we are uncomplicated, we can properly receive direct instructions from a qualified guru, a genuine and mature teacher. These precious instructions don't bounce off our assumptions—our messy ball-of-yarn of a mind—but go straight to our heart, where we can enshrine them for as long as we breathe.

Devotion and Trust

Devotion is an important aspect of Tibetan Buddhism but is often misunderstood, especially in the West. Devotion can come in all shapes and sizes. While all theistic religions include an aspect of devotion, this influences the way Westerners perceive the Buddhist notion of devotion. However, since Buddhism is a non-theistic tradition, its concept of devotion is a little different.

Interestingly, the Tibetan term we often translate as "devotion," *mögü*, actually encompasses two concepts: interest (*mös pa*) and humility (*gus pa*). This is why Traleg Kyabgon often translates it as "interested humility." It comes from recognising the limitations of a life devoid of spiritual practice and from a genuine eagerness to continue learning without becoming arrogant.[117] Traleg Kyabgon adds:

> If we wish to make any real progress on the spiritual path, we must become worthy vessels for the precious nectar of the Dharma. A practice that is sustained by interested humility will have more depth, breadth, and longevity than one punctuated by sporadic and undisciplined bursts of enthusiasm. Without curiosity and humility nothing can be retained or absorbed, because our minds are already too full of judgments and prejudices.[118]

This is a general approach to devotion in the Mahayana Buddhist context. Vajrayana takes devotion to a whole other level, which involves a kind of surrender. However, this type of devotion is even more misunderstood than the type found in the Mahayana. Some time ago, I heard an interesting comment from Dzigar Kongtrul Rinpoche: to paraphrase, he said that since a lot of practitioners leave Christian and Protestant religions, they expect Buddhism to be completely different. Since their former religion was all about faith, they expect Buddhism to be all about reasoning; this makes it very difficult to talk about Vajrayana.[119] We will return to Vajrayana in the next section, but my understanding is that second-guessing one's own experience (by always feeling the need to refer everything to reason and to intellectually established frameworks) can become a conceptual habit for many of us. This makes it hard for us to stay relaxed and trust ourselves. It's as if our spiritual sensor were malfunctioning. I suppose it is also a "throwing the baby out with the bathwater" kind of situation.

However, it is important to acknowledge that devotion is not limited to religious pursuits. We are devoted to our friends, our work, our pet projects, and our institutions. If any endeavour is to bring about some kind of fruition, there has to be some level of effort, some level of commitment, or some level of appreciation. Of course, distinctions can be made between enjoying a hobby, focusing on one's art or career, or being involved in any kind of temporal project, and devoting oneself in the religious sense. But the idea with how devotion works is that, to a large extent, mind becomes what it contemplates. There's a causal process, one that we can use to our advantage. This also involves a process similar to what we've seen in the section on empathetic joy (as part of the four immeasurables): if we delight in the positive qualities of others, we will develop a taste for these qualities and the inclination to develop them, whether consciously or not. In other words, we come to share in the merits of others through the power of appreciation.

As Orgyen Chowang Rinpoche often says, if you want to become extraordinary, you have to focus on something extraordinary. This is why so many teachings and texts encourage us to recall the buddhas and their enlightened qualities as much as possible. This is also a form of mindfulness (remember, the Sanskrit term usually translated as "mindfulness" connotes "recalling something" or remembering). As much as we can think of the buddhas, as much as we imbue our minds with bodhicitta, as much as we can recall the openness of the meditative state—to that extent, our experience changes. So a practitioner of Tibetan Buddhism will be devoted to the Buddha, but also to the Dharma, to the Sangha, and to the qualities of liberation. It is a way to connect with, and eventually embody, the heart of the teachings.

Of course, misunderstandings can occur, especially when it comes to devotion to a specific, living teacher. This can vary greatly depending on culture and context. In any case, it is good to take some time, first seeing the teacher as an *elder*, someone who simply knows more on the subject of Dharma; then as a *spiritual friend*, with a somewhat deeper level of mutual commitment; then perhaps someday the relationship will evolve beyond elder and spiritual friend to *master*. But as Samuel Bercholz likes to say, it is not a one-way street. The teacher should not be in it for personal profit, and both sides should assess each other before making a commitment. There should be actual communication. Just as there are some deceitful teachers, there are also deceitful students. So, it is advised to proceed slowly and to consider the qualifications of both.

Generally speaking, the rarer, higher, and more powerful the teachings, the more prepared one must be. However, for the foundational teachings of the Hinayana and the common teachings of the Mahayana, it is safe to say that a good student is simply one who is honest, or at least trying to be. They should be willing to see through their own bullshit (pardon my French). Additionally, they should be open to taking advice and applying what makes sense to their own situation. It's not necessary to report back every week like in a military or business environment, nor to bother the teacher about every little detail relating to one's own life; but it is the student's responsibility to ask questions and seek clarifications. As professor Greg Seton likes to point out, asking good questions is in itself a skill that can be honed, and an important one at that. It's wonderful to be able to really see where our confusion lies. Sometimes, when we ask for advice, we try to smuggle our assumptions into the conversation in an attempt to seek reassurance, or frame our questions in such a way that hides our discomfort and confusion. Good teachers see through this, but some self-awareness helps. Lastly, don't approach teachers with blatantly materialistic intentions. Nowadays, some people attend a few workshops and then create new sidelines based on spiritual ideas. That's not at all the approach here.

When it comes to teachers, the ideal scenario is to find one who possesses 1) vast learning, 2) deep, genuine meditative realisation (not just some fleeting experience), and 3) the blessings of an authentic lineage. One's gender, age, nationality, looks, and personality do not matter. However, finding someone who has perfected these three elements is quite rare. Generally speaking, what matters is that the teacher has 1) more knowledge than the student, 2) wisdom and bodhicitta in their mindstream, and 3) a connection to an actual lineage. We should be wary of self-proclaimed teachers who have merely read some books and attended a couple of conferences. There must be some kind of actual transmission for the tradition to continue. Buddhism is a living tradition, and its transmission should not be like presenting a folkloric artifact or a mere set of fun facts; it is more akin to learning how to bake good, nourishing bread, where the freshness is constantly present, generation after generation. It's also important that the teacher has a positive, pure motivation. Of course, some teachers have specific areas of expertise and may not be able to answer all of your questions, and that is perfectly fine. We should also be careful not to project too many assumptions and personal concepts onto the teacher, expecting them to be perfect all the time, or to fit our current, limited notion of perfection. But we should find a teacher who is ethical and caring, who embodies what they're teaching (or who is at least honestly trying), and who is not in it for personal gain.

There's no need to complicate things when it comes to devotion to a specific teacher. We can simply rely on the Triple Gems and see how things evolve. Importantly, being devoted doesn't mean abandoning our discernment, quite the contrary; in fact, we are devoted to deep wisdom. There are many beautiful praises and verses of homage in Indo-Himalayan Buddhism celebrating enlightened qualities. It is also interesting to note that all the great masters are exemplary in their great devotion towards their own lineage and masters, to the point that there seems to be a powerful correlation between devotion and realisation. In fact, devotion at such a level becomes complete, irreversible trust. We may see that the more accomplished a spiritual teacher is, the humbler and more devoted they become. Perhaps it's also the other way around: the humbler, the wiser. One becomes more open to receiving blessings and better equipped to keep cultivating wisdom. The true devotee can then learn to trust their own deep, primordial awareness, not their usual, dualistic consciousness. In doing so, they're less prone to taking their own concepts and discursiveness too seriously, which allows them to keep progressing, quite simply, for the benefit of themselves and others. At that point, one gains confidence, and the path becomes increasingly clear.

Simplicity in Vajrayana

The Vajrayana, or Indestructible Vehicle, is central in Himalayan Buddhism. It builds upon the renunciation of samsaric neuroses and their causes, as espoused in the foundational vehicle or Hinayana, and the cultivation of bravery, compassion, and wisdom taught in the Mahayana. From the perspective of the "three turnings of the wheel of Dharma,"[120] the Vajrayana integrates the second turning teachings on emptiness-openness and the third turning teachings on buddha nature. While discussing the Vajrayana in detail here would be inappropriate (as this vehicle relies on actual transmission from teacher to disciple), I would like to briefly explore how it ties in with the main concerns of this book: finding true ease of mind, simplifying our lives in a way that is oriented towards genuine wisdom, and reconnecting with fundamental sanity despite our current overload.

Vajrayana offers an integrated path that encompasses all aspects of our experience. One of its distinctive features is its ability to turn absolutely anything into the path of awakening from the samsaric nightmare—sometimes, if necessary, in a shocking manner. Accommodating all aspects of our experience involves *pure perception*, also known as *sacred outlook*. This outlook is not a denial of the ruggedness of life as it is ordinarily experienced; yet, as Trungpa Rinpoche explains, "We find that life can be an easy, natural process. [...] The idea of purity [in 'pure perception'] here refers to an absence of imprisonment. Sacred outlook means perceiving the world and oneself as intrinsically good and unconditionally free."[121]

On this sacred path, we learn to perceive things in a wholly different way, fostering gratitude, relaxation, clarity, alertness, and responsiveness, whatever the situation requires. We can learn to play with the different energies and textures of any given situation without losing our fundamental dignity and without losing sight of others' fundamental dignity. This doesn't mean becoming a doormat or encouraging people's maleficence or harmful behaviour towards themselves and others. Specifically, in our practice, we integrate the senses instead of blocking them. We use positive images (such as visualisations of enlightened figures), positive sounds and words, and positive meditative experiences, but without clinging to them. The Vajrayana incorporates teachings on shunyata in a very refined way, teaching us that we don't have to struggle all the time. Instead of using countless antidotes to forcefully counter specific emotions, we use the emotions themselves on the path; this is why it is said that in the Vajrayana, the problem becomes the solution. These noble practices—received from a qualified lineage holder—provide powerful means to purify and simplify our minds.

Among these means are deity practices focused on buddhas associated with specific enlightened qualities. For example,

Avalokiteshvara is associated with love and compassion; Manjushri is associated with wisdom; Bhaisajya-Guru or the Buddha of Medicine is associated with healing; and some, like Tara and Vajrapani, are associated with protection and enlightened activity. Practices involving such representations are not about idol worship or venerating an individual. Rather, they focus on relying on extraordinary, enlightened qualities to overwhelm our ordinary, deluded consciousness. Because we all possess different personalities and qualities, we may develop a closer relationship with one representation of enlightenment compared to another. Regardless of which buddhas we form a closer relationship with, two things help us appreciate "simplicity" in Vajrayana. The quotation marks are deliberate: while some practices are particularly straightforward and unelaborate, others are highly complex and codified. Vajrayana, as a whole, has an unfathomable richness that cannot even be conceived of with an ordinary mindset. Such practices are powerful means that bypass our conceptual barriers, leading to an unfettered, unfabricated, unbounded mind. In the following section, we'll explore two notions that can help us make sense of the richness of the Vajrayana, find clarity, and relax into our practice: firstly, the three main qualities of the buddhas and secondly, the view that one buddha contains all buddhas.

The Three Main Qualities of the Buddhas

As bodhisattvas progress along the path, they develop a vast number of qualities that further propel them towards buddhahood and reinforce their capacity to help sentient beings. These qualities and abilities include courage, compassion, resilience, determination, equanimity, stability, vastness of mind, analytical power, communication skills, and so on. When they fully awaken and become actual buddhas, even the subtlest obscurations are removed, and their measureless qualities of enlightened body, speech, and mind become manifest.

However, for us, a useful way to consider this is to appreciate that each buddha embodies three main qualities: unconditional love, omniscient wisdom, and boundless power. Concerning omniscient wisdom, it doesn't matter whether or not the Buddha knows how many pebbles there are on the banks of the St. Lawrence River; what matters is that he knows everything necessary to reach full liberation. Similarly, the quality of power does not mean that Buddhists rely on an all-powerful external entity, as is common in eternalistic religions. Instead, Buddhism acknowledges the need to work with our own karma, habits, and obscurations; in other words, we have to do our part.

There is tremendous, unfathomable wisdom, love, and power in all buddhas: a buddha knows, cares, and has unimpeded capacity. All buddhas possess these qualities—Avalokiteshvara, most often associated with love, also has fully realised wisdom; Vajrapani, predominantly associated with power or enlightened capacity, is just as compassionate and caring. The different names and forms serve the different needs and profiles of practitioners. Interestingly, each deity's specificity depends on each buddha's past aspirations when they became bodhisattvas, vowing to assist with specific situations. We can derive great comfort, trust, and ease in knowing that all buddhas perfectly embody these three main qualities: love, wisdom, and power.

One Buddha, All Buddhas

One particular aspect of the Vajrayana is that each buddha contains all buddhas. This is a very subtle point that can only be fully understood with time and practice, but it holds significant power. It doesn't imply that we lose the capacity to appreciate the different manifestations of enlightenment or reduce everything into a bland uniformity. Nor does it mean that all buddhas are representatives of some kind of unitary, autonomous, God-like figure. Rather, it suggests that, on a subtle level, each buddha's wisdom body is a ceaseless, spontaneous manifestation of ultimate reality and atemporal enlightened mind. Each buddha is truly boundless. Admittedly, such a notion can rapidly exhaust our conceptual mind, but there is a connection, a natural, inherent simplicity.

We don't need to wrestle with these ideas too much; knowing that one buddha embodies all buddhas can be enough. As the venerable Nyingma master Lama Sonam Tsering Rinpoche explains, understanding that each buddha contains all buddhas, our mind is more relaxed: we can practice Vajrayana knowing that nothing is missing. This engenders confidence and encourages one to practice more, with a sense of relaxed focus. Otherwise, while meditating on one buddha, our minds might become distracted by thoughts of needing to complement our practice with another.

In the Nyingma tradition of Himalayan Buddhism, we often invoke Guru Rinpoche, Padmasambhava, the Lotus-Born, who is also called "the second Buddha," due to his central role in firmly establishing Buddhism, especially Vajrayana and Dzogchen teachings, in Tibet and neighbouring regions. His enlightened power is still palpable today, and through various means, he continues to play a vital role in transmitting fresh and authentic Buddhadharma in this world. Many great lamas consider him to be the buddha for our time, his teachings being all the more powerful amid chaos, confusion, and turmoil. We view Guru Rinpoche as the quintessential enlightened master, embodying all sources of refuge. With the right understanding, receiving blessings and inspiration from Guru Rinpoche is like receiving blessings and inspiration from all buddhas, bodhisattvas, lamas, and deities. It is so powerful, and in a way, so simple. It helps clear away mental pollution and provides great ease, protection, and clarity on the path.

Boundless Joy and Clarity

Our usual experience of love is conditional. It varies according to circumstances, and it depends on several factors, such as our subjective concepts concerning closeness and enmity. But, by familiarizing ourselves with bodhicitta (both relative and absolute bodhicitta), we move towards developing truly unconditional love: a deep, ceaseless, spontaneous caring for all, regardless of time, distance, and other conceptual categories. Likewise, other qualities such as joy and clarity can evolve similarly. Over time, our joy becomes less and less dependent on outer circumstances and temporal factors, and our clarity becomes less and less impeded by thoughts, concepts, and emotions.

Moreover, when we start to feel a profound respect for all things, we begin to experience a unique type of happiness—a deep contentment that is perspicacious. This profound happiness is not necessarily expressed loudly, but there is great comfort in knowing that it is always within reach. We may experience anger or sadness on occasion, but knowing how to return to fundamental sanity helps us maintain an elevated, wholesome baseline. This is not mere elation or some kind of "high." We become more supple, appreciative, and resilient. It is a kind of satisfaction more in line with the nature of reality and thus much more stable than any mundane satisfaction derived from crossing off everything on a to-do list.

Freedom from the bondage of discursive thinking also fosters a sense of fundamental dignity. We feel dignified within, naturally, without making a big deal about ourselves, and we recognise dignity in all beings as well. We see things more clearly because our perceptions are less clouded by our own conceptual biases and self-centred habits. This type of freedom relates to the notion of "pure perception" in Vajrayana: we catch a glimpse of the boundless, open qualities of the world when our view is not tainted by our hang-ups, assumptions, and habits; we begin to glimpse primordial purity, unscathed by the projections, fantasies, preferences, and delirium of our own mind.

This doesn't mean that all's well and good in the world or that we should allow tyrants and criminals to do their thing, nor does it imply that rose bushes suddenly lose their thorns. We still have a finger on the pulse of the world; we can still feel the suffering of the world and know when others have gone astray, lost in delusion due to not recognising their fundamental dignity. The skin of a peach is still soft, and a knife remains sharp. We stay connected with the earthly aspects of situations. In fact, in Vajrayana Buddhism, it is believed that natural elements hold great wisdom and energy. Thus, behaving respectfully and humbly adhering to the principles of causality are also part of cultivating a sacred outlook.

Raising One's Energy Level

Most of us, when we start to meditate, seek tranquillity—peace of mind. This involves slowing down and learning to relax at a deeper level. But Buddhism does not suggest that we should become lifeless or apathetic. On the contrary, it is sometimes important to generate momentum and cultivate inspiration. Vigour, or diligence, is one of the six paramitas, which are important aspects of the bodhisattvas' sixfold training. Shantideva defines it in this way:

Diligence means joy in virtuous ways.
Its contraries have been defined as laziness,
An inclination for unwholesomeness,
Defeatism and self-contempt.[122]

Delighting in virtue fosters perseverance, enthusiasm, and fearlessness—strength in the face of adversity. Interestingly, the word "courage" is etymologically related to the French word *cœur*, meaning "heart." We should put our hearts into our practice, particularly when it has a twofold goal: truly benefitting oneself and others.

The Tibetan Buddhist tradition speaks of *lungta*, often translated as "windhorse." Windhorse is also related to the notion of the "subtle body" found in tantric Buddhism and traditional medical systems. The subtle body includes channels and energies referred to as "winds." Physical imbalance can occur due to improper circulation of these winds. To some extent, a comparison can be made between the Tibetan medical system and other systems (such as the meridians and chi, central to traditional Chinese medicine, or the structure of the energetic body as found in Ayurveda), but the Tibetan system has its own specificities.

In the Buddhist context, some practices are meant to "raise the lungta," allowing positive qualities in one's life to flourish, especially one's strength and resilience. Such practices are often coupled with altruistic means in order to balance the outer environment and heal our relationship with the elements and different forces involved in interdependent existence.[123] In particular, there is a famous prayer composed by the great nineteenth-century Nyingma master, Mipham Rinpoche, that includes offerings and mantras to raise the windhorse and dispel obstacles. The prayer does not represent an "I can do this!" kind of attitude based on egocentric pride. Rather, it is based on dignity. Often people enter into a conflictual relationship with the energies of their world in a misguided attempt to repel interferences that arise. Here, if we generate lungta, we find that we can be both direct and respectful, incisive and tender, strong and humble, energised and clear-headed, active and at ease. Ideally, specific practices related to lungta are received directly from a teacher; but the general idea with lungta here is that we can always pick ourselves up through making offerings and reconnect with a sense of strength and purpose.

In addition to practices specifically designed to raise lungta, there are various ways to achieve balance, alertness, and resilience. Engaging in regular exercise and stretching, eating wholesome foods, and adopting a generally healthy lifestyle all contribute significantly to these qualities. Additionally, creative pursuits and healthy habits enhance our overall well-being.

Meditative practices also play a crucial role. One effective method is visualising an enlightened figure, such as Guru Rinpoche. We can visualise him in the sky before us, as clearly and in as much detail as possible, but in a relaxed manner. We can imagine him not as a statue or a being of flesh and bones but as a form made of subtle, brilliant, beautiful light. We can reflect on his qualities of love, wisdom, and power and invoke his blessings with a humble mindset. While imagining that nectar or light rays emanate from him and purify us entirely, we feel our qualities increasing, fostering our spiritual realisations, and dispelling obstacles—ours and those of all beings. As we feel this in our body and mind, we pick ourselves up, readjusting our posture, and we experience a sense of dignity and upliftedness. Then we can relax in openness, and finally dedicate the positive energy generated to all beings.

Such practices are profound and go beyond merely raising our current energy levels. They help dissipate depression, foster clarity and bravery, and enhance our capacity for compassionate actions.

Taking Heart: Additional Bits of Advice

You may have gained an appreciation of how the themes that we've covered in this book converge towards an integrated path. For many of us, this is just the beginning; but we can face future challenges with a sense of humour, trust, dignity, and openness. With that goal in mind, and as we near the end of this book, I'd like to offer some additional pieces of advice.

Kindly Learn to Recognise Addictions and Habits

We all have some form of habit or addiction, whether subtle or not-so-subtle. A slogan from the *Seven Points of Mind Training*, the classic collection of lojong instructions mentioned earlier, suggests that we should work with our greatest defilements or obscurations first. This is sound advice. However, even if we manage to relinquish our most destructive habits, we may start to recognise subtler ones as we progress along the path, such as clinging and self-centredness. We should acknowledge them. Just like with the teaching on the four truths of the noble ones, we need to recognise suffering and its causes, even our most intimate forms of suffering, which are less obvious, such as our tendency to grasp at thoughts and concepts.

We can do this in a kind, compassionate manner. There's no need to beat ourselves up. Yet, every day, we can increase our determination to get to the bottom of our neuroses and confusion. The great masters of the past, such as Patrul Rinpoche, were unequivocal when they caught themselves entertaining harmful habits; that's how they made real progress. Remember, it's not so much oneself as a person who is to blame (although we definitely have to face up to our responsibilities when we screw up), but more to the point, it's the result of self-centredness and delusion. So keep cultivating bodhicitta, no matter what.

Do Not Underestimate the Importance of Relaxation

In my teenage years, when I first started meditating, I had a narrow understanding of the term "meditation." I found it irksome when people referred to meditation when they simply meant relaxation. I valued effort and structure and disliked the vague way in which the term "meditation" was being thrown around. That attitude was just a manifestation of attachment to my own ideas, of course.

Years later, I started to recognise the importance of relaxation for meditators. This is something I have had to rediscover time and time again. While relaxation is important for meditators of all schools and traditions, it is particularly important in Mahamudra and Dzogchen forms of meditation practice. To recognise the true nature of the mind, one has to let go and settle. Just one caveat: if you have a tendency to sink into torpor whenever you want to "relax," understand that the relaxation we are referring to here goes hand in hand with presence and awareness. It has nothing to do with the darkness of sleep or drug-induced stupor; rather, it has everything to do with the brightness of wakefulness. You can be both very relaxed and totally aware, with a fresh mind—a truly delightful combination.

Beginners and intermediate students might find inspiration in Dza Kilung Rinpoche's *The Relaxed Mind* in this regard. However, I believe that nearly everyone, regardless of their level of experience with meditation, will benefit from occasionally checking in with tensions, whether physical, mental, emotional, or spiritual.

Do Not Grasp at Experiences

There is a crucial difference between mere experience and actual realisation. Many interesting and unusual things can happen during our meditation sessions, as well as during post-meditation. Mistaking these fleeting, conditioned sensations for spiritual accomplishment is deluded and a major hindrance on the path.

Generally speaking, three types of experiences are likely to appear: the experiences of bliss, clarity, and non-conceptuality. Each has both a mundane and a transcendent aspect. As Traleg Kyabgon explains in a brilliant footnote in *Moonbeams of Mahamudra*:

> Anyone who has meditated for some time can have these experiences to some extent. A general sense of physical and mental well-being is the experience of bliss. Being focused with a sense of sharpness is the experience of clarity. When thoughts and concepts subside and we experience a spaciousness that is free from mental agitation, we are experiencing non-conceptuality. [...] To experience them properly, you need to relate them to realisation, rather than remaining on the level of experience without realisation. We have to understand that distinction. You will also become caught in your meditative experiences if you become attached or fixated on them.[124]

If we become attached to these experiences, we'll see meditation as a means to recreate a specific mental state. As a result, we'll begin to have expectations, and our practice will become fabricated and unnatural. This kind of pitfall can be quite subtle. Traleg Rinpoche adds that "some experiences can be quite strong and have powerful emotional overtones, which may be mistaken for realisation."[125] So, whatever happens in meditation, stay open, relaxed, and humble. We can enjoy an experience without fixating on it.

To paraphrase the great enlightened master from the eighteenth century, Rigdzin Jigme Lingpa, who himself was quoting timeless, perfect teachings:

> Understanding is like a patch that will soon fall off.
> Experiences are like mist—they will vanish.
> Realization is like the sky that never changes.[126]

Acknowledge the Spirally Nature of Spiritual Development

Spiritual progress is not exactly like climbing a ladder. It is more spirally, as we continually unveil nuances to instructions that we thought we had fully understood or that initially seemed redundant. Therefore, it is often worthwhile to review the material we have encountered in the past, looking at it from different angles, with fresh eyes. We may occasionally notice that some of our interpretations were incorrect or that translations we had read or heard were inaccurate. Moreover, we may realise that a teaching we thought was simple is, in fact, astonishingly profound. (Then again, as I hope I've made clear throughout this book, profundity and simplicity are not necessarily antithetical.)

Seek a Reliable Teacher

If, like me, you feel inspired to maintain a connection with the Buddha and Guru Rinpoche, then pray that their timeless wisdom and compassion guide and inspire you. If you take the teachings of the Buddha to heart and wish to further explore Buddhadharma, seek out an authentic, living teacher. Proceed carefully, but remain open and discerning. Don't get derailed by romantic notions or unrealistic hopes, nor let doubt and fear prevent you from embarking on and treading an authentic path towards fundamental sanity.

— —

Conclusion

The French translator and teacher Philippe Cornu talks of Buddhism as a "path of deconditioning" that has a lot to offer, given that our predominant materialistic model has run out of steam.[127] I wholeheartedly agree, and hope that this book contributes to greater understanding of what Buddhism actually is and of how it can help us in our current predicament. Buddhism is not just for Eastern people and Westerners who have a particular affinity with Eastern cultures, although some level of humility and openness are necessary, while arrogance and subtle forms of prejudice can and do get in the way.

Rather, Buddhism has to do with one's wish to see things clearly and to see through self-deception. It requires acknowledging the causes of suffering—especially the poisonous quality of self-centredness—and glimpsing the possibility of liberation, through personal insight and the examples of wondrous beings who have been there. Not only that, it involves a commitment to getting to the root of one's own confusion and adopting a way of life that is simple, open, courageous, compassionate, and perceptive.

To paraphrase the contemporary teacher Khenpo Tsewang Dongyal Rinpoche: between birth and death, when you have the opportunity to practice, there's a space, a window of light. It is not going to last very long, so take advantage of it.

Use that window.

If you do so, you will be able to gradually transform an overload into an overflow: a simple, responsive, wise heart that is overflowing with love.

— Postscript —

Clarity, Tenderness, and Integrity in an Era of Unbridled AI

MY FRIEND AND PUBLISHER, Matthew Dawson, suggested I write a postscript on generative artificial intelligence, ChatGPT, and similar technologies. It is a tricky subject: by the time you read this, a lot will have changed in the development of AI systems and in the world at large. It is even challenging to accurately determine the *current* state of AI, as it evolves at a dizzying pace. That's the nature of the beast. In an increasingly interconnected world—and by "connected" I refer to technology rather than actual human relationships—so-called progress is exponential.

Let's consider a few examples of this rapid progress.

Not long ago, business websites that implemented automated chatbots to carry out their first-line customer service merely provided stock answers—a slightly more interactive version of a FAQ webpage. Now, with the rapid development of conversational and speech synthesis systems, we will soon reach a point where we can call a company and not be able to tell whether we are speaking to a human being or an AI. Nothing to do with our old GPSs that had the stupidest, most robotic voices!

Not long ago, we all had a friend who would be all proud and excited when asking Alexa or Google for the weather. Now, teachers worldwide tear their hair out because students can ask ChatGPT to write their entire essays.

And the AI generated "art?" It is both exhilarating and frightening! You can also use AI tools to create a marketing campaign structure, brainstorm slogans with varying styles and levels of creativity, write social media content and blog posts, rewrite them concisely or idiomatically, translate them into several languages, and schedule their publication at optimal times depending on market segments—all in an extremely short period of time if you know how to prompt the system effectively.

You can upload a book and interact with its content—in doing so, you can converse with your favourite fictional characters! I am even told of a pornographic entertainer who is offering a troubling twist on the old concept of prostitution: fans can interact with one of her avatars as their own "girlfriend." It's a crude example, but it shows how weird and possibly psychotic things could get. As more and more of what we read, see, and hear is AI-generated (at the time of writing this, hundreds of books co-authored by ChatGPT are available on Amazon), it is imperative that we scrutinise our relationship with content and make an effort to heal this relationship.

The exponential nature of technological advancement brings widespread increases in uncertainty and anxiety and a feeling that time is contracting. Some people will experience a sense of being left out or feel alienated. It is not unlike when the internet and social media reached global audiences, and older or less tech-savvy folks felt excluded—there will be this sort of feeling, to the tenth power. My bet is that many people will soon start to feel insidiously disempowered and deprived of their sense of agency. For now, some are in denial, many are scared, and most don't understand the implications of the unbridled development of AI: how could we possibly understand *all* the implications anyway?

Generally speaking, the Buddhist approach is to find and tread the middle way, questioning extreme scenarios that are either overly pessimistic or overly hopeful. We need to remain inquisitive and open, without taking our understanding for granted. We can analyse the processes and mechanisms at play with a sense of wonder if that's what it takes, but we also need discernment and we must remember the indubitable—though sometimes unfathomable—connections between causes and effects. There are different ways to look at the generative AI phenomenon, and enquiring into the benefits of such technology for humankind certainly seems worthwhile. However, there appears to be a lot of naivety involved, and that is very much part of the problem.

We need to assess the potential risks. I am not just referring to a potential weakening of one's memory, job losses in certain domains, or newsworthy deepfakes. AI will rapidly impact *all* areas of our lives.

The troubling thing is that the gap between the political apparatuses and the technological sphere is wider than ever. Governments have been lagging behind for years, and now we need them to be wise yet agile. They must stand up to corporate greed (as industry giants are bound to make their plea) and refrain from taking the easy route, which could bring marginal benefits in the short term but result in utter chaos and suffering in the long run (and this may well come sooner rather than later).

Additionally, we must understand that our behaviour as customers, voters, and global citizens does have an impact. I am not necessarily suggesting that we should never use any AI tools whatsoever; only that if we do use them, it should be with clarity, discernment, and integrity. In any event, it is our duty to make responsible choices, to use new products and services wisely (or refrain from using them if necessary), to steer discussions with friends and colleagues in a positive and productive direction, and so forth. Then, come what may, we'll be at ease knowing that we've lived an ethical life and have done our best to bring happiness and warmth to those around us, or at least that we have not added more suffering and confusion to the world.

To give an analogy, it is like when self-serve checkout systems appeared in stores. Perhaps, sympathising with those human cashiers who were at risk of losing their jobs, you made an effort to go to them as much as possible and ditch the machine. But over time, there were fewer and fewer cashiers and more and more self-serve systems. At that point, some cynics may have thought, "going to a human cashier is pointless, I'm not making a difference here." But even if choosing the traditional lane only *delayed* the job losses a tiny bit, it did make a difference for the people affected, at least during that time. And that's not insignificant.

— —

Unawareness and greed have always caused tremendous suffering for oneself and others. This is nothing new: ignorance and the erratic, egocentric emotions that ensue are tied to the very process of samsara.

We can look at different problems through the lens of this understanding. For example, if we consider the housing market craze or our addiction to plastic or fossil fuels, we can see that such situations are connected in one way or another to egoism, self-centredness, and lack of insight. This is something to keep in mind as we consider the development of AI.

Of course, we can acknowledge that a lot of good can come from such technological advances. I marvel at their potential uses in healthcare, natural resource management, emergency response, and language learning. But it would be naïve to claim that it is all very promising and believe that it will all just turn out nicely. We need to make a conscious, deliberate decision to reorient our efforts towards positive goals and halt irresponsible and greedy uses of AI as much as possible. We will also need ethics professors, perhaps now more than ever.

In any event, this is not a book about politics or technology specifically; so let's see more precisely how it all relates to the main themes that we have been exploring throughout.

New, unforeseen phenomena are bound to occur in all areas of our lives and at a dizzying scale. When paradigm shifts like this happen, it is even more important to cultivate tranquillity and the capacity to abide peacefully so that we are not constantly carried away. It is also important to cultivate patience and be kind towards ourselves, especially when we notice that our practice is still challenged by outer circumstances, or when we face inner turmoil. We'll need more bodhisattva apprentices, but these bodhisattva apprentices will need to learn to be at ease with themselves, abide peacefully, and balance their inner practice with their engagement with the world.

It is said that accomplished bodhisattvas plunge into hell realms like "swans plunging into a lake." The fact that they maintain grace, dignity, and composure in all situations doesn't mean that they are not moved by the suffering and confusion they witness. Quite the contrary. This gentle yet fearless approach can also apply to the social and economic upheavals that we are likely to face in the near future. When we commit to a path on which we can learn to thrive amidst chaos and adversity and use every situation to nourish compassion, joy, and wisdom, then egotistic fears lose their grip. They surface every now and then, but they don't stick.

Even if the bodhisattva ideal seems remote to you, there is no need to lose hope. Once you connect with an authentic lineage and learn how to relate to it, you can always find inspiration, clarity, and protection. This emphasises the importance of an actual, genuine lineage in Buddhism: asking AI for guidance does not count as an actual transmission. At some point, there needs to be heart-to-heart communication—a true meeting of minds.

This brings us to another interesting notion related to AI, one that will be of paramount importance for spiritual seekers. When we interact with a machine, no matter how learned it is in theory, we have an opportunity to truly discern between mere knowledge (in the sense of "information") and actual awareness. Between data and mind—and, from a Buddhist point of view, between deluded mind and enlightened mind. Recognising this distinction between knowledge and awareness is also connected to the threefold aspects of practice: study, contemplation, and meditation. "Study" is often translated as "hearing," which involves receiving a teaching from an actual lineage holder. It can include personal study through books and so on, but as precious as this is, it is not enough. We need reflection, or contemplation—really spending time with the material to further familiarise ourselves with it, discern areas of confusion, and clear away any lingering doubts. Then we need actual meditation, which leads to realisation. Nowadays, there is a tendency to overemphasise study. But intellectual understanding alone does not suffice, and just thinking about things a little is also not enough to develop certainty and true wisdom. What we need is actual realisation and accomplishment.

— —

Given the alarming number of people at risk of losing their jobs in fields such as graphic design, concept art, translation, journalism, writing, coding, customer service, and secretarial work, and the widespread anxiety caused by rapid AI development, it will be important now more than ever to cultivate warmth and empathy. We need to care for each other, learn to listen, and be both at ease and responsive to others. However, to avoid becoming overwhelmed or ineffective, it's important to remember that compassion must always be coupled with understanding and true wisdom. One of the beautiful things about the Buddhist path is that kindness and discernment, or compassion and wisdom, always go hand in hand.

It is comforting to remember that the buddhas have provided means to address all situations, including the current upheavals we experience throughout the world. Personally, I have faith in Guru Rinpoche, Padmasambhava, and his enlightened lineages, whose greatest masters periodically reveal timely practices that align with Buddhism's timeless principles but are also incredibly fresh and potent.

In any case, clarity, tenderness, integrity, wisdom—all the qualities that this book aims to foster—will remain relevant in the era of unbridled AI, perhaps more so than ever. It will also be essential to cultivate a joyful and courageous heart, learn to be flexible, serene, and open, which does not mean being weak—quite the contrary. The confidence that comes from a balanced, non-materialistic spiritual development brings much power, and this wonderful energy can and should be put to good use.

— —

One last thing. The sense of exponential "progress" comes with a feeling that time is contracting, exacerbated by our fast-paced lives. This feeling of acceleration or "time-shrinking" presents a significant opportunity for spiritual seekers, who need to ascertain what it means to truly experience the present moment. On one hand, there is a sense of urgency; we need to examine how we interact with the world and demand better treatment and protection for people, nations, and the natural environment. On the other hand, each one of us must also take care of our own spiritual practice and not neglect it.

Many great Buddhist masters have written about our relationship with time. The great thirteenth-century Zen master, Dōgen Zenji, wrote that "each moment is the universe," to paraphrase the contemporary Zen teacher Dainin Katagiri. In the Nyingma tradition, as taught by Kunkhyen Longchenpa and others, there is the notion of a "timeless time," a pure experience unaffected by our ordinary, linear approach to time. Also, as I have quoted in this book, Trungpa Rinpoche has pointed out that "one's whole practice should be based on the relationship between you and nowness."

These are just a few pithy insights from the great masters—extraordinarily profound teachings on healing our relationship with time, thus fostering a sense of being fully alive and present for others. Each teaching requires a lot of unpacking. So I will simply end on this note: Trungpa Rinpoche also liked to remind us that *the future is open.*

I agree and I believe that we must take responsibility, joyfully and resolutely.

Vincent Thibault
4th July, 2023

Acknowledgments

I WOULD LIKE TO EXPRESS MY DEEP, heartfelt gratitude to Tulku Thondup Rinpoche for his indelible inspiration, and to Samuel Bercholz for his generous guidance and selfless companionship. I also wish to thank Lama Sonam Tsering Rinpoche, Orgyen Chowang Rinpoche, Dza Kilung Rinpoche, Khenpo Sonam from Lhundrup Choling, Chakung Jigme Wangdrak Rinpoche, Tulku Thadral Rinpoche and Greg Seton. Likewise, I pay my respects to Dzigar Kongtrul Rinpoche and Shechen Rabjam Rinpoche.

This is an unusual and deeply personal book, and I have tried my best to convey what I have learned in a fresh and relatable way. I bow to the lineage holders, enlightened ones, and Dharma protectors, and apologize if any inaccuracies or misinterpretations have crept in while discussing Buddhadharma.

Thankfully, the writer was not alone; creating a book takes teamwork. I thank my publisher Matthew Dawson for his vision, trust, patience, and integrity, and Annelise Roberts for her skilful preliminary editing. Heartfelt thanks go to editor Dee Collings for challenging me on several fronts and inspiring me to deliver a book that is hopefully more impactful and coherent, as well as to Paul Croucher for the final round of edits. With gratitude, I bow to Traleg Khandro, who kindly wrote the foreword. I'm also grateful to Hazel Bercholz for her gracious feedback on an early version of the manuscript; to Émilie Côté for her support when I was going through the first drafts; to my family who has always been there in one way or another; and to Alice, for being who she is.

Last but not least: thank you, dear readers.

— —

To end on an auspicious note, here is a beautiful prayer of aspiration by Kyabje Dudjom Rinpoche, Jikdral Yeshe Dorje (1904–1987), translated by Adam Pearcey:

འཛམ་གླིང་སྤྱི་དང་ཡུལ་ཁམས་འདི་དག་ཏུ། །
ནད་མུག་མཚོན་སོགས་སྡུག་བསྔལ་མིང་མི་གྲགས། །
ཆོས་ལྡན་བསོད་ནམས་དཔལ་འབྱོར་གོང་དུ་འཕེལ། །
རྟག་ཏུ་བཀྲ་ཤིས་བདེ་ལེགས་ཕུན་ཚོགས་ཤོག །

Throughout these lands and everywhere upon the earth in general,
May the sufferings of disease, famine and warfare be entirely unknown,
so that not even their names occur.
May observance of the Dharma, merit, and prosperity increase,
And may there always be good fortune and well-being in abundance.

Notes

1 I mention this out of respect for my main teachers, but it should be noted that much of this book is written from a general Mahayana perspective.

2 Daniel J. Levitin, *The Organized Mind* (Toronto: Penguin, 2014), p. xx.

3 Johnson, D. "SMS open rates exceed 99%." *Tatango SMS Marketing Blog* (2013). This data has been referenced in Hall AK, Cole-Lewis H, Bernhardt JM, "Mobile text messaging for health: a systematic review of reviews," *Annu Rev Public Health* 2015 Mar 18;36:393-415. doi: 10.1146/annurev-publhealth-031914-122855. PMID: 25785892; PMCID: PMC4406229. It has also been quoted more recently (April 21, 2023) by Kiltesh Patel in *Forbes*.

4 Exceeding a billion websites: Netcraft, *September 2014 Web Server Survey*, https://news.netcraft.com/archives/2014/09/24/september-2014-web-server-survey.html. As of February 16, 2023, Siteefy says 1.13 billion (https://siteefy.com/how-many-websites-are-there/); in its *March 2023 Web Server Survey*, Netcraft received responses from 1,116,018,952 sites (https://news.netcraft.com/archives/category/web-server-survey/).

5 Levitin, *The Organized Mind*, p. 6.

6 *Ibid.*, pp. 6–7.

7 See, for example, WordsRated, "Number of Books Published Each Year" (February 2, 2022), https://wordsrated.com/number-of-books-published-per-year-2021/.

8 See https://blog.youtube/press/ (last consulted as of April 26, 2023). In 2014, Levitin mentioned "6,000 hours of video every hour" (*The Organized Mind*, p. 6). I suppose that the overall quantity of content has greatly increased since then, but it may also be that the number provided by YouTube includes audio-only content that is not counted as "video" in Levitin's book. In any case, the numbers are dizzying!

9 See www.who.int/europe/health-topics/noise, and https://www.who.int/tools/compendium-on-health-and-environment/environmental-noise. For a fun (though less scientifically precise) article on the subject of silence, see Anne Bokma and Alexandra Caufin, "Quiet, Please! How Staying Silent Can Boost Your Health," *Reader's Digest Canada*, 2018, www.readersdigest.ca/health/healthy-living/embracing-silence-tips/.

10 "The Benefits of Silence", excerpt from an interview directed and produced by Maya van der Meer for The Yogini Project, https://www.youtube.com/watch?v=MxeDYz4cZoY (accessed July 2019).

11 Seneca, *Moral letters to Lucilius (Epistulae morales ad Lucilium)*, translated by Richard M. Gummere (London: William Heinemann, 1917), Letter 2: "On discursiveness in reading." https://en.wikisource.org/wiki/Moral_letters_to_Lucilius/Letter_2.

12 See, for example, https://en.wikipedia.org/wiki/Flow_(psychology) and https://en.wikipedia.org/wiki/Mihaly_Csikszentmihalyi.

13 Matthieu Ricard, *Happiness: A Guide to Developing Life's Most Important Skill* (New York: Little, Brown and Company, 2006), p. 227.

14 Jigme Lingpa and Longchen Yeshe Dorje, Kangyur Rinpoche, *Treasury of Precious Qualities*, revised edition (Boston: Shambhala Publications, 2010), p. 22. In Matthieu Ricard's aforementioned book (opening of chapter 20), a similar quote is attributed to Buddha Shakyamuni, but this is possibly a mistake and Matthieu himself refers to Jigme Lingpa's *Treasury* elsewhere. I thank our editor Annie for bringing this to my attention.

15 https://en.wikipedia.org/wiki/Dunbar%27s_number (accessed April 27, 2023).

16 Josh Kaufman, *The Personal MBA* (New York: Portfolio/Penguin, 2012), pp. 240–241. An online version of the article "Cognitive Scope Limitation" can be found online here: https://personalmba.com/cognitive-scope-limitation/.

17 *Ibid.*, p. 241.

18 Dza Kilung Rinpoche, *The Relaxed Mind: A Seven-Step Method for Deepening Meditation Practice* (Boston: Shambhala Publications, 2015), pp. xxii–xxiii.

19 To be more precise, Mahayana Buddhism even refers to a state that is beyond both samsara and nirvana, in which one does not simply hang out forever in some static paradise, but spontaneously and ceaselessly manifests enlightened energies and activities to benefit beings. They call that full awakening—but more on that later.

20 His Eminence the Third Jamgon Kongtrul Rinpoche, Karma Lodrö Chökyi Senge, *The Four Dharmas of Lha-je Gampopa*, commentary on the fourth verse, http://www.dharmadownload.net/pages/english/Natsok/0010_Teaching_English/Teaching_English_0005.htm (last accessed April 28, 2023).

21 I thank Chakung Jigme Wangdrak Rinpoche for his January 4, 2023 teaching on the eight worldly concerns, in which he shared profound insights and clarifications on the "age of degenerations." I have slightly adapted some of this information to make it relatable for our readers, some of which may be non-Buddhists. A more traditional explanation can be found in Dilgo Khyentse Rinpoche's book, *Guru Yoga* (Boulder: Snow Lion, 1999), p. 50. As for Guru Rinpoche's predictions, examples can be found in the seventh chapter of the *Le'u Dünma* (especially in the prologue to the "Sampa Lhundrupma" section).

22 A vocal example: Harry Oldmeadow, *Timeless Truths & Modern Delusions: The Perennial Philosophy as a guide for contemporary Buddhists* (Melbourne: Platform Publications, 2021).

23 For more on the subject of hope in this day and age, please refer to my short book, *The Sensible Optimist Manifesto* (Melbourne: Platform Publications, forthcoming). I also warmly recommend Matthieu Ricard's previously quoted book on *Happiness*.

24 Orgyen Chowang, *Our Pristine Mind: A Practical Guide to Unconditional Happiness* (Boulder: Shambhala Publications, 2016), p. 117.

25 U.S. Departments of the Army and Air Force, *Survival at Sea* (Washington: United States Government Printing Office, 1950), p. 58.

26 Georges Simenon, *La Fuite de Monsieur Monde*, in *Tout Simenon 1* (Paris: Omnibus, 2002), p. 196. Loosely translated by myself.

27 Longchen Rabjam (1308–1363), quoted by Matthieu Ricard in *Happiness*, prev. quoted.

28 Ultimately, the truth of buddhahood, or enlightenment, is uncompounded. A discussion of the vehicles or "yanas" can also be found in chapter 5 under "Mahayana Buddhism and Bodhicitta."

29 Chögyam Trungpa, *Cutting Through Spiritual Materialism*, in *The Collected Works of Chögyam Trungpa*, volume 3 (Boulder: Shambhala Publications, 2003), p. 119.

30 *Ibid.*, p. 117.

31 Occasionally, for some people, bits of insight might come first; but the stability that tranquillity meditation provides still proves essential, otherwise the initial insight may quickly vanish.

32 Jamgön Mipham Rinpoche, from the *Khenjuk* (Tib. *mkhas 'jug*), quoted by Rigpa Wiki and translated by Rigpa Translations. Mipham's original text has also been translated by Erik Pema Kunsang. See *Gateway to Knowledge*, volume 1 (Hong Kong: Rangjung Yeshe Publications, 2013), p. 24.

33 Traleg Kyabgon, *The Practice of Lojong: Cultivating Compassion through Training the Mind* (Boulder: Shambhala Publications, 2007), p. 39.

34 One of the "three baskets" into which the traditional Buddhist teachings are divided, the Abhidharma is associated with wisdom. Since it provides frameworks to understand all experience, we could say that one of its main themes is psychology.

35 Nyoshul Khen Rinpoche, *Mindfulness: The Mirror of the Mind* (Tib. *drenpa sems kyi me long bzhugs*), translated by Adam Pearcey/Rigpa Translations (Lotsawa House, 2013).

36 Thich Nhat Hanh, *Peace Is Every Step* (New York: Bantam Books, 1991), p. 45.

37 See *Tricycle*, "Give Yourself a Breathing Room," March 14, 2021, https://tricycle.org/trikedaily/thich-nhat-hanh-breathing-room/.

38 In the West, we often relate this notion to Cartesian dualism, which was defended by the French philosopher and mathematician René Descartes in the first half of the seventeenth century. An oversimplification at best would be to claim that body and mind are two distinct, separate substances. However, according to Buddhism, substance dualism is extremely frequent, regardless of time, place, and culture. While it can be used temporarily, in certain contexts, the notion ultimately has limits.

39 *Dharmapada* as quoted by Tulku Thondup in *The Healing Power of Mind* (Boston: Shambhala Publications, 1998), p. 25.

40 Gyalse Tokme Zangpo, *The Thirty-Seven Practices of All the Bodhisattvas*, translated by Adam Pearcey (Lotsawa House, 2006).

41 Nagarjuna's *Letter to a Friend*, translated by the Padmakara Translation Group (Ithaca: Snow Lion, 2005), verse 38.

42 For example, the classic, sixteenth-century meditation manual, *Moonbeams of Mahāmudrā*, says:

> If we eat only a very small amount of food, we will feel hungry and weak. If we consume too much, our body will feel heavy and our drowsiness and dullness will

> increase. Indigestible or unwholesome food provokes new or old illnesses. All of those will make our body unsuitable for spiritual practices. (Dakpo Tashi Namgyal, *Moonbeams of Mahāmudrā* with Wangchuk Dorke's commentary, translated by Elizabeth M. Callahan [Boulder: Snow Lion, 2019], pp. 170–171)

It even adds, referencing the fourth century Indian saint Asanga:

> We should reflect upon how enjoying moderation benefits our patrons, nourishes the microorganisms in our body, and enables us to work for the welfare of sentient beings. These points are discussed by the Noble Asanga. (*Ibid.*, p. 171)

On the relationship between Buddhist practice, food and compassion more specifically, see Shabkar, *Food of Bodhisattvas: Buddhist Teachings on Abstaining from Meat* (Boston: Shambhala Publications, 2004). It is also worth noting that the great master Dudjom Rinpoche, Jikdral Yeshe Dorje (1904–1987), who is revered as an enlightened teacher in the Nyingma tradition of Tibetan Buddhism, was unequivocal about the ravages of tobacco.

When it come to *how* we eat, a more contemporary reference that is likely to be helpful for the general public is provided by Zen master Thich Nhat Hanh and Dr. Lilian Cheung: see *Savor: Mindful Eating, Mindful Life* (New York: HarperOne, 2011). On the Indian yoga side, André Van Lysebeth's classic *Yoga Self-Taught* (York Beach: Weiser, 1999) also contains some good elements.

43 For example, see Tulku Thondup Rinpoche's excellent books, *The Healing Power of Mind* and *Boundless Healing*. In *Integral Buddhism*, Traleg Kyabgon devotes two chapters to health and well-being, and includes a succinct presentation of fundamental notions of Tibetan medicine. Anyen Rinpoche and Allison Choying Zangmo also wrote a helpful guide titled *The Tibetan Yoga of Breath* (Boulder: Shambhala Publications, 2013).

44 In some variants, the hands simply rest on the knees. This relaxed posture is said to have been particularly used by Longchenpa, a great fourteenth-century master of the Nyingma tradition of Tibetan Buddhism.

45 See, for example, the Glossary entry "Sevenfold Vairochana Posture" in Tulku Thondup's *The Heart of Unconditional Love* (Boston: Shambhala Publications, 2015), or the article "Seven-point posture of Vairochana" on Rigpa Wiki.

46 If you find that your breathing is often restricted, not just due to mental stress, but to physical tension in the upper body, you might want to consider adding to your daily routine some gentle self-massage (belly and diaphragm area, chest and back muscles) followed by some stretching and some deep, relaxed breathing. Don't hesitate to consult a physical therapist.

47 More on refuge in chapters 4 and 7.

48 Interestingly, the Nyingma and Kagyu traditions don't necessarily emphasise all nine levels, as some may lead to absorptive states that are unhelpful to developing awareness. In these traditions, practitioners are more concerned with cultivating awareness rather than strict concentration.

49 In fact, there is a beautiful interplay between shamatha training and thematic contemplations: the former fosters stability, which gives more power to the latter. Another way to look at it is to consider that all meditations, including contemplations on impermanence, love, or any other topic, must have an element of calm, stability, and accuracy; so, in a sense, they all have a quality of shamatha. Still, so as to not take this element for granted, it is healthy training to allow regular sessions for shamatha per se (using the breath or any other method).

50 More on nihilism and eternalism in chapters 6 and 7.

51 Here and for the lines that follow, we have used Philippe Cornu's excellent article, "karma," in his wonderful *Dictionnaire encyclopédique du bouddhisme* (Paris: Seuil, 2001), pp. 286–289.

52 A buddha has freed herself from karma. This does not mean that enlightenment is death; that would be a dangerously nihilistic idea, turning spirituality into some kind of suicidal path. Full awakening is the death of false conceptions—the exhaustion of ignorance, confusion, self-cherishing patterns, and skewed views. And so an enlightened person can still walk in this world, often rather joyfully, acting for the benefit of beings in whatever form or way situations call for; but that person is free from the chain reactions of karma, in the sense of being free from the habits of mind—both in the intentions that imply clinging and their correlated imprints.

53 See, for example, Dudjom Rinpoche, *Counsels from My Heart* (Boston: Shambhala Publications, 2003), p. 13.

54 A more traditional approach to the "four contemplations that turn the mind towards Dharma" could be much vaster, in that it could put into perspective previous and future lives as well, with an emphasis on the correlation between dharmic practice and happiness, liberation and enlightenment, on the one hand, and between non-dharmic behavior and suffering on the other.

55 From Andrew Colman, *A Dictionary of Psychology* (New York: Oxford University Press, 2006, p. 670): "A decision-making procedure or cognitive heuristic that entails searching through the available options just long enough to find one that reaches a preset threshold of acceptability." The Wikipedia article "Satisficing" (consulted May 9, 2023 and referencing an 1979 issue of *The American Economic Review*) also quotes Herbert A. Simon's 1978 Nobel Prize in Economics speech: "decision makers can satisfice either by finding optimum solutions for a simplified world, or by finding satisfactory solutions for a more realistic world. Neither approach, in general, dominates the other, and both have continued to co-exist in the world of management science."

56 Shantideva's *Bodhicaryāvatāra*, 8.13. Adapted from *La Marche vers l'Éveil* (Peyzac-le-Moustier: Éditions Padmakara, 1992).

57 Levitin, *The Organized Mind*, pp. 6–7.

58 Dzigar Kongtrul, *The Intelligent Heart: A Guide to the Compassionate Life* (Boulder: Shambhala Publications, 2016), p. 131 (commentary on slogan 28, "Abandon any expectation of fruition").

59 Nagarjuna's *Letter to a Friend*, verse 34.

60 André Comte-Sponville, *Le bonheur, désespérément* (Éditions Pleins feux, 2000, réédition Librio).

61 More on this crucial distinction in chapter 6.

62 For more on *satisficing*, see the section entitled "The Power of Small Things," as well as note 55.

63 Christophe André, *Looking at Mindfulness* (New York: Blue Rider Press, 2016), pp. 219–220. Translated by Trista Selous and originally published in French under the title *Méditer, jour après jour* (Paris: L'Iconoclaste, 2011).

64 Chögyam Trungpa, *Cutting Through Spiritual Materialism* in *The Collected Works of Chögyam Trungpa*, volume 3, pp. 142–143.

65 Tulku Thondup, *Boundless Healing: Meditation Exercises to Enlighten the Mind and Heal the Body* (Boulder: Shambhala Publications, 2001), p. 29.

66 Thich Nhat Hanh, *Peace Is Every Step*, p. 6.

67 Traleg Kyabgon, *Mind at Ease* (Boulder: Shambhala Publications, 2004), p. 12.

68 More on emptiness (*shunyata*) in the next chapter.

69 Traleg Kyabgon, *Integral Buddhism* (Victoria: Shogam Publications, 2018), pp. 84–85.

70 Patrul Rinpoche (*rdza dpal sprul o rgyan 'jigs med chos kyi dbang po*), "An Essential Instruction on Refuge and Bodhicitta," translated by Adam Pearcy (Lotsawa House, 2004).

71 Often, the contemplation on suffering is the third one, and reflection on karma is the fourth. The idea is that we contemplate the defects of cyclic existence—we develop the conviction that any life based on delusion, clinging, and egotistic patterns is bound to produce suffering and can never bring any lasting satisfaction—and then we eagerly learn what to do and what to avoid, as we become acquainted with the unfailing principles of karma. But we can combine the "four contemplations" in any way we see fit. For example, we can meditate on the preciousness of human life when we are depressed, or on impermanence when we are elated, naïve, or overly attached. In this chapter, our contemplations of suffering will naturally connect with another set of four meditations, called the four boundless attitudes.

72 "Consciousness here refers to the consciousness of impressions from the five senses, and also consciousness of mental objects, like thoughts, ideas and emotions." (Rigpa Wiki, article "Five skandhas"). For some excellent, succinct, and complementary explanations of the functions of ordinary consciousness (and its sensory, intentional, and cognitive aspects), see Traleg Kyabgon, *Mind at Ease*, pp. 74–76; for an overview of the eight levels of consciousness and their relationship with karma, see *Mind at Ease*, pp. 81–84.

73 When we examine what we typically call "I," we see that it includes several elements, and not just our physical body. "I" is a mere label for a dynamic, ever-changing set of impermanent and interdependent factors. It is important to remember that Buddhism is not nihilism: understanding that the "self" is but a bundle of divisible, subjective, and transitory components does not mean that there is nothing whatsoever, or that we should despise all conventions that involve a certain continuum or a causal relationship between the person we were yesterday and the person we are today: we are still responsible for our actions, and so on. As well, Buddhism can recognise the value of what we could call a "healthy ego" or an "integrated personality." It is *clinging*—and not the proper and inevitable use of labels—as well as our basic ignorance about the reality of things that underlie suffering. More on the distinction between ego-grasping and a healthy sense of personhood in the next chapter.

74 See, for example, Traleg Kyabgon, *Mind at Ease*, p. 63. We could also compare Chögyam Trungpa's fascinating "tour" in *Cutting Through Spiritual Materialism* (chapter "The Six Realms"), and Patrul Rinpoche's moving (and graphic) descriptions in *The Words of My Perfect Teacher* (Boston: Shambhala Publications, 1998, chapter 3: "The defects of samsara").

75 This is the translation provided by Tulku Thondup in *The Heart of Unconditional Love*, p. 62.

76 Tulku Thondup, *The Heart of Unconditional Love*, p. 61.

77 If you have read them a while ago, now would be a good time to read again the sections "Mahayana Buddhism and Bodhicitta," "Spiritual Clarity: Finding the Essence of All Teachings," and "Compassion, Courage, and Complexity."

78 Slightly adapted from the translation by the Padmakara Translation Group: Shantideva, *The Way of the Bodhisattva* (Boulder: Shambhala Publications, 2008), I, 15–16.

79 Padmakara Translation Group: Shantideva, *The Way of the Bodhisattva*, V, 13.

80 Chögyam Trungpa, *The Heart of the Buddha* (Boston: Shambhala Publications, 1991), p. 108, quoted by Reginald A. Ray in *Indestructible Truth: The Living Spirituality of Tibetan Buddhism* (Boston: Shambhala Publications, 2002), p. 332.

81 Ray, *Indestructible Truth*, pp. 332–333.

82 Dzigar Kongtrul, *The Intelligent Heart*, prev. quoted, pp. 130–131 (commentary on slogan 28, "Abandon any expectation of fruition").

83 Translation by the Padmakara Translation Group: Shantideva, *The Way of the Bodhisattva*, VIII, 129–30.

84 These and many other references are listed in the following Reader's Guide: https://www.shambhala.com/lojong-mind-training/.

85 Traleg Kyabgon, *Moonbeams of Mahamudra* (Victoria: Shogam Publications, 2015), p. 211.

86 Chögyam Trungpa Rinpoche, "A Meditation Instruction by Chögyam Trungpa Rinpoche," *Lion's Roar*, January 2012. See also the original instructions: https://www.chronicleproject.com/meditation-the-path-of-the-buddha/ (Talk One).

87 I'm thinking of Patrul Rinpoche's summary of the instructions of Aro Yeshe Jungne.

88 Here one might wonder whether Buddhism is a religion. Actually, it depends on our definition of the word "religion." But one thing is certain: it is non-theistic. Now, most of the religions we know are either monotheistic or polytheistic. If our idea of a religion inevitably implies theism, the use of the word "religion" to refer to Buddhism is likely to confuse us. Personally, I see it as a non-theistic religion and spirituality. It does have an element of faith. In any case, I prefer to say "non-theistic" rather than "atheist." I have nothing against the word "atheist," but it sometimes connotes a rather aggressive position, where one feels the need to deny the beliefs of others and to stick to one's own point of view. Here, we are not trying to denigrate other religions. This is why I speak of "non-theism," even if it may sound a bit dubious, linguistically. Of course, not all atheists are bellicose; I just wanted to emphasize the nuance. In any event, Dharma must be practiced with respect for other traditions and other points of view.

89 I use the word "possibilities" in the plural, because the "middle" is not a fixed point. That is key. If we've fixated on a specific middle point, we've erred from the true middle way.

90 As pointed out on the Shambhala Publications website, in "The Heart Sutra: A Reader's Guide," part of a series of articles on the arc of Zen thought, practice, and history as presented in Barbara O'Brien's book, *The Circle of the Way* (Boulder: Shambhala Publications, 2019).

91 Karl Brunnhölzl, *The Heart Attack Sūtra: A New Commentary on the Heart Sūtra* (Boston: Snow Lion, 2012), p. 12.

92 I'm grateful to Greg Seton, professor at Dartmouth College and collaborator of Mangala Shri Bhuti, for the very helpful classes he's given on these subjects. A book reference would be *Progressive Stages of Meditation on Emptiness* (translated and arranged by Lama Shephen Hookham, Shrimala Trust, 2016), in which the great Khenpo Tsultrim Gyamtso Rinpoche offers experiential training following a fivefold sequence, starting with the Shravaka meditation on no-self, all the way to the Shentong "emptiness-of-other."

93 See note 53.

94 As part of the 2022 Nyingma Summer Seminar, organized by Mangala Shri Bhuti, Dzigar Kongtrul Rinpoche's organization.

95 See also the nuance between *prajna* and *jnana* as summarized in chapter 5, under "The Sixfold Training of a Bodhisattva."

96 Traleg Kyabgon, *The Practice of Lojong*, p. 34.

97 *Ibid.*

98 I'm grateful to Dza Kilung Rinpoche for helping me see, in a more intuitive and experiential way, the connection between tranquillity, clarity, and insight. The following exercise is partly inspired by some of his teachings contained in *The Relaxed Mind.*

99 Dharmakirti, translated by Ari Goldfield and quoted by Andy Karr in *Contemplating Reality: A Practitioner's Guide to the View in Indo-Tibetan Buddhism* (Boston: Shambhala Publications, 2007), p. 5.

100 From Chandrakirti's "Entering the Middle Way," verse translated by Ari Goldfield and quoted by Andy Karr in *Contemplating Reality*, p. 40.

101 See *Integral Buddhism*, p. xi. That book, which is subtitled *Developing All Aspects of One's Personhood*, tackles this issue from different angles.

102 See the section titled "The Turbulence That Arises from the Aggregates," in chapter 5.

103 To be more precise, the term "skandhas" can be understood in two different ways: on a general level, it comprises all conditioned phenomena that could ever be found in the universe; on an individual level, it refers to the foundations on which we mistakenly establish some kind of personal soul or inherent identity. Both are linked, considering that mind is involved in any experience of the "outer world" and that we have a tendency to believe that subjective phenomena are objective; nonetheless, in this chapter we mostly refer to the skandhas as the basis on which we project an autonomous self, the so-called "real me."

104 In fact, we could and should investigate that too. We aim to explore all logical possibilities (searching to find out whether the self can be found within the aggregates, outside of the aggregates, in a combination of both inside and outside, or apart from both). My point, in emphasising that the skandhas include all possible aspects of one's experience, is that as we investigate, we should not be led to think that maybe the self is to be found somewhere else, in a category that is somehow not covered by this system of classification, which would be way off the mark. We should have confidence that the omniscient Buddha did not simply forget a category.

105 Tulku Thondup, *The Heart of Unconditional Love*, pp. 144–145.

106 *Ibid.*, p. 146.

107 Traleg Kyabgon, *The Practice of Lojong*, pp. 54–55.

108 Atiśa Dīpaṃkara Śrījñāna, *Lamp for the Path to Enlightenment,* translated by Patrick Dowd (Lotsawa House, 2021), verse 54.

109 On the other hand, lack of understanding of the second turning teachings might lead one to grasp at these qualities when they arise, which is also off. This all relates to the eternalism/nihilism distinction.

110 Traleg Kyabgon, *Integral Buddhism*, pp. 128–130.

111 Traleg Kyabgon, *Moonbeams of Mahamudra*, p. 216.

112 There are many excellent biographies out there. A few that come to mind are *The Spirit of Tibet: The Life and Work of Khyentse Rinpoche, Spiritual Teacher* and *Enlightened Vagabond: The Life and Teachings of Patrul Rinpoche*, both by Matthieu Ricard; *Old Path, White Clouds: Walking in the Footsteps of the Buddha*, by Thich Nhat Hanh; and *Masters of Meditation and Miracles*, by Tulku Thondup.

113 Tulku Thondup, *The Heart of Unconditional Love*, p. 135.

114 For a humorous and thought-provoking explanation of the four hallmarks, see *What Makes You Not a Buddhist*, by Dzongsar Jamyang Khyentse (Boston: Shambhala Publications, 2008), based on this very subject. For a considerably abbreviated version, see the article titled "The Four Seals of Dharma are Buddhism in a Nutshell" by the same author, published in *Lion's Roar* on January 12, 2017 (available online here: https://www.lionsroar.com/buddhism-nutshell-four-seals-dharma/).

115 Khenchen Palden Sherab, *Mipham's Sword of Wisdom: The Nyingma Approach to Valid Cognition*, translated by Ann Helm with Khenpo Gawang (Somerville: Wisdom Publications, 2018), p. 143. The author quotes, among other texts, the wondrous eighth-century translator Kawa Paltsek's *Dictionary of Dharma Terminology.*

I have also seen a mention of four reliances in the *Noble Mahāyāna Sūtra titled "The Teaching of Akṣayamati"* (Toh 175). See, for example, the following quote:

> Furthermore, Venerable Śāradvatīputra, the bodhisattvas four reliances are also imperishable. What are these four? They are the reliance on the meaning but not on the letter, the reliance on wisdom but not on consciousness, the reliance on the sūtras of definitive meaning but not on the sūtras of implicit meaning, and the reliance on the true state of phenomena but not on the person. (1.236)
>
> (transl. by Prof. Jens Braarvig, 84000, https://read.84000.co/translation/toh175.html)

116 Oral teachings, September 4, 2022, Source of Mahamudra program, year 5.

117 See Traleg Kyabgon, *Mind at Ease*, glossary entry "Interested humility," p. 242.

118 Traleg Kyabgon, *The Practice of Lojong*, p. 16.

119 Oral teachings, July 24, 2022, as part of the Nyingma Summer Seminar, Vajrayana section.

120 See the previous chapter, under "Freedom from Bondage."

121 Chögyam Trungpa, *The Heart of the Buddha*, in *The Collected Works of Chögyam Trungpa*, volume 3, pp. 419–420.

122 Translation by the Padmakara Translation Group: Shantideva, *The Way of the Bodhisattva*, VII.2.

123 As a side note, the colourful prayer flags that can be seen around temples or occasionally near a practitioner's house are generally meant to foster peace, harmony, and auspiciousness, and they often include prayers and iconography related to lungta.

124 Traleg Kyabgon, *Moonbeams of Mahamudra*, p. 439 (note 7).
125 *Ibid.*
126 See Rigdzin Jigme Lingpa, "The Lion's Roar" in Thinley Norbu, *Sunlight Speech that Dispels the Darkness of Doubt* (Boston: Shambhala Publications, 2015), pp. 77–85.
127 Philippe Cornu and Louise Bressollette, *Manuel de bouddhisme: Philosophie, pratique et histoire*, tome 1 (Éditions Rangdröl, 2019), p. 28.

Vincent Thibault is a Canadian writer who has published twenty books in French with various publishing houses in Quebec. From novels to travel memoirs and philosophical essays, his work is surprisingly varied but keeps exploring key themes—the meaning of kindness; the quest for clarity and wisdom in a hectic and noisy world; courage in the face of uncertainty; and the reconciliation of tradition and modernity. He is also a screenwriter.

A proponent of what he calls "clear-sighted optimism," Vincent has been studying Buddhism for nearly twenty-five years. His practice is mostly focused on the Nyingma tradition, but he has also received teachings from other lineages. He has translated (from English to French) more than three hundred texts for Lotsawa House, a digital library of Tibetan Buddhism, as well as books by the prominent Buddhist teachers Tulku Thondup Rinpoche, Traleg Kyabgon, and Dza Kilung Rinpoche. He regularly organizes friendly activities to foster a deeper understanding and appreciation of the Indo-Himalayan Buddhist traditions.

For more information, visit www.vincentthibault.com.